T0221063

Cognitive Engineering for Next Generation Computing

Scrivener Publishing
100 Cummings Center, Suite 541J
Beverly, MA 01915-6106

Next Generation Computing and Communication Engineering

Series Editors: Dr. G. R. Kanagachidambaresan and Dr. Kolla Bhanu Prakash

Developments in artificial intelligence are made more challenging because the involvement of multi-domain technology creates new problems for researchers. Therefore, in order to help meet the challenge, this book series concentrates on next generation computing and communication methodologies involving smart and ambient environment design. It is an effective publishing platform for monographs, handbooks, and edited volumes on Industry 4.0, agriculture, smart city development, new computing and communication paradigms. Although the series mainly focuses on design, it also addresses analytics and investigation of industry-related real-time problems.

Publishers at Scrivener
Martin Scrivener (martin@scrivenerpublishing.com)
Phillip Carmical (pcarmical@scrivenerpublishing.com)

Cognitive Engineering for Next Generation Computing

A Practical Analytical Approach

Edited by

Kolla Bhanu Prakash,
G. R. Kanagachidambaresan,
V. Srikanth, E. Vamsidhar

Scrivener
Publishing

WILEY

This edition first published 2021 by John Wiley & Sons, Inc., 111 River Street, Hoboken, NJ 07030, USA and Scrivener Publishing LLC, 100 Cummings Center, Suite 541J, Beverly, MA 01915, USA
© 2021 Scrivener Publishing LLC
For more information about Scrivener publications please visit www.scrivenerpublishing.com.

All rights reserved. No part of this publication may be reproduced, stored in a retrieval system, or transmitted, in any form or by any means, electronic, mechanical, photocopying, recording, or otherwise, except as permitted by law. Advice on how to obtain permission to reuse material from this title is available at http://www.wiley.com/go/permissions.

Wiley Global Headquarters
111 River Street, Hoboken, NJ 07030, USA

For details of our global editorial offices, customer services, and more information about Wiley products visit us at www.wiley.com.

Limit of Liability/Disclaimer of Warranty
While the publisher and authors have used their best efforts in preparing this work, they make no representations or warranties with respect to the accuracy or completeness of the contents of this work and specifically disclaim all warranties, including without limitation any implied warranties of merchantability or fitness for a particular purpose. No warranty may be created or extended by sales representatives, written sales materials, or promotional statements for this work. The fact that an organization, website, or product is referred to in this work as a citation and/or potential source of further information does not mean that the publisher and authors endorse the information or services the organization, website, or product may provide or recommendations it may make. This work is sold with the understanding that the publisher is not engaged in rendering professional services. The advice and strategies contained herein may not be suitable for your situation. You should consult with a specialist where appropriate. Neither the publisher nor authors shall be liable for any loss of profit or any other commercial damages, including but not limited to special, incidental, consequential, or other damages. Further, readers should be aware that websites listed in this work may have changed or disappeared between when this work was written and when it is read.

Library of Congress Cataloging-in-Publication Data

ISBN 978-1-119-71108-7

Cover image: Pixabay.Com
Cover design by Russell Richardson

Set in size of 11pt and Minion Pro by Manila Typesetting Company, Makati, Philippines

Dedicated to our parents, family members, students and the Almighty.

Contents

2   Machine Learning and Big Data in Cyber-Physical System: Methods, Applications and Challenges   49

Janmenjoy Nayak, P. Suresh Kumar, Dukka Karun Kumar Reddy, Bighnaraj Naik and Danilo Pelusi

Preface

Cognitive computing is a hardware and software element which is presently being used mainly in smart system development. Technologies such as artificial intelligence, machine learning, advanced analytics, natural language processing, big data analytics, and distributed computing come under the umbrella of cognitive computing. The impact of this technology can be seen in areas such as healthcare, business, decision-making, personal lives, and many more. Cognitive engineering is commonly used in analysis, design, decision-making, and sociotechnical systems; and cognitive physical systems are used in applications such as human–robot interactions, transport management, industrial automation, healthcare, agriculture, etc. Human individual interactions and group behavior are important to all these applications. Cognitive cyber-physical systems are applied in different areas such as smart manufacturing, agriculture, education, energy management, security, environmental monitoring, transportation systems, process control, smart cities and homes, medical healthcare devices, etc. The increasing complexity of cognitive computing also includes the security problems confronted by such networks. This rise of the Internet of Things (IoT) network complexity is due to too many devices being interconnected with each other through the internet along with the enormous amount of data originating from these devices. Also, novel security issues arise relating to the development of the IoT while conventional security issues become more severe. The major reasons for this are the heterogeneity and the substantially large scale of the objects. As the threats to IoT devices are increasing and the security metrics are based on the developmental aspects of software as well as network, the hackers can expand control and carry out malicious activities and attacks on other devices close to the compromised one. Due to the natural significance of the low-power and low-memory nature of these devices, these devices do not have malware protection or virus protection software. The cognitive approach to the IoT provides connectivity to everyone and everything since IoT connected devices are known to increase rapidly. When the IoT is integrated with cognitive technology, performance is improved, and smart intelligence is obtained. Different types of datasets with structured content are discussed based on cognitive systems. The IoT gathers the information from the real-time datasets through the internet, where the IoT network connects with multiple devices.

This book mainly concentrates on providing the best solutions to existing real-time issues in the cognitive domain. Healthcare-based, cloud-based and smart transportation-based applications in the cognitive domain are addressed. The data integrity and security aspects of the cognitive computing domain are also thoroughly discussed along with validated results.

Editors
Kolla Bhanu Prakash
G. R. Kanagachidambaresan
V. Srikanth
E. Vamsidhar

Acknowledgment

We would like to thank the Almighty and our parents for their endless support, guidance and love throughout all the stages of our lives. We are grateful to our beloved family members for standing beside us throughout our careers, which are advanced with the editing of this book.

We would especially like to thank Sri. Koneru Satyanarayana, president of K.L. University, India, and Vel Tech Rangarajan Dr.Sagunthala R&D Institute of Science and Technology for their continuous support and encouragement throughout the preparation of this book. We dedicate this book to them.

Many thanks go to our students and family members who have put in their time and effort to support and contribute in some manner. We would like to express our gratitude to all who supported, shared, talked things over, read, wrote, offered comments, allowed us to quote their remarks and assisted in the editing, proofreading and design of this book throughout the journey to its completion. We also give our sincere thanks to the open dataset providers.

We believe that the team of authors provided the perfect blend of knowledge and skills that went into authoring this book. We thank each of the authors for devoting their time, patience, perseverance and effort towards this book; we think that it will be a great asset to all researchers in this field!

We are grateful to Martin Scrivener and all other members of the publishing team, who showed us the ropes to creating a book. Without that knowledge we would not have ventured into such a project. Their trust in us, guidance and the necessary time and resources afforded us, gave us the freedom to manage this book.

Last, but definitely not least, we'd like to thank our readers, and we hope our work inspires and guides them.

Editors
Kolla Bhanu Prakash
G. R. Kanagachidambaresan
V. Srikanth
E. Vamsidhar

Introduction to Cognitive Computing

Vamsidhar Enireddy*, Sagar Imambi† and C. Karthikeyan‡

Department of Computer Science and Engineering, Koneru Lakshmaiah Education Foundation, Guntur, India

Abstract

Cognitive computing is an interdisciplinary subject that brings under its umbrella several techniques such as Machine learning, big data analytics, artificial intelligence, analytics, natural language processing, and probability and statistics to gather information and understand it using different senses and learning from their experience. Cognitive computing helps humans in taking the right decisions at a right time helping the people to grow in their respective fields. In this chapter, we are going to discuss cognitive computing and the elements involved in it. Further, we will learn about the components and hypothesis generation and scoring of it.

Keywords: Artificial intelligence, cognition, cognitive computing, corpus, intuitive thinking, hypothesis generation, machine learning

1.1 Introduction: Definition of Cognition, Cognitive Computing

The term Cognition is defined as "The procedure or the method of acquiring information and understanding through experience, thought and the senses" [1]. It envelops numerous parts of procedures and intellectual functions, for example, development of information, thinking, reasoning, attention, decision making, evaluating the decisions, problem-solving, computing techniques, judging and assessing, critical thinking, conception,

*Corresponding author: enireddy.vamsidhar@gmail.com

†Corresponding author: simambi@gmail.com

‡Corresponding author: ckarthik2k@gmail.com

Kolla Bhanu Prakash, G. R. Kanagachidambaresan, V. Srikanth, E. Vamsidhar (eds.) Cognitive Engineering for Next Generation Computing: A Practical Analytical Approach, (1–48) © 2021 Scrivener Publishing LLC

and creation of language. This process produces new information using existing information. A large number of fields especially psychology, neuroscience, biology, philosophy, psychiatry, linguistics, logic, education, anesthesia, and computer science view and analyze the cognitive processes with a diverse perspective contained by dissimilar contexts [2].

The word cognition dates to the 15th century, derived from a Latin word where it meant "thinking and awareness" [3]. The term comes from cognitio which means "examination, learning or knowledge", derived from the verb cognosco, a compound of con ('with'), and gnōscō ('know'). The latter half, gnōscō, itself is a cognate of a Greek verb, gi(g)nósko (γι(γ)νώσκω, 'I know', or 'perceive') [4, 5].

Aristotle is probably the first person who has shown interest to study the working of the mind and its effect on his experience. Memory, mental imagery, observation, and awareness are the major areas of cognition, hence Aristotle also showed keen interest in their study. He set incredible significance on guaranteeing that his examinations depended on exact proof, that is, logical data that is assembled through perception and principled experimentation [6]. Two centuries later, the basis for current ideas of comprehension was laid during the Enlightenment by scholars, like, John Locke and Dugald Stewart who tried to build up a model of the psyche in which thoughts were obtained, recalled, and controlled [7].

As Derived from the Stanford Encyclopedia of Philosophy the Cognitive science can be defined as "Cognitive science is the interdisciplinary study of mind and intelligence, embracing philosophy, psychology, artificial intelligence, neuroscience, linguistics, and anthropology."

The approach for cognitive computing depends on understanding the way how the human brain can process the information. The main theme or idea of a cognitive system is that it must able to serve as an associate for the human's rather than simply imitating the capabilities of the human brain.

1.2   Defining and Understanding Cognitive Computing

Cognitive computing can be defined as hardware and software to learn so that they need not be reprogrammed and automate the cognitive tasks [11]. This technology brings under its cover many different technologies such as Artificial Intelligence, Machine Learning, Advanced Analytics, Natural Language Processing, Big Data Analytics, and Distributed Computing. The impact of this technology can be seen in health care, business, decision making, private lives, and many more.

Two disciplines are brought together with cognitive computing

    i.   Cognitive Science
   ii.   Computer Science.

The term cognitive science refers to the science of mind and the other is a computational approach where the theory is put into practice.

The ultimate objective of cognitive computing is that it must able to replicate the human thinking ability in a computer model. Using technologies like machine learning, natural language processing, advanced analytics, data mining, and statistics had made these things possible where the working of the human brain can be mimicked [8].

From a long back, we can construct the computers which perform the calculations at a high speed, also able to develop supercomputers which can do calculations in a fraction of second, but they are not able to perform the tasks as humans do like the reasoning, understanding and recognizing the objects and images.

Cognitive researchers discover the mental capability of humans through an examination of the aspects like memory, emotion, reasoning, perception, and language [12]. Figure 1.1 shows the Human centered cognitive cycle. On analysis, the human being's cognitive process can be divided into two stages. One is the humans use their sensory organs to perceive the information about their surrounding environment and become aware of

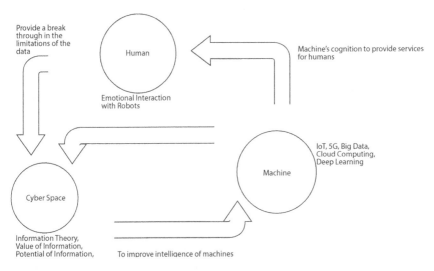

Figure 1.1 Human-centered cognitive cycle.

it, in this manner humans gather the input from the outside environment. The second stage is that this information is carried by the nerves to the brain for processing and the process of storing, analyzing, and learning takes place [13].

Many researchers and scientists from many years had tried to develop the systems that can mimic the human thoughts and process, but it is relatively complex to transform the intricacy of thinking of humans and actions into systems. Human beings have a lot of influence on them such as perception, culture, sentiment, lifestyle, and implicit beliefs about their surrounding environment. Cognition is the basic framework that not only leverages the way we imagine but also the way we behave and the way we make decisions. To understand this let us consider some examples that we see around us. Why there are different recommendations and approaches between the treatments for the same disease with different doctors? Why do people with the same background born and brought up in the same family have different views and opinions about the world?

Dr. Daniel Kahneman is a Nobel Prize winner in economic sciences in 2002 had paved a way for the cognitive computing approach. He had made a lot of research in the area of psychology of judgment and decision making [11]. The approach is divided into two systems: 1. Intuitive thinking and 2. Controlled andrulecentric thinking.

System 1: Intuitive thinking

In this system, reasoning occurs in the human brain naturally. The conclusions are drawn using our instincts. In System 1 human thinking begins the moment they are born. Humans learn to notice and recognize the things and their relationship by themselves. To illustrate this we consider some examples for better understanding. The children correlate their parent's voices with safety. People correlate strident sound with danger. At the same time, we can see that children with a harsh mother are not going to have a similar experience with the voice of the mother as the child with a good mother. Humans learn more things over time and continue assimilating their thoughts into their mode of working in the world. The chess grandmaster can play the game with their mind anticipating their opponent's move and also they can play the game entirely in their mind without any need to touch the chessboard. The surrounding environment plays a major role in a person's behavior, it affects their emotions and attitudes. A person brought up in treacherous surroundings, have a different attitude about the people compared to a person brought up in healthy surroundings. In System1 using the perception, we gather the data about the world and connect the events. In the cognitive computing point of view, this System 1 had taught the way how we gather information from the surroundings helps us to conclude. Figure 1.2 shows collaboration between the Intuitive thinking and analysis.

System 2: Controlled and rulecentric thinking.

In this process, the reasoning is based on an additional premeditated process. This conclusion is made by taking into consideration both observations and test assumptions, rather than simply what is understood. In this type of system the thinking process to get a postulation, it uses a simulation model and observes the results of that particular statement. To do this a lot of data is required and a model is built to test the perceptions made by System 1. Consider the treatment of cancer patients in which a large number of ways and drugs are available to treat the patients. The cancer drugs not only kill the cancer cells but also kill the healthy cells, making the patient feel the side effects of it. When a drug company comes with any novel drug it tests on animals, records its results, and then it is tested on humans. After a long verification of the data checking the side effects of the drug on the other parts of the body, the government permits to release the drug into the market where it takes a long time from research to availability of that drug. In System 1 when a drug can destroy the cancer cells it determines it can be put onto the market. It is completely biased. System 2 will not conclude as of System 1, it collects the data from various sources, refines it, and then it comes to a conclusion. Although this process is slow it is important to study all the things before jumping to a conclusion. One

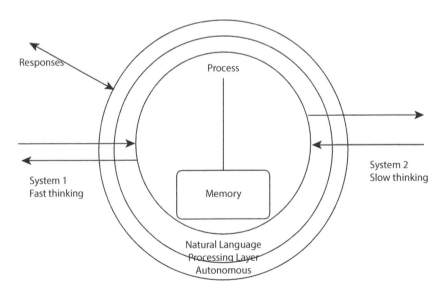

Figure 1.2 Intuitive thinking and analysis [11].

of the most complex problems is predicting the outcomes as many factors can affect the outcomes. So, it is very important to merge the spontaneous thinking with the computational models.

The cognitive system is based on three important principles

1. Learn
2. Model
3. Hypothesis generation.

1. Learn: The cognitive framework must be able to learn. The framework use information to make inductions about an area, a theme, an individual, or an issue dependent on preparing and perceptions from all assortments, volumes, and speed of information.
2. Model: To learn, the framework it requires to make a model or portrayal of a domain which incorporates interior and conceivably exterior information and presumptions that direct what realizing calculations are utilized. Understanding the setting of how the information fits into the model is critical to a cognitive framework.
3. Generate hypotheses: A cognitive framework expects that there will be several solutions or answers to a question. The most fitting answer depends on the information itself. In this way, an intellectual framework is probabilistic. A theory is an up-and-comer clarification for a portion of the information previously comprehended. A cognitive framework utilizes the information to prepare, test, or score speculation.

1.3   Cognitive Computing Evolution and Importance

The basis for cognitive computing is artificial intelligence. Artificial Intelligence has roots back at least 300 years ago, but in the last 50 years, there is much research and improvement in this field which has impacted the development of cognitive computing. The combined work of the mathematicians and scientists in converting the working of a brain into a model such that it mimics the working of the brain, but it has taken a long time to make them work and think like a human brain. During WW-II England has achieved victory due to the decoding of the messages of the opponent and this is achieved by the great work of Alan Turing who worked on the cryptography. Later Turing worked on machine learning and published a paper "Computing Machinery and Intelligence" in which he put up a question "Can machines think", he greatly believed that machines can think and also throw away the argument that the machines cannot think as they do not have any emotions like the human beings. In the later years, he came up with the famous Turing test to prove that machines can think as human beings do. From ten many scientists had contributed to the development of artificial intelligence and can be termed as modern artificial intelligence. The cognitive computing is still evolving. Figure 1.3 shows how the evolution of Cognitive Computing had taken place over the years.

The main focus of cognitive computing is on processing methods, here the data that is to be processed need not be big. The most important thing in understanding the working of the brain is how a brain can decode the image and it is well known that 20% of the brain working function is allocated for the vision and the working of the brain in the image processing is highly efficient. The brain can do things with limited data and even the limited memory is not affecting the cognition of image information. Cognitive science helps to develop the algorithms required for cognitive computing, making the machines to function like a human brain to some degree of extending [14]. The only way to build up the computers to compute as a human brain is to understand and cognize the things and surroundings in the perspective of how a human brain thinks. The cognitive computing is very much important and critical to building up the cognition of a machine and thereby making it to understand the requirements of humans [15]. There is a necessity to make the machines think like humans and they must be able to make decisions and have some intelligence as of humans, of course, a lot of improvement is to be made in this field. With the help of the present techniques, it is possible to make machines think like humans, as they involve reasoning, understanding complicated emotions.

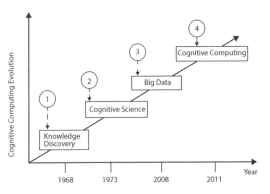

Figure 1.3 Showing the evolution of Cognitive Computing [13].

Cognitive computing had made tremendous progress and also exceeded the conventional machine learning. Internet of Things is one technology that had made very good progress and helping the people in many ways and now IoT is embedded with cognitive computing developing a smarter Internet of Things systems assisting the humans in many ways like providing vital suggestions and helping in the decision making [16].

In today's world with a lot of sensors around a lot of data is being generated all the time in many forms. The evolution of cognitive computing is to make a sense in this multifaceted world with this large volume of data. The older technologies have been developed to make sense with the structured data and machines, software is also developed to deal with such type of data and gathering information from the structured data. The growth of social site and apps have impacted the growth in the unstructured and semi-structured data and these older technologies are no more a way to handle these types of data and the cognitive computing helps in gathering the information from all types of data Unstructured, Semi-structured, and Structured data. Without the handling of these different types of data, a lot of information can be missed and the cognitive computing is going to help the humans to collaborate with the machines so that a maximum gain can be extracted from them. In the past also we have seen the technology had transformed the industries and also the human way of living from the last decades. Transactional processing had started in the 1950s had brought a lot of transformation in government operations and also in business transactions, giving a lot of efficient ways to deal with the operations. During that time the data was limited and major data is structured data and tools are developed to handle this type of data and many mining tools are developed to extract the information from that data. A large amount of data cannot be handled by the traditional tools and methods, so we need a mixture of traditional methods with traditional technical models with the innovations to solve the niggling problems.

1.4   Difference Between Cognitive Computing and Artificial Intelligence

Although it was stated that the foundation for cognitive computing is artificial intelligence there is a lot of difference between the two.

The basic use of artificial intelligence is to solve the problem by implementing the best algorithm, but cognitive computing is entirely different from artificial intelligence as cognitive computing adds the reasoning, intelligence to the machine and also analyzes different factors to solve the problem.

Artificial Intelligence mimics the human intelligence in machines. This process comprises making the machines learn constantly with the changing data, making sense of the information, and taking decisions including the self-corrections whenever needed.

Human beings use the senses to gather information about the surrounding environment and process that information using the brain to know about the environment. In this context, we can define that artificial intelligence can also include replicating the human senses such as hearing, smelling, touching, seeing, and tasting. It also includes simulating the learning process and this is made possible in the machines using machine learning and deep learning. Last but not least is human responses achieved through the robotics [18].

The cognitive computing is used to understand and simulate the reasoning and human behavior. Cognitive Computing assists humans to take better decisions in their respective fields. Their applications are fraud detection, face and emotion detection, sentiment analysis, risk analysis, and speech recognition [17].

The main focus of cognitive computing includes

    i.   To solve complex problems by mimicking human behavior and reasoning.
   ii.   Trying to replicate the humans in solving the problems
  iii.   Assists the human in taking decisions and do not replace humans at all.

Artificial Intelligence focus includes

    i.   To solve complex problems it augments human thinking, it tries to provide accurate results.
   ii.   It tries to find new methods to solve problems which can potentially be superior to humans
  iii.   The main intent of AI is to solve the problem utilizing the best algorithm and not simply mimicking the human brain.
  iv.   The human role is minimized in taking the decisions and artificial intelligence takes over the responsibility.

The main advantage that needs to be highlighted is that Cognitive Computing does not pose any threat to humans. Cognitive computing helps in assisting human beings in taking better decisions in their tasks, endowing human beings with high precision in analyzing the things, same time having everything under their control. In the case of the health care system, cognitive computing assists the specialists in the diagnosis of the disease using the data and advanced analytics, by which it helps to take quality decisions by the doctors [10]. In Figure 1.4 we can see the growth of Cognitive Computing in various continents. In Figure 1.5 we can see the growth of revenue in the various locations of the world.

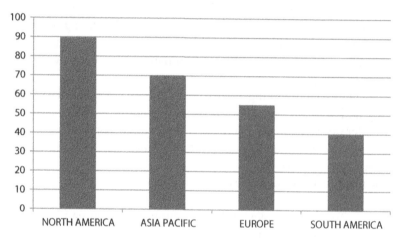

Figure 1.4 Global cognitive market [17].

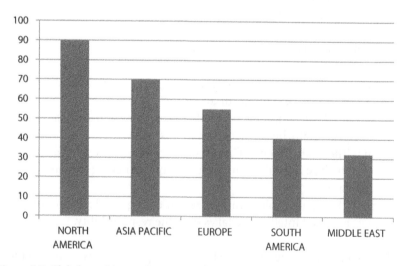

Figure 1.5 Global cognitive market revenue, by geography [17].

1.5   The Elements of a Cognitive System

Several different elements constitute the cognitive system, starting from hardware and operational prototypes to modern machine learning algorithms and applications. Figure 1.6 gives a general design for building a cognitive system.

1.5.1   Infrastructure and Deployment Modalities

The system needs to meet the demands of the industries as they continuously grow and the infrastructure should be flexible to carry on the applications required for the industry. A large amount of data is required to be processed and managed; this data consists of both public and private data. Cloud infrastructure services are required and constant support should be given, providing a highly parallel and distributed computing environment.

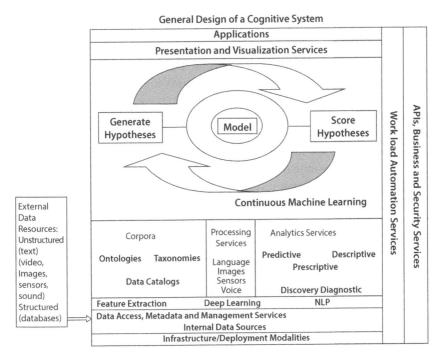

Figure 1.6 The general design of a cognitive system [11].

1.5.2   Data Access, Metadata, and Management Services

Data is the most important point where cognitive computing revolves around, so the data collection, accession, and maintaining it must have a very important role. A lot of essential services are required for adding the data and also using it. To ingest the data utmost care should be taken to check the source from which the data is originated. As a result, there is a requirement that data should be classified based on the origin of data, as it is required to check the data source was trusted or not. The most important thing to learn here is that the data is not static as it is required to update the data from the sources and upload it into the systems. The corpus is the one that holds the data and it relies on various internal and external sources. As a large data is available, a check should be done on data sources, data should be verified, cleaned, and check for accuracy so that it can be added into the corpus. This is a mammoth task as it requires a lot of management services to prepare the data.

1.5.3   The Corpus, Taxonomies, and Data Catalogs

Firmly connected with the information access and the other executive layer are the corpus and data analytics administrations. A corpus is the information base of ingested information and is utilized to oversee classified information. The information required to build up the area for the framework is incorporated in the corpus. Different types of information are ingested into the framework. In numerous cognitive frameworks, this information will principally be text-based (records, patient data, course books, client reports, and such). Other cognitive frameworks incorporate numerous types of unstructured and semi-structured information, (for example, recordings, pictures, sensors, and sounds). What's more, the corpus may incorporate ontologies that characterize explicit elements and their connections. Ontologies are regularly evolved by industry gatherings to arrange industry-specific components, for example, standard synthetic mixes, machine parts, or clinical maladies and medicines. In a cognitive framework, it is frequently important to utilize a subset of an industry-based ontology to incorporate just the information that relates to the focal point of the cognitive framework. A taxonomy works inseparably with ontologies. It also provides a background contained by the ontology.

1.5.4   Data Analytics Services

These are the methods used to increase the comprehension of the information ingested and managed inside the corpus. Ordinarily, clients can take a bit of leeway of structured, unstructured, and semi-structured information that has been ingested and start to utilize modern calculations to anticipate results, find designs, or decide the next best activities. These administrations don't live in separation. They constantly get to new information from the information get to layer and pull information from the corpus. Various propelled calculations are applied to build up the model for the cognitive framework.

1.5.5   Constant Machine Learning

Machine learning is a strategy that gives the ability to the information to learn without being unequivocally modified. Cognitive frameworks are dynamic. These models are ceaselessly refreshed dependent on new information, examination, and associations. This procedure has two key components: Hypothesis generation and Hypothesis evaluation.

A distinctive cognitive framework utilizes machine learning calculations to construct a framework for responding to questions or conveying insight. The structure requires helping the following characteristics:

1. Access, administer, and evaluate information in the setting.
2. Engender and score different hypotheses dependent on the framework's aggregated information. The framework may produce various potential arrangements to each difficult it illuminates and convey answers and bits of knowledge with related certainty levels.
3. The framework persistently refreshes the model dependent on client associations and new information. A cognitive framework gets more astute after some time in a robotized way.

1.5.6   Components of a Cognitive System

The framework has an interior store of information (the corpus) and also communicates with the exterior surroundings to catch extra information, to possibly refresh external frameworks. Cognitive frameworks may utilize NLP to get text, yet additionally need another handling, profound learning capacities, and instruments to apprehend images, voice, recordings, and position. These handling capacities give a path to the cognitive framework to comprehend information in setting and understand a specific domain area. The cognitive framework creates hypotheses and furnishes elective answers or bits of knowledge with related certainty levels. Also, a cognitive framework should be able to do deep learning that is explicit to branches of knowledge and businesses. The existing pattern of a cognitive framework is an iterative procedure. The iterative procedure requires the amalgamation of best practices of the humans and also training the system with the available data.

1.5.7   Building the Corpus

Corpus can be defined as a machine-readable portrayal of the total record of a specific area or theme. Specialists in an assortment of fields utilize a corpus or corpora for undertakings, for example, semantic investigation to contemplate composing styles or even to decide the credibility of a specific work.

The information that is to be added into the corpus is of different types of Structured, Unstructured, and Semi-structured data. It is here what makes the difference with the normal database. The structured data is the data which have a structured format like rows and column format. The semi-structured data is like the raw data which includes XML, Jason, etc. The unstructured data includes the images, videos, log, etc. All these types of data are included in the corpus. Another problem we face is that the data needs to be updated from time to time. All the information that is to be added into the corpus must be verified carefully before ingesting into it.

In this application, the corpus symbolizes the body of information the framework can use to address questions, find new examples or connections, and convey new bits of knowledge. Before the framework is propelled, in any case, a base corpus must be made and the information ingested. The substance of this base corpus obliges the sorts of issues that can be tackled, and the association of information inside the corpus significantly affects the proficiency of the framework. In this manner, the domain area for the cognitive framework has to be chosen and then the necessary information sources can be collected for building the corpus. A large of issues will arise in building the corpus.

What kinds of issues would you like to resolve? If the corpus is as well barely characterized, you may pass up new and unforeseen insights.

If information is cut from outside resources before ingesting it into a corpus, they will not be utilized in the scoring of hypotheses, which is the foundation of machine learning.

Corpus needs to incorporate the correct blend of applicable information assets that can empower the cognitive framework to convey exact reactions in normal time. When building up a cognitive framework, it's a smart thought to decide in favor of social occasion more information or information because no one can tell when the disclosure of an unforeseen affiliation will lead to significant new information.

Accorded the significance set on obtaining the correct blend of information sources, several inquiries must be tended to right off the bat in the planning stage for this framework:

> Which interior and exterior information sources are required for the particular domain regions and issues to be unraveled? Will exterior information sources be ingested in entire or to some extent?
> How would you be able to streamline the association of information for effective exploration and examination?
> How would you be able to coordinate information over various corpora?
> How would you be able to guarantee that the corpus is extended to fill in information gaps in your base corpus? How might you figure out which information sources need to be refreshed and at what recurrence?

The most critical point is that the decision of which sources to remember for the underlying corpus. Sources running from clinical diaries to Wikipedia may now be proficiently imported in groundwork for the dispatch of the cognitive framework. It is also important that the unstructured data has to be ingested from the recordings, pictures, voice, and sensors. These sources are ingested at the information get to layer (refer figure). Other information sources may likewise incorporate subject-specific organized databases, ontologies, scientific classifications, furthermore, indexes.

On the off chance that the cognitive computing application expects access to exceptionally organized information made by or put away in different frameworks, for example, open or exclusive databases, another structure thought is the amount of that information to import at first. It is additionally essential to decide if to refresh or invigorate the information intermittently, consistently, or in light of a solicitation from the framework when it perceives that more information can assist it with giving better answers.

During the plan period of an intellectual framework, a key thought is whether to build a taxonomy or ontology if none as of now exists for the specific domain. These types of structures not only streamline the activity of the framework, but they also make them more productive. In any case, if the designers are accountable for guaranteeing that an ontology and taxonomy is absolute and fully updated, it might be progressively viable to have the framework constantly assess connections between space components rather than have the originators incorporate that with a hard-coded structure. The performance of the hypothesis generation and scoring solely depend on the data structures that have been chosen in the framework. It is in this manner prudent to demonstrate or reenact regular outstanding tasks at hand during the planning stage before focusing on explicit structures. An information catalog, which incorporates metadata, for example, semantic data or pointers, might be utilized to deal with the basic information all the more productively. The list is, as a deliberation, progressively smaller what's more, for the most part, quicker to control than a lot bigger database it speaks to. In the models and outlines, when alluding to corpora, it ought to be noted that these can be coordinated into a solitary corpus while doing so will help disentangle the rationale of the framework or improves execution. Much like a framework can be characterized as an assortment of littler incorporated frameworks, totaling information from an assortment of corpora brings about a solitary new corpus. Looking after isolated corpora is ordinarily accomplished for execution reasons, much like normalizing tables in a database to encourage inquiries, instead of endeavoring to join tables into a solitary, progressively complex structure.

1.5.8   Corpus Administration Governing and Protection Factors

Information sources and the development of that information are progressively turning out to be intensely managed, especially for by and by recognizable data. Some broad issues of information approach for assurance, security, and consistency are regular to all applications, however, cognitive computing applications be trained and infer new information or information that may likewise be dependent upon a developing collection of state, government, furthermore, global enactment.

At the point when the underlying corpus is created, almost certainly, a ton of information will be imported utilizing extract–transform–load (ETL) apparatuses. These devices may have risk management, security, and administrative highlights to enable the client to make preparations for information abuse or give direction when sources are known to contain sensitive information. The accessibility of the said instruments doesn't clear the developers from a duty to guarantee that the information and metadata are consistent with material rules and guidelines. Ensured information might be ingested (for instance, individual identifiers) or produced (for instance, clinical findings) when the corpus is refreshed by the cognitive computing framework. Anticipating great corpus the executive sought to incorporate an arrangement to screen applicable strategies that sway information in the corpus. The information gets to layer instruments depicted in the following area must be joined by or implant consistence strategies and techniques to guarantee that imported and determining information and metadata stay consistent. That incorporates the thought of different sending modalities, for example, distributed computing, which may disperse information across geopolitical limits.

1.6   Ingesting Data Into Cognitive System

In contrast to numerous customary frameworks, the information that is added into the corpus is always dynamic, which means that the information should be always updated. There is a need to fabricate a base of information that sufficiently characterizes your domain space and also start filling this information base with information you anticipate to be significant. As you build up the model in the cognitive framework, you refine the corpus. Along these lines, you will consistently add to the information sources, change those information sources, and refine and purge those sources dependent on the model improvement and consistent learning.

1.6.1   Leveraging Interior and Exterior Data Sources

Most associations as of now oversee immense volumes of organized information from their value-based frameworks and business applications, and unstructured information, for example, the text contained in structures or notes and conceivably pictures from archives or then again corporate video sources. Albeit a few firms are composing applications to screen outer sources, for example, news and online life channels, numerous IT associations are not yet well prepared to use these sources and incorporate them with interior information sources. Most subjective registering frameworks will be created for areas that require continuous access to coordinated information from outside the association.

The person figures out how to recognize the correct sources to sustain his statements or his decision, he is normally based on social media, news channels, newspapers, and also on different web resources. Similarly, the cognitive application for the most part needs to get to an assortment of efficient sources to keep updated on the topic on which the cognitive domain operates. Likewise, similar to experts who must adjust the news or information from these exterior sources in opposition to their understanding, a cognitive framework must figure out how to gauge the external proof and create trust in the source and also on the content after some time. For instance, one can find an article related to medicine in a famous magazine, which can be a good source of information but if this article is contrary to an article published in a peer-reviewed journal, then the cognitive system must able to gauge the contradicting positions. The data that has to be ingested into the corpus must be verified carefully. In the above example, we may find that all the information sources that might be helpful ought to be thought of and conceivably ingested. On the other hand, this doesn't imply that all sources will be of equivalent worth.

Consider the case of the healthcare in which we can see that an average person meets several doctors or specialists for any health issue. A large number of records will be generated each time he meets the doctors, so Electronic Medical Records (EMRs) help to place all the records in one place and also help to refer them whenever required and doctors can map easily on verifying these records. This helps the specialist to find the association between the blends of side effects and disorders or infections that would be missed if a specialist or scientist approached uniquely to the records from their training or establishment. This cannot be done manually by a person as he may miss or forget to carry all the records with him while meeting the doctor.

A communications organization using the cognitive approach wants to improve its performance to capture or improve their market share. The cognitive system can foresee ant failures in the machine by calculating the inner variables, for example, traffic and traditional patterns; they also calculate the external components, for example, extreme climate threats that are probably going to cause over-burdens and also substantial damage.

1.6.2   Data Access and Feature Extraction

In the diagram data access level has portrayed the principle interface connecting the cognitive system and the external world. Any information that is needed has to be imported from outer sources has to go through the procedures inside this layer. All types of structured, semi-structured, and unstructured data are required for the cognitive application is collected from different resources, and this information is arranged for processing using the machine learning algorithms. To put an analogy to the human way of learning is that it represents the senses. There are two tasks that the feature extraction layer needs to complete. One is identifying the significant information and the second is to extract the information so that it can be processed by the machine learning algorithms. Consider for instance with image processing application where the image representation is in pixels and it does not completely represent an object in the image. We need to represent the things in a meaningful manner as in the case of the medical images, where a dog or dog scan is not useful to the veterinary doctor until the essential structure is captured, identified, and represented. Using Natural Language Processing the meaning in the unstructured text can be identified. The corpus is dynamic hence the data is added or removed from it constantly by using the hypotheses score.

1.7   Analytics Services

The term Analytics alludes to an assortment of procedures used to discover and provide details regarding fundamental qualities or associations inside a dataset. These techniques are very helpful in guiding us by providing knowledge about data so that a good decision can be taken based on the insights. Algorithms such as regression analysis are most widely used to find the solutions. In cognitive systems, a wide scope of sophisticated analytics is accessible for descriptive, predictive, and prescriptive tasks in many commercial library packages in the statistical software. In further to support the cognitive systems tasks a large number of supporting tools are available. In the present time analytics role in the market has changed a lot. Table 1.1 gives us a view of the analytics role that many organizations are experiencing. These analytics helps to learn and understand things from the past and thereby predict future outcomes. Most of the data collected from the past are utilized by business analytics and data scientists to come up with a good prediction. The main important thing in these days is that the technology is growing and it is meeting all levels of the people in the whole world and world has itself become a small global village due to the information technology, so the organizations should learn that they are many dynamic changes in the behavior and taste of the people. Using the advanced analytics it is necessary to build better predictive models so that for any small change in the trade environment these models can react to them.

Figure 1.7 gives a brief look at how analytics and artificial intelligence technologies are converged. In the competitive world, operational changes and planning should be done at a quick rate to survive in the market. A decision should be taken fast and it can happen when the tools used for the prediction can give us a result in no time otherwise it may become a disaster for the company if it takes decisions a late as the competitor can overtake the market within no time. Many big and reliable companies have lost the market for taking late decisions it has happened in the past and can happen in the future also. For instance, consider a client relationship

Table 1.1 Different types of analytics and their examples [11].

S. no.	Analytics type	Description	Examples
1	Descriptive Analytics	Realize what transpires when using analytic procedures on past and present data.	Which item styles are selling better this quarter as analyzed to last quarter? Which districts are displaying the most elevated/least development? What components are affecting development in various areas?
2	Predictive Analytics	Comprehend what may happen when utilizing statistical predictive modeling capabilities, that includes both data mining and AI. Predictive models use past and current data to forecast forthcoming outcomes. Models search for patterns, clusters of behavior, and events. Models recognize outliers.	What are the forecasts for next quarter's sales by items and territory? How does this affect unprocessed acquisitions, human resources and inventory Management?

(Continued)

Table 1.1 Different types of analytics and their examples [11]. (*Continued*)

S. no.	Analytics type	Description	Examples
3	Prescriptive Analytics	Use to create a framework for deciding what to do or not do in the future. The "prescient" component ought to be tended to in prescriptive examination to help recognize the overall outcomes of your activities. Utilize an iterative procedure so that your model can gain from the relationship among activities and results	What is the best blend of items for every locale? In What Way the consumers in each zone respond to marketing promotions and deals? What type of the offer ought to be made to each client to fabricate dependability and increment deals?
4	Machine Learning and Cognitive Computing	A coordinated effort among people and machines to take care of complicated issues. Incorporate and evaluate different sources of data to anticipate results. Need relies upon the issues you are attempting to understand. Improve adequacy of critical thinking and decrease blunders in predicting outcomes.	In What Manner the city environment is secure? Are there any cautions from the immense the measure of data spilling from checking gadgets (video, sound, and detecting gadgets for smoke or harmful gases)? Which blend of drugs will furnish the best result for a particular cancer patient based on precise attributes of the tumor and genetic sequencing?

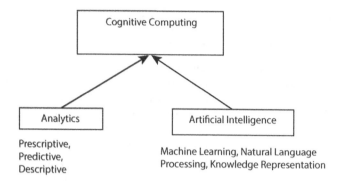

Figure 1.7 Figure showing the convergence of technologies.

application in which the customer calls the executive for some reason, and in this interaction, with the customer, the executive must clear the doubts of the client and satisfy him by deciding in a short time. This helps the organization to retain the customer and helps to add more clients to them when the service provided to them is done in no time. The problem is that there is a large amount of data available and to process it also is difficult. As the data contains structured, semi-structured, and unstructured a large number of analytical models are need to be incorporated so that the prediction can be improved.

1.8 Machine Learning

Machine learning is the logical control that rose out of the general field of Artificial Intelligence. It is an interdisciplinary field where insights and information speculations are applied to discover the connections among the information and to build up programs by adapting consequently without human intercession. This procedure looks like the human learning process. Analysts are as yet attempting to make machines smart and act like people. This learning procedure begins with accessible information. Information assumes an essential job in the machine learning process. ML is also being utilized for information examination, such as identifying regularities in the information by fittingly managing incomplete information and the transformation of constant information.

Machine learning is multidisciplinary and is a subset of AI. However, it additionally consolidates the methods from statistics, control hypothesis, Cognitive Science as shown in Figure 1.8. The subsequent explanation is the exponential development of both accessible information and computer

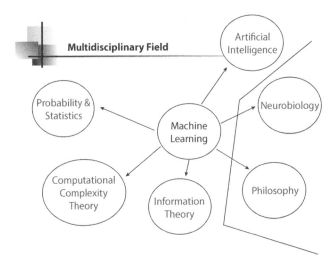

Figure 1.8 Machine learning.

processing power. The order of AI additionally joins other information investigation disciplines like data mining, probability and statistics, computational complexity theory, Neurobiology, philosophy, and Information theory.

Cognitive computing models use machine learning techniques dependent on inferential insights to identify or find designs that direct their behavioral patterns. Picking the fundamental learning way to deal with model recognition versus disclosure of examples ought to be founded on the available information and nature of the issues to be unraveled. AI regularly utilizes inferential insights (the reason for prescient, instead of precise examination) methods.

One of the more important uses of AI is to mechanize the procurement of information bases utilized by supposed master frameworks, which plans to imitate the dynamic procedure of human aptitude in a field. Be that as it may, the extent of its application has been developing.

The significant methodologies incorporate utilizing neural systems, case-based learning, hereditary calculations, rule enlistment, and analytical learning. While in the past they were applied autonomously, as of late these ideal models or models are being utilized in a crossbreed design, shutting the limits among them and empowering the improvement of increasingly compelling models. The blend of analytical techniques can guarantee compelling and repeatable and reliable outcomes, a necessary part for practical use in standard business and industry arrangements.

1.9 Machine Learning Process

1.9.1 Data Collection

- The quantity and quality of data decide how our model performs. The gathered data is represented in a format which is further used in training
- We can also get preprocessed data from Kaggle, UCI, or from any other public datasets.

1.9.2 Data Preparation

Data preparation of machine learning process includes

- Arranging information and set it up for preparing.
- The cleaning process includes removing duplicate copies, handling mistakes, managing missing qualities, standardization, information type changes, and so on.
- Randomizing information, which eradicates the impacts of the specific samples wherein we gathered or potentially, in any case, arranged our information.
- Transforming information to identify pertinent connections between factors or class labels and characteristics (predisposition alert!), or perform other exploratory examination.
- Splitting data set into training and test data sets for learning and validating process.

1.9.3 Choosing a Model

Choosing the model is crucial in the machine learning process as the different algorithms are suitable for different tasks. Choosing an appropriate algorithm is a very important task.

1.9.4 Training the Model

- The goal of training is to learn from data and use it to predict unseen data. For example in Linear, the regression algorithm would need to learn values for m (or W) and b (x is input, y is output)

- In each iteration of the process, the model trains and improves its efficiency.

1.9.5   Evaluate the Model

Model evaluation is done by a metric or combination of metrics and measures the performance of the model. The performance of the model is tested against previously unknown data. This unknown data may be from the real world and used to measure the performance and helps in tuning the model. Generally, the train and the split ratio is 80/20 or 70/30 depending on the data availability.

1.9.6   Parameter Tuning

This progression alludes to *hyperparameter* tuning, which is a "fine art" instead of a science. Tune the model boundaries for improved execution. Straightforward model hyperparameters may include the number of preparing steps, learning rate, no of epochs, and so forth.

1.9.7   Make Predictions

Utilizing further (test set) information which has, until this point, been retained from the model (and for which class names are known), are utilized to test the model; a superior estimate of how the model will act in reality.

1.10   Machine Learning Techniques

Machine learning comes in many different zests, depending on the algorithm and its objectives. The learning techniques are broadly classified into 3 types, Supervised learning, unsupervised, and reinforcement learning. Machine learning can be applied by specific learning strategies, such as:

1.10.1   Supervised Learning

It is a machine learning task of inferring function from labeled data. The model relies on pre-labeled data that contains the correct label for each input as shown in Figure 1.9. A supervised algorithm analyses the training example and produce an inferred function that can be used for mapping new examples. It is like learning with a teacher. The training data set is considered as a teacher. The teacher gives good examples for the student to

Supervise Learning Process: Two Steps

Learning(Training): Learn a model using the training data

Testing: Test the model using unseen test data to assess the model accuracy

$$Accuracy = \frac{No.\ of\ correct\ classifications}{Total\ no\ of\ test\ cases}$$

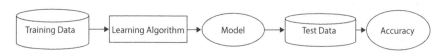

Figure 1.9 Supervised model.

memorize, and guide the student to derive general rules from these specific examples.

In the Supervised learning technique, an algorithm learns from historical data and the related target labels which may consist of numeric values or string, as classes. And the trained model predicts the correct label when given with new examples.

The supervised approach is generally similar to human learning under the supervision of a teacher. There is a need to distinguish between regression problems, whose target is a numeric value, and classification problems, whose target is a qualitative variable, such as a class or a tag. A regression task determines the average prices of houses in the Boston area, and a classification task distinguishes between kinds of iris flowers based on their sepal and petal measures. A supervised strategy maps the data inputs and models them against desired outputs.

The supervised learning technique can be further divided into regression and classification problems.

- *Classification*: In the classification problem, the output variable is a category, such as "red" or "blue" or "disease" and "no disease". Classification emails into 'spam' or 'not spam' is another example.
- *Regression*: In the regression problem, the output variable is a real value, such as "price" or "weight" or "sales".

Some famous examples of supervised machine learning algorithms are: SVM, Bayes, KNN, Random forest, Neural networks, Linear regression, Decision tree, etc.

1.10.2   Unsupervised Learning

An unsupervised strategy used to map the inputs and model them to find new trends. Derivative ones that combine these for a semi-supervised approach and others are also be used. Unsupervised learning is another form of machine learning algorithm which was applied to extract inferences from the large number of datasets consisting of input data without labeled responses.

Unsupervised learning happens when a calculation gains from plain models with no related reaction, leaving for the calculation to decide the information designs all alone. This sort of calculation will, in general, rebuild the information into something different, such as new highlights that may speak to a class or another arrangement of uncorrelated qualities. They are accommodating in giving people bits of knowledge into the significance of information and new valuable contributions to administered machine learning techniques.

The most widely recognized unsupervised learning technique is cluster analysis, which is utilized for exploratory information investigation to discover hidden examples or gathering in the information. It is like learning without a teacher. The machine learns through observation and finds structures in data.

Clustering and Association rule the two techniques that come under unsupervised learning.

Hierarchical clustering, K mean clustering, Markov models.

As a part of learning, it takes after the strategies people use to make sense of those specific articles or occasions are from a similar class, for example, by watching the level of similitude between objects. Some suggestion frameworks that find on the web through promoting robotization depend on this sort of learning.

This opens the entryway onto a huge number of utilizations for which AI can be utilized, in numerous territories, to depict, endorse, and find what is happening inside enormous volumes of assorted information.

1.10.3   Reinforcement Learning

Reinforcement Learning involves the mechanism of reward and punishment for the process of learning. In this type of learning, the objective is to maximize the reward and minimize the punishment. In Reinforcement Learning Errors help you learn because they have a penalty added (cost, loss of time, regret, pain, and so on).

Ex. when computers learn to play video games by themselves.

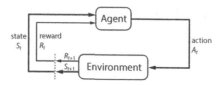

Figure 1.10 Reinforcement learning.

Reinforcement learning is connected to the applications for which the algorithm must make decisions and where the decisions held consequences. In the human world, it is similar to learning by trial and error. In cognitive computing, reinforcement learning is mostly used where numerous variables in the model are difficult to represent and the model has to do a sequence of tasks. For example Self-driving cars.

In reinforcement learning, we have an agent that acts in the environment as shown in Figure 1.10. The agent can take action and this action can impact the environment. In a particular stage, the agent takes an action and the environment goes to a new state and gives some reward to the agent, that reward may be positive can be a negative reward or penalty or can be nothing at that particular time step. But the agent is continually acting in this world.

The model finds a relation between the reward and the sequence of tasks, which lead to getting a reward.

1.10.4   The Significant Challenges in Machine Learning

- Identifying good hypothesis space
- Optimization of accuracy on unknown data
- Insufficient Training Data.

It takes a great deal of information for most Machine Learning calculations to work appropriately. For underlying issues, regularly need a vast number of models, and for complex issues, for example, picture or discourse recognition you may require a great many models.

- Representation of Training Data
  It is critical, to sum up, the preparation of information on the new cases. By utilizing a non-representative preparing set, we prepared a model that is probably not going to make precise forecasts, particularly for poor and rich nations. It is essential to utilize a preparation set that is illustrative of the cases you need to generalize to. This is frequently harder than it sounds:

if the example is excessively small, you will have inspecting clamor. However, even extremely enormous examples can be non-representative of the testing technique is defective. This is called sample data bias.

- Quality of Data

If the preparation of information is loaded with mistakes, exceptions, and clamor it will make it harder for the framework to distinguish the basic examples, so your framework is less inclined to perform well. It is regularly definitely justified even despite the push to invest energy tidying up your preparation information. In all actuality, most information researchers spend a noteworthy piece of their time doing only that. For instance: If a few occurrences are exceptions, it might help to just dispose of them or attempt to fix the blunders physically. If a few examples are feeling the loss of a couple of highlights (e.g., 5% of your clients did not determine their age), you should choose whether you need to overlook this characteristic altogether, disregard these occasions, fill in the missing qualities (e.g., with the middle age), or train one model with the component and one model without it, etc.

- Unimportant Features

The machine learning framework might be fit for learning if the preparation information contains enough significant features and not very many unimportant ones. Now days Feature engineering, became very necessary for developing any type of model. Feature engineering process includes choosing the most helpful features to prepare on among existing highlights, consolidating existing highlights to deliver an increasingly valuable one (as we saw prior, dimensionality decrease calculations can help) and then creating new features by social event new information.

- Overfitting

Overfitting implies that the model performs well on the preparation information, yet it doesn't sum up well. Overfitting happens when the model is excessively mind boggling comparative with the sum and din of the preparation information.

The potential arrangements to overcome the overfitting problem are

- To improve the model by choosing one with fewer boundaries (e.g., a straight model instead of a severe extent polynomial model), by lessening the number of characteristics in the preparation of data.
- To assemble all the more preparing information

- To lessen the commotion in the preparation information (e.g., fix information blunders and evacuate anomalies)
- Constraining a model to make it more straightforward and decrease the danger of overfitting is called regularization.

1.11 Hypothesis Space

A hypothesis is an idea or a guess which needs to be evaluated. The hypothesis may have two values i.e. true or false. For example, "All hibiscus have the same number of petals", is a general hypothesis. In this example, a hypothesis is a testable declaration dependent on proof that clarifies a few watched marvel or connection between components inside a universe or specific space. At the point when a researcher details speculation as a response to an inquiry, it is finished in a manner that permits it to be tested. The theory needs to anticipate a predicted result. The ability to explain the hypothesis phenomenon is increased by experimenting the hypothesis testing. The hypothesis may be compared with the logic theory. For example, "If x is true then y" is a logical statement, here x became our hypothesis and y became the target output.

Hypothesis space is the set of all the possible hypotheses. The machine learning algorithm finds the best or optimal possible hypothesis which maps the target function for the given inputs. The three main variables to be considered while choosing a hypothesis space are the total size of hypothesis space and randomness either stochastic or deterministic. The hypothesis is rejected or supported only after analyzing the data and find the evidence for the hypothesis. Based on data the confidence level of the hypothesis is determined.

In terms of machine learning, the hypothesis may be a model that approximates the target function and which performs mappings of inputs to outputs. But in cognitive computing, it is termed as logical inference. The available data for supporting the hypothesis may not always structured. In real-world applications, the data is mostly unstructured. Figure 1.11 shows an upright pattern of hypothesis generation and scoring. Understanding and traversing through the unstructured information requires a new computing technology which is called cognitive computing. The intellectual frameworks can create different hypotheses dependent on the condition of information in the corpus at a given time. When all the hypotheses are generated then they can be assessed and scored. In the below fig of, IBM's Watson derives the responses questions and score each response. Here 100 autonomous hypothesis might be produced for a question after parsing

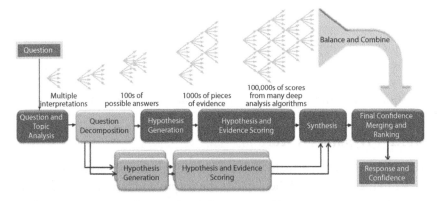

Figure 1.11 Hypotheses generation IBM Watson.

the question and extracting the features of the question. Each generated hypothesis might be scored using the pieces of evidence.

1.11.1   Hypothesis Generation

The hypothesis must be generalized and should map for the unseen cases also. The experiments are developed to test the general unseen case. There are two key ways a hypothesis might be produced in cognitive computing systems. The first is because of an express inquiry from the user, for example, "What may cause my fever and diarrhea?" The system generates all the possible explanations, like flu, COVID where we can see these symptoms. Sometimes the given data is not sufficient and might require some additional input and based on that the system refines the explanations. It might perceive that there are such a large number of answers to be valuable and solicitation more data from the client to refine the arrangement of likely causes.

This way to deal with hypothesis generation is applied where the objective of the model is to recognize the relations between the causes and its effects ex. Medical conditions and diseases. Normally, this kind of psychological framework will be prepared with a broad arrangement of inquiry/answer sets. The model is trained using the available question and answer sets and generates candidate hypotheses.

The second sort of hypothesis generations doesn't rely upon a client inquiring. Rather, the system continually searches for atypical information patterns that may demonstrate threats or openings. In this method, hypotheses are generated by identifying a new pattern. For example to detect unauthorized bank transactions the system generated those fraudulent transaction patterns, which became the hypothesis space. Then the cognitive computing model has to find the evidence to support or reject the hypothesis. The hypothesis space is mostly based on assumptions.

The two kinds of hypothesis generation methods produce at least one theory given an occasion, however in the primary case, the event is a client question, and in the second it is driven by similar pattern data.

1.11.2   Hypotheses Score

The next step is to evaluate or score these hypotheses based on the evidence in the corpus, and then update the corpus and report the findings to the user or another external system. Now, you have perceived how hypotheses are generated and next comes scoring the hypothesis scoring. In the scoring process, the hypothesis is compared with the available data and check whether there is evidence or not. Scoring or assessing a hypothesis is a procedure of applying measurable strategies to the hypothesis evidence sets to dole out a certain level to the theory and find the confidence level to each hypothesis. This confidence level weight might be updated based on the available training data. The threshold score is used to eliminate the unnecessary hypothesis. On the off chance that none of the hypothesis scores over the threshold the system may need more input which may lead to updating the candidate hypothesis. This information may be represented in a matrix format and several tools are available to manipulate these matrices. The scoring process is continued until the machine learns the concept.

1.12   Developing a Cognitive Computing Application

Cognitive computing is evolving at a good pace and in the next decade, a large number of applications can be built using this technology.

The organizations of different sectors are in the premature stages in developing the cognitive applications; its applications are from healthcare to production industries to governments, making a decision using the huge variety and volumes of data. There are some issues to be noted in the process of building the application [11].

a. A good decision can be taken if large volumes of data can be analyzed

b. There will be a change in decisions dynamically with the frequently varying data, obtaining data from the latest sources and also from the other forms of data

c. There should be a transfer of knowledge by the domain experts to the junior trainees through the training and mentoring process.

d. In the process of decision making a large amount of data is analyzed, several options and solutions to a problem are obtained.

To develop the cognitive application the first step is to define the objective, which requires understanding the types of problems the application can solve. It also has to consider the different types of users using the application. The most important thing is that it also has to take care of the types of issues the user is interested in and also what they are looking for and need to know. The next step is to define the domain, it is important because we need to identify and also assess the different data sources that match to build the application. Defining the domain helps to identify the subject experts.

In training the cognitive application the domain helps in identifying the subject experts that will be useful in training the cognitive application. Table 1.2 gives the examples of the Cognitive application domains.

Characterizing Questions and Exploring Insights

The cognitive applications that are developed in the early stages for customer engagement can be divided into two types:

i.   Discovery and Exploration
ii. Using sophisticated question and response mechanisms to
iii. respond to inquiries as part of continuous exchange with the client.

The cognitive framework can build a relationship between questions, answers, and information to enable the client to better grasp the topic at a more profound level. The inquiries clients will pose can be set in two general classifications (Table 1.3):

a. Question–Response pairs: The responses to the inquiries can be unearthed in an information resource. There might be clashing responses inside the information resources, and

Table 1.2 Examples of cognitive application domains [11].

S. no.	Domain	Data requirements to be selected	Subject experts
1	Medical	Electronic medical health records, International classification of diseases (ICD) Codes, Research journals	Experienced specialists, doctors, and specialists.
2	Airplane Manufacturing and Maintenance	List of complete parts, spare parts inventory and maintenance records of each plane	Skilled and qualified technicians, preservation staff, and trained and experienced pilots. These persons are capable of anticipating the failures and fix them
3	Trade	Client and product information	Skilled and qualified Salespersons

Table 1.3 Question–response pairs for different types of users.

S. no.	Question	Answer
1	Health Consumer: What Did You Say about a morcellator	A morcellator is a tool that consists of a spinning blade that is utilized to destroy a fibroid through an opening on a female's stomach. The power and speed of the tool may make cell particles from the fibroid become scattered in the stomach.
2	Gynecologist: What are the consequences and advantages of utilizing a morcellator for careful treatment of fibroids?	Consequences incorporate likely spread of an occult uterine sarcoma. Advantages incorporate little incisions for the patient, lowblood loss, and faster healing and recovery.

the framework will break down the choices to furnish various reactions with related certainty levels.

b. Anticipatory analytics: The client takes part in an exchange with the cognitive application. The client may pose a few inquiries however not all the inquiries. The subjective application will utilize prescient models to envision the client's next inquiry or arrangement of inquiries.

Along with the things we discussed above the following requirements are also needed to build the application

- ➢ Creating and Refining the Corpora
- ➢ Preparing the Data
- ➢ Ingesting the Data
- ➢ Refining and Expanding the Corpora
- ➢ Governance of Data
- ➢ Training and Testing

To understand the way to build a cognitive application here we discuss with the health care application.

1.13   Building a Health Care Application

To develop a cognitive health care application, the system has to incorporate differing associations, where each association commits to growth, funding, service provision, products, and procedures. The listing shows the various group of people required for the system.

i.   Patients
ii.   Health care Practitioners
iii.   Pharmaceutical Companies
iv.   Players
v.   Governance bodies
vi.   Data service providers.

1.13.1   Healthcare Ecosystem Constituents

The Healthcare environment as shown in Figure 1.12 incorporates the information utilized by various constituents and these are:

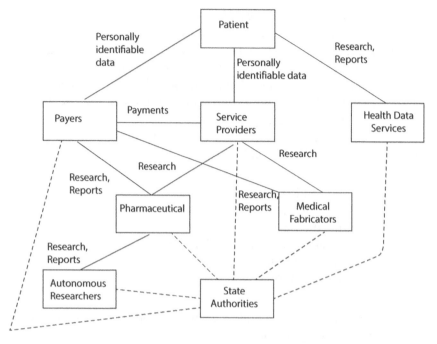

Figure 1.12 Healthcare ecosystem.

i.   Patients: With family backgrounds and research behaviors, people participation in the health care ecosystem creates individually identifiable results Information, which may be anonymously aggregated, if allowed; direct treatment of people with identical qualities.

ii. Providers: Information covers a wide scope of unstructured and organized sources. A few models incorporate patient clinical records (EMR, specialists' office notes, and lab information), information from sensors and clinical gadgets, consumption records from the emergency clinic, clinical course readings, diary articles, clinical exploration examines administrative reports, charging information, and operational cost information.

iii. Pharmaceutical organizations: Data to help research in pharmacy, taking up the clinical trials, testing the drug, and verifying the side effects, competitive information, and prescriptions provided by the clinical suppliers.

iv. Payers: Data incorporates charging information and use audit information.

v. Administrative agencies: Regulating the information.

vi. Data service providers: Taxonomies and ontologies of healthcare terminology, Usage of prescription drugs, and adequacy information providing software to analyze.

1.13.2 Beginning With a Cognitive Healthcare Application

In the previous stages, cognitive healthcare application is based on the cognitive platform. To build up an application you have to start by characterizing your objective clients and afterward train the cognitive framework to address the issues of your client base. The following questions are important to note to develop the application. Define your general branch of knowledge for your application? List out the requirements of the clients and their expectations of the application and also find out the knowledge levels of the clients on this subject?

1.13.3 Characterize the Questions Asked by the Clients

This can be started by collecting the sorts of inquiries that will be posted by a delegate gathering of clients. On collecting this information an information base can be constructed to respond to the inquiries and train the framework successfully. Although you might be enticed to start by looking into information resources, as a result, you can fabricate your insight base or corpus for your framework, best practices demonstrate that you have to make a stride back and characterize your general application technique. The problem to start with corpus is it is likely to aim to the inquiries to sources that have been already assembled. If you start with the corpus, you may discover you can't address the issues of your end clients when you move to an operational state.

These underlying inquiries need to speak to the different kinds of clients that always question the application. What would clients like to ask and by what means will they ask inquiries?

While building the application we need to consider whether it is a consumer-based application utilized by an all-inclusive community of clients, or are you building up a framework that is destined to be utilized by technicians? The future performance of the application depends on gathering the right questions. A large number of these questions and answers pairs should be collected and used in the system as machine learning algorithms are used to train it. We need at least 1,000 to 2,000 question–answer pairs to kick start the procedure. The subject expert's help should be taken and the questions are posed by the clients using their voice to the system.

1.13.4   Creating a Corpus and Ingesting the Content

The corpus gives the base of information utilized by the psychological application to respond to questions and give reactions to inquiries. All the reports the cognitive application needs to access will be remembered for the corpus. The Q–A sets you have made assistance to drive the way toward gathering the content. By starting with the inquiries, you have a superior thought of the substance that will be required to fabricate the corpus. List the contents required to answer the questions precisely? All the resources required for answering the questions are needed to be identified and should be added to the corpus. For instance, these resources include research articles, medical textbooks, pharmaceutical research data, ontologies, taxonomies, health dictionaries, clinical studies, and patients' records.

1.13.5   Training the System

To train the system the key point is analyzing the question and answer pairs. Even though it is significant for delegate clients to produce inquiries, specialists need to produce the appropriate responses and settle the inquiry/answer sets. The inquiries should be predictable with the degree of information on the end client. In any case, the specialists need to guarantee that the appropriate responses are exactly what's more, following the substance in the corpus. Table 1.4 gives you an example that covers some questions or inquires. The system learns from the questions.

Table 1.4 Sample questions to train the application [11].

S. no.	Question
1	What is the difference between whole and skim milk?
2	Is low-fat milk unique with whole milk?
3	Which is better skim milk or whole milk?

1.13.6   Applying Cognition to Develop Health and Wellness

The main challenging task is that these applications don't generally give the customized reactions and motivating forces that their individuals need to change conduct and optimize the results. The compensation of helping people to shed weight, increment work out, eat a well-balanced diet, quit smoking, and make sound decisions generally is immense.

Medicinal services payers, governments, and associations all get an advantage if communities are healthy and people able to manage recently analyzed conditions. These conditions are premature death, Diabetics, High blood pressure, Heart disease, stroke, high cholesterol, hypertension, sleep apnea, Asthma, Osteoarthritis, Gall bladder disease, and certain types of cancer. Discovering approaches to improve the associations and correspondence of people and the medicinal services is a need for various developing organizations.

1.13.7   Welltok

It has developed a proficient healthcare concierge—CaféWell—that keeps in touch with the clients and updates their relevant health information by processing a vast amount of medical data. This is a health tool used by insurance providers to provide relevant information to their customers to improve their health. This application is smart in answering the queries of the clients and it gathers the information from various sources and offers customized heath proposals to their clients to improve their health (Figure 1.13), (Table 1.5).

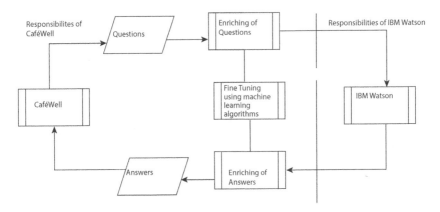

Figure 1.13 Welltok training architecture [11].

Table 1.5 Sample of Welltok question/answer pairs [11].

S. no.	Question	Answer
1	What are some way of life changes that I ought to make on the off chance if I have high blood pressure?	Way of life changes is similarly as significant as taking prescriptions. Lessening your weight by only 10 pounds might be sufficient to bring down your blood pressure. Shedding weight can assist with upgrading the impacts of high blood pressure prescription and may likewise decrease other risk factors, such as diabetes and high bad cholesterol
	How can you decide about the calories burned by the body?	Basal Metabolic Rate (BMR) is calculated using the Harris–Benedict equation. This equation use3 variables: weight, height, and age to calculate the total energy expenditure by multiplying BMR by an activity factor. **Equation For Men:** BMR = 88.362 + (13.397 × weight in kg) + (4.799 × height in cm) – (5.677 × age in years)
	Do my dietary needs differ all through life?	Dietary needs change all through life. From early stages through adulthood, great nourishment is fundamental to growth and development, and to keeping up wellbeing in the later years.
	For what reason should I read the labels on packaged foods? Particularly on a low-sodium diet, you have to take a gander at the food name to constrain sodium admission.	Almost all of the packaged foods have a list of ingredients and their nutrition. In the United States, Food and Drug Administration (FDA) look over the nutrition fact of a processed food using the food label. The reason for this is to assist the buyers with making fast, informed food decisions that add to a healthy diet. Particularly on a low-sodium diet, you have to take a gander at the food name to constrain sodium intake.

(Continued)

Table 1.5 Sample of Welltok Question/Answer Pairs [11]. (*Continued*)

S. no.	Question	Answer
	I have a grain hypersensitivity, what food would it be advisable for me to stay away from? What sort of food are considered grains?	Any food produced using wheat, rice, oats, cornmeal, grain, or another oat grain is a grain item. Bread, pasta, cereal, breakfast oats, tortillas, and cornmeal are instances of grain items. There are entire grains, containing the grain piece, also, refined grains, which have been processed to evacuate bran and germ. There are numerous advantages to an eating routine wealthy in grains.

1.13.8   CaféWell Concierge in Action

The intention of this is to assist the people in understanding their health position and guide them with the customized methods to accomplish good health and also encouraging them by giving rewards to them on meeting their goals. Suppose that a person went to a doctor for a diagnosis of diabetics and taken some tests after the examination. After receiving the results doctor advises losing your weight, by changing the diet and also asks to increase the physical activity. On the other hand, your job makes you travel a lot and also making you take the diet in the outside restaurants. You also don't have enough time to increase physical activity by spending some time at the gym. Now the question arises what I have to do now? With the increase in technology and the availability of information on the internet, a search can be made on the diabetics. A lot of information, methods, and applications are found on the net and it leads to confusion and also makes us scary. The main important point to note here is a need for personalized support and it can be made possible with the help of the cognitive application because it can provide a better insight with the personal information making it customized to the needs of the person rather than going in a generalized method.

Using IBM Watson's cognitive capability CafeWell Concierge (Figure 1.14) built a health application with a lot of support for the people who use it. Using the tracking devices helps to reduce your weight, reminds you to take pills on time, customize your diet based on the BMI, gives information about the restaurants around you with the food choices and also

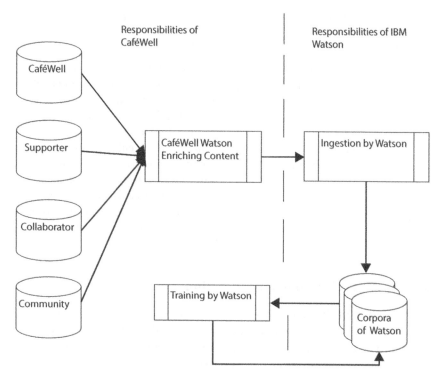

Figure 1.14 Content acquisition.

other community support. The main advantage of this is that it will give a tailored and constant support to the user.

1.14 Advantages of Cognitive Computing

There is a revolution in the automation process in every organization and the pace has increased these days. The organizations have realized that if they do not do it they will be lost in the competition. Cognitive computing helps organizations to take decisions by their executives as it can analyze a large volume of all types of data.

Cognitive computing has a host of benefits including the following:

Precise Data Analysis

These systems are highly productive in analyzing a situation efficiently as they can gather and analyze a large volume of data. In the event we take the instance of the health care industry, these cognitive systems play an important role in assisting the doctors and making things easy for deciding so that life can be saved in time. The cognitive systems gather and dissect the information from different resources for example past clinical reports, past information from the clinical organizations, medical journals, and diagnostic tools that assist the doctors in giving a suggestion based on an information-based treatment that benefits the patients and also the doctors. One important point to know here is that cognitive computing is not going to replace the doctors, but assist them to take decisions faster.

Leaner & More Efficient Business Processes

In real-time the cognitive computing can access the large volume of data and analyze it thereby it can find new business opportunities and also can deal with the basic procedure is driven issues progressively. With the help of IBM Watson, the system can simplify the lengthy process, decrease the risk factors, and guides to take the right path with the varying conditions.

Enhanced Client Interaction

The cognitive computing can assist humans while interacting with clients to provide a better answer to the question posed by him. It can be utilized to automate the client interaction process and provide a better service to the clients. This technology can provide a solution to the client without the need for interaction with the staff. It can provide better relevant information to the customer so that it increases client satisfaction, improve the client experience, and considerably more betrothed with the organization.

1.15   Features of Cognitive Computing

The motivation behind cognitive computing is the making of processing structures that can take care of confusing issues without consistent human intercession. To execute these functions in business and across the board applications, Cognitive Computing consortium has suggested the features as Adaptive, Interactive, Iterative and stateful, and Contextual.

Adaptive: It is the initial step for building a cognitive application. The system should learn to adapt from the surroundings as humans do. It should be dynamic and always well prepared to gather information, learning the objectives, and updating the requirements and goals. This type of system cannot be designed for a single assignment.

Interactive: In human beings, the brain controls the body by connecting with different and gathering information using the senses. In the same manner, the cognitive application should be able to interact with different elements such as processors, gadgets, databases, users, and cloud services. It should make use of various technologies like natural language processing, machine learning, advanced analytics, deep learning probability and statistics, and big data analytics. For interaction with the users, it uses chatbots.

Iterative and stateful: The framework must be able to recall the past interactions in a procedure and return the information whenever necessary. It ought to have the option to characterize the issue by posing inquiries or finding an extra source. This element needs a cautious utilization of the information quality and approval procedures to guarantee that the framework is constantly furnished with enough data and that the information sources it works on to convey solid and state-of-the-art input.

Contextual: They should comprehend, distinguish, and extract relevant components, for example, implications, suitable domains, position, time, guidelines, client's profile, procedure, errand, and objective. They may draw on various wellsprings of data, including both organized and unstructured computerized data, just as tactile sources of information.

1.16   Limitations of Cognitive Computing

Limited Analysis of Risk

The cognitive applications fail flat when examining the unstructured data. There will be a risk with the unstructured data as it incorporates politics, finance, culture, economy, and public. For instance, there is a prescient model that finds an area for oil investigation even though a lot of people objecting it. Yet, if the nation is experiencing a complete change in the government, then human intervention is required as the cognitive system should also consider this and it cannot be done on its own [9].

Rigorous Training Process

These systems require a lot of training initially to comprehend the procedure and improve, but to do this a lot of data is required at the initial stage itself. The adoption is slow because of this lengthy process of collecting the data and training the system. One fine example of this is the training of IBM Watson by WellPoint's financial management. When the user uses the Watson the text has to be inspected on each medical policy by the company engineers. The medical staff like the nurses has to upload the data regarding the cases until the cognitive system understands the specific medical situation. Also, the mind-boggling and costly procedure of utilizing cognitive frameworks aggravates it even.

More Knowledge Enlargement Instead of Artificial Intelligence

The extent of present cognitive innovation is constrained to commitment and choice. Most of these systems are best as assistants which are increasingly similar to knowledge growth and not as popular as the artificial intelligence applications. It supplements human reasoning and examination however relies upon people to take the final decision. Chatbots and smart assistants becoming popular these days are some fine examples. As opposed to a big business wide selection, such particular activities are a viable path for organizations to begin utilizing cognitive models. In the process of automation, the subsequent step in processing is cognitive computing and it has become popular in every field. The cognitive computing will set standards for the systems to arrive at the degree of the human brain. In the case of innovation, dynamic changes, a significant level of uncertainty it is difficult to apply in these circumstances. The multifaceted nature of the issue develops with the number of information sources. It is trying to total, coordinate, and break down such unstructured information. A complex cognitive arrangement ought to have numerous innovations that exist together to give profound area bits of knowledge.

The enterprises looking to adopt cognitive solutions should start with a specific business segment. These segments should have strong business rules to guide the algorithms, and large volumes of data to train the machines. In the cognitive system more technological advancements should be included so that they can take care of changing real-time data, past data, and also the different types of data (Unstructured, structured, and semi-structured). It will be better if the Kafka, Elasticsearch NoSQL, Hadoop, Spark, etc. become a part of the cognitive systems so that they handle the data problems easily. Any enterprise having a protocol, business domain and huge volumes of company data can adopt these cognitive systems as they are useful in training the system.

Issues With Cognitive Computing: Challenges for a Better Future

Each innovation faces a few issues at some stage in its lifecycle. Technology has a lot of potentials to make an impact on the lives of people, but humans are resisting this innovative technology owing to fear of transform. Individuals are thinking of a few cognitive computing detriments tossing huge difficulties in the way towards more noteworthy implementation, which are given below:

Security

At the point when computerized gadgets oversee basic data, the subject of security naturally comes into the image. With the ability to deal with a lot of information and break down the equivalent, psychological figuring has a critical test concerning information security and encryption. With an ever-increasing number of associated gadgets coming into the scene, cognitive processing should consider the issues identified with security penetrate by building up a full-confirmation security plan that likewise has a system to apprehensive actions to encourage integrity.

Adoption

The greatest obstacle in the way of accomplishment for any innovation is adopting it voluntarily. To make this technology effectively, it is fundamental to build up a future vision of how innovation will improve procedures and organizations. Through a coordinated effort between different partners, for example, innovation engineers, ventures, government, and people, the reception procedure can be smoothed out. Simultaneously, it is basic to have an information protection system that will additionally help the selection of technology.

Change Management

People are resistant to change because of their natural human behavior & as cognitive computing have the power to learn like humans, people are fearful that machines would replace humans someday. This has gone on to impact the growth prospects to a high level. Change the board is another pivotal test for cognitive computing need to overcome for survival. Individuals are impervious to change in light of their normal human conduct and as the technology can be trained like people, individuals are frightful that machines would supplant people sometime in the not so distant future. This has proceeded to affect the development possibilities to a significant level. The technology can work in synchronization with the people and can help them in taking the wise decision sat the right time.

Extensive Advancement Cycles

Probably the best test is the time to put resources into the improvement of situation-based applications through the cognitive approach. It is at present being created as a universal arrangement—this implies the arrangement can't be executed over different industry fragments without development groups and a lot of time to develop the application.

Extensive advancement cycles make it harder for small organizations to create cognitive capacities all alone. With time, as the improvement lifecycles will in general abbreviate, this technology will gain a greater stage in the future.

1.17   Conclusion

Cognitive computing is a subject which helps to make better decisions by humans. It involves machine learning, big data analytics, and advanced analytics to make better decisions. It builds a corpus to keep all the data in it and also it updates it all the time. It takes data from the different sources and also it can read the structured, unstructured, and semi-structured data models. Cognitive computing does not make any disturbances in the hiring market since it cannot replace humans but it helps and assists them to do better in their fields.

References

1. *Cognition*, Lexico, Oxford University Press and Dictionary.com, https://www.lexico.com/definition/cognition. Retrieved 6 May 2020.
2. Von Eckardt, B., *What is cognitive science?*, pp. 45–72, MIT Press, Princeton, MA, 1996.
3. Revlin, R., *Cognition: Theory and Practice*. Worth Publishers, 2012. https://books.google.co.in/books?id=tuCBGepl2VMC
4. Liddell, H.G. and Scott, R., γιγνσκω, *A Greek-English Lexicon*, revised by H.S. Jones and R. McKenzie, Clarendon Press.—via Perseus Project, Oxford, 1940, Retrieved 6 May 2020.
5. Stefano, F. and Bianchini, F., On The Historical Dynamics Of Cognitive Science: A View From The Periphery, in: *The Search for a Theory of Cognition: Early Mechanisms and New Ideas*, p. XIV, Rodopi, Amsterdam, 2011.
6. Matlin, M., *Cognition*, p. 4, John Wiley & Sons, Inc., Hoboken, NJ, 2009.
7. Eddy, M.D., The Cognitive Unity of Calvinist Pedagogy in Enlightenment Scotland, in: *Reformed Churches Working Unity in Diversity: Global Historical, Theological, and Ethical Perspectives*, Á. Kovács (Ed.), pp. 46–60, l'Harmattan, Budapest, 2016.
8. Marr, B., What Everyone Should Know About Cognitive Computing https://www.forbes.com/sites/bernardmarr/2016/03/23/what-everyone-

should-know-about-cognitive-computing/? sh=30f75db65088, 2016, March 23.

9. https://marutitech.com/cognitive-computing-features-scope-limitations/.

10. Mukadia, M. What is Cognitive Computing? How are Enterprises benefitting from Cognitive Technology? Towardsdatascience.Com. https://towardsdatascience.com/what-is-cognitive-computing-how-are-enterprises-benefitting-from-cognitive-technology-6441d0c9067b, 2019.

11. Hurwitz, J. S., Kaufman, M., Bowles, A., Cognitive Computing and Big Data Analytics. John Wiley & Sons, 2015, https://www.wiley.com/en-us/Cognitive+Computing.

12. Mundt, C., Why We Feel: The Science of Human Emotions. *Am. J. Psychiatry*, 157, 1185–1186, 2000. https://doi.org/10.1176/appi.ajp.157.7.1185.

13. Chen, M., Herrera, F., Hwang, K., Cognitive Computing: Architecture, Technologies, and Intelligent Applications. *IEEE Access*, 6, 19774–19783, 2018.

14. Appel, A.P., Candello, H., Gandour, F.L., Cognitive computing: Where big data is driving us, in: *Handbook of Big Data Technologies*, pp. 807–850, 2017.

15. Chen, M., Tian, Y., Fortino, G., Zhang, J., Humar, I., Cognitive Internet of vehicles. *Elsevier Comput. Commun.*, 120, 58–70, 2018. https://doi.org/10.1016/j.comcom.2018.02.006

16. Hwang, K. and Chen, M., *Big-Data Analytics for Cloud, IoT, and Cognitive Learning*, Wiley, London, U.K, 2017.

17. https://www.newgenapps.com/blog/what-is-cognitive-computing-applications-companies-artificial-intelligence/.

18. https://towardsdatascience.com/ai-and-cognitive-computing-fc701b4fbae7.

Machine Learning and Big Data in Cyber-Physical System: Methods, Applications and Challenges

Janmenjoy Nayak[1]*, P. Suresh Kumar[2], Dukka Karun Kumar Reddy[2], Bighnaraj Naik[3] and Danilo Pelusi[4]

[1]*Department of Computer Science and Engineering, Aditya Institute of Technology and Management (AITAM), K Kotturu, India*
[2]*Dept. of Computer Sc. & Engg., Dr. Lankapalli Bullayya College of Engineering, Visakhapatnam, India*
[3]*Dept. of Computer Application, Veer Surendra Sai University of Technology, Burla, India*
[4]*University of Teramo, Agostino Campus, Teramo, Italy*

Abstract

One of the most considerable and emerging methodologies, defined by the integration of physical and computational processes as cyber-physical systems. These systems are emphasized to supervise the data processing and synchronize it among the cyber computational processes and physically connected systems. Machine learning crafts the intelligent control process by instilling astute self-learning processes with automated and indicative capabilities. The main point of this literature is to give overall survey of cyber-physical system challenges and to accomplish the ideal degree of integration in automation and intelligence in diverse domains for the progress of emerging systems. This chapter aims to provide the advances and challenges for significant research and development of existing and future cyber physical-based technologies using machine learning methods. The research challenges are primarily summarized as i) large-scale data collection, in

---

Corresponding author: mailforjnayak@gmail.com

Kolla Bhanu Prakash, G. R. Kanagachidambaresan, V. Srikanth, E. Vamsidhar (eds.) Cognitive Engineering for Next Generation Computing: A Practical Analytical Approach, (49–92) © 2021 Scrivener Publishing LLC

the integration of systems from IoT, smart cities as well as industries, ii) the synchronization of interconnectivity and intelligence of these frameworks requires a shared perspectives model with decision making, iii) control technique, management service, model-based design, network security, and resource allocation, iv) safety, security, robustness, and reliability is a vital challenge because of errors, security attacks, improbability in the environment, security, and protection of physical systems.

Keywords: IoT, cyber-physical system, machine learning, big-data

2.1   Introduction

Cyber-physical systems (CPS) are physically designed engineered systems, where the operational models are supervised, synchronized, regulated, and incorporated through computing and communication core. Numerous constraints lie ahead on the economically important areas of health-care, aerospace, transportation, agriculture, manufacturing, buildings, defense, and energy. The scheme of design, the architecture building, and the authentication of cyber-physical systems propound numerous technical issues and challenges, which must be taken into consideration by a multi-disciplinary community of educators and researchers [1]. CPS entail enhanced design tools that facilitate design methodology that supports scalability and complexity management. They require cybersecurity to avoid malicious attacks and intrusion detection. CPS is smart, intelligent, and real-time feedback systems, which support validation and verification like assurance, simulation, certification, etc. They are networked and distributed systems possibly through wireless sensing and actuation. In expansion to the challenging constraints of scope, control and scale of CPS give growth to an additional major challenge concerning the confidentiality of the people who make use of the systems [2].

The increasing complexity of IoT networks also focuses on the security problems confronted by such networks. The rise of IoT network complexity is due to too many devices are interconnected with each other through the internet at the side with enormous data originated by these devices. At the side, the development of IoT, novel security issues arise while conventional security issues become more severe. The major reasons are the heterogeneity and the substantially large scale of the objects [3]. As the threats on IoT devices are flattering in a common fashion and the security metrics are based on the developemental aspects of software as well as network, so the hackers can expand control and transmit out malicious activities and attack other devices close to the compromised systems or nodes [4]. Due to the natural significance of its low-power and low-memory nature of these devices, these devices do not comprise of malware protection or virus protection software. The inexistence of malware and virus defense system in IoT devices make them extremely vulnerable to turn into bots and bring out the malicious movement to other devices in the network. When an IoT device is hacked, the invader will be capable of taking control on forwarding and routing operations of the hijacked device. In accumulation to various other devices in the network by attacking, the attackers preserve the gain to access, for sensitive information transmitted and collected by the IoT devices. This absence of integrity, confidentiality, and security of data in IoT has the impending nature to disrupt the pervasive implementation of this technology. These technological constraints are typically correlated to wireless technologies, energy, scalability, and distributed in nature. At the same time, security hurdles require the capability to make sure by confidentiality, authentication, integrity, end-to-end security, etc.

The advancement and operational lifecycle of all IoT hubs and devices must enforce the complete security in all aspect. The distributed system has exceptional factors of threat for devices. The existing distributed systems offer considerable opportunities for the introduction of malicious or insecure software. They have the capacity for browsing and hacking. Indeed distributed systems are proposed to sustain a medium or low area of risk in business, but still, need to be cautious today and not to put down unprotected. These attacks do not imperil data integrity but lead to expensive and inconvenient. So, the critical characteristic nature of these applications performed in real-time existing systems and security for distributed systems is an inherent requirement [4].

The main contribution of this chapter are:

i. A brief overview to the CPS mechanism with the integration of physical processes, computation, and networking.

ii. Importance of Human-in-the-loop connected to CPS, with emphasis on the functionality of human in cooperation with CPS.

iii. Analytical study about the research of decision making through machine learning (ML) algorithms applied in CPS and other research works of CPS related to IoT and

Big-data through computational methods and frameworks for sensing, processing, and storage of substantial amount of data.
iv. Understanding the technology possesses of CPS in various application fields.

This paper is structured as follows: Section 2.2 elaborates the CPS architecture with its components. Section 2.3 provides a brief human-in-loop cyber-physical systems description. Sections 2.4, 2.5, and 2.6 discusses a brief study of major-related research in the area of ML Section 2.7 summarizes the critical analysis with analyzing the impact of ML and big data approaches in CPS. Section 2.8 illustrates the conclusion with future concerns.

2.2 Cyber-Physical System Architecture

CPS is a promising and exploring area which deals with the integration and overlapping of numerous fields of science and technology. The architectural design of CPS as shown in Figure 2.1. The operations of engineered and physical systems are integrated, coordinated, controlled, monitored by a communication and computing system. CPS comprises the communication by a set of networked agents with the physical world. The network agents incorporate devices like actuators, sensors, communication devices, and control processing units.

The CPS interacts through networks of a physical system with wireless sensors intelligently composed and embedded computing systems with securely coupled. The collective intelligence system functions to coordinate for knowledge integration and data pre-processing across heterogeneous, multidisciplinary domains of sensors. The real-time systems feedback control is held by the computation process with support to different time scale asynchronous event processing. In the architecture of computation and controller, the computation process is used to hold feedback control of real-time event triggered systems. This suits the asynchronous realtime event dispensation with variation time scale. The architecture of the controller assures the security of cyber networks, through taking apart reliable tasks from unreliable tasks with considerations on the safety and latency. The actuator network is self-possessed with control nodes, which receives control instructions from computation control and sends the instructional control to consequent nodes with a collaborative design of scheduling and feedback control [5].

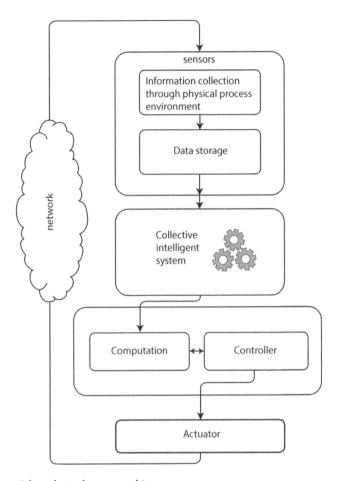

Figure 2.1 Cyber-physical system architecture.

2.3 Human-in-the-Loop Cyber-Physical Systems (HiLCPS)

The rapid technological advancement in embedded systems and communication technologies and the availability of low-cost sensors has to lead to the development of next-generation hardware/software systems called CPS. These systems interact with the physical world to support human–machine interaction. Moreover, the development of HiLCPS consists of more powerful applications with enormous latent for the daily routine of human life. A HiLCPS system (Figure 2.2) consists of some components of real-time security-based activities, the involvement of humans in a loop, cyber-based components (CPS), and the physical environment. With the use of body

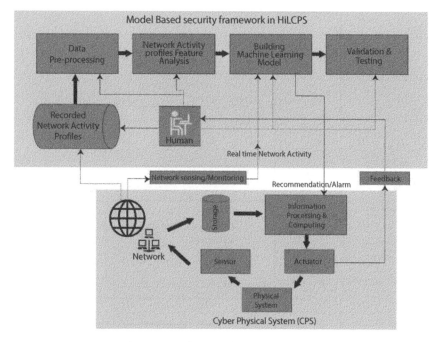

Figure 2.2 Integration of ML with HiLCPS.

and brain interface (brain sensors), HiLCPS is can infer the user's objective for the measurement of cognitive capabilities. The features like control of physical processes by monitoring variables and obtaining broad knowledge of controlled environment using ML to furnish timely and specific decisions have made CPS more popular to meet the requirements of new challenging applications and future smart services. Moreover, the increased use of CPS may result in challenges such as security, performance, stability, reliability, and robustness that could have major consequences on society, economy, and environment. Therefore designing accurate, secure, and efficient CPS in applications such as transportation, energy, medical and healthcare, defense, manufacturing, and agriculture is emerging as an interesting area of research. However, the use of intelligent based methods in security systems or to design a perfect secured system has always been a challenging aspect for the researchers. Also, issues like arbitrary failures and various cyber-attacks in CPS make those more vulnerable. If any sort of unusual activity is detected by the intrusion detector, apposite action needs to be taken for minimizing the risk to harm the system. The unintended activity caused by the random failures or repeated cyber-attacks results smashes up to the physical objects as well the users who are dependent on it. So, protecting CPS from vulnerable attacks and repeated failures has always been an important measure. Various approaches based on rule integration [6, 7], statistics [7, 8], data mining [9, 10] and cryptography [11, 12] are developed to handle the aforementioned problems. However, different limitations [13] such as the requirement of prior knowledge in case of rule integration and statistics based approaches; high complexity in case of data mining based approaches; lesser capability to handle the malicious attacks with legal privileges in case of cryptography-based approaches, give a new direction for the scope of advance research. By using the combination of qualitative and quantitative techniques, ML techniques can find the approximate and efficient solution in an affordable time. Several hybrid ML based approach is developed to provide a unique high-end solution for the large scale CPS, which cannot be achieved by a single method.

2.4 Machine Learning Applications in CPS

In this section various ML approaches such as k-nearest neighbors, decision trees, Naïve Bayes, support vector machine, random forest, multi-layer perceptron, linear regression, and their studies in the CPS have been studied.

2.4.1 K-Nearest Neighbors (K-NN) in CPS

K-NN is a straight forward supervised ML algorithm classifier. Classification is achieved by identifying the nearest neighbors from the samples. To evaluate a data point in a sample, its neighbor sample points are considered and recurrently 'K' number of values may be determined. This is the reason it is named as the K-NN algorithm [14]. There are various methods to calculate the distance between testing and training point such as Euclidian distance, Manhattan distance, and hamming distance (Equations (2.1)–(2.3)). Classification of testing is completely based on the training examples and it is also named as the lazy learning algorithm. Classification purely depends on the value of 'K' and different 'K' values will produce variation in results.

$$\sqrt{\sum_{i=1}^{k}(x_i - y_i)^2} \tag{2.1}$$

$$\sum_{i=1}^{k} |x_i - y_i| \qquad (2.2)$$

$$D_H \sum_{i=1}^{k} |x_i - y_i| \qquad (2.3)$$

de Mello and Stemmer [15] investigated K-NN classifier in golden images and some background samples to inspect surface mounted devices. From the investigated results such as confusion matrix, kappa statistics, MAE, RMSE, it proves the features that are related to the histogram is the perfect method to differentiate various components from images. So that it will classify missing, shifting, identify rotation or wrong devices. Table 2.1 shows various studies of CPS using K-NN.

Table 2.1 Various applications in CPS using K-NN.

S. No.	Application	Dataset	Method	Evaluation factor	Ref.
1	Cellular connectivity of CPS	Massive measurement data	KNN, NB, RF	Accuracy	[16]
2	Cyber-Physical Social Systems	Corpus	NB, KNN, DT, SVM	MAE, RMSE, RAE, RRSE, SSE, SST, D2	[17]
3	CIoT-based cyber-physical system	CASIA, TIDE	NB, SVM, LR, J48, KNN	Accuracy, Precision, Recall, F-Measure, ROC	[18]
4	CPS for Stroke Detection	EEG	KNN, SVM, MLP	Precision, Recall	[19]
5	CPS of an offshore gas turbine	PI system	MLP, DT, RF, KNN, LR, NB	MAE, RMSE, RAE, Accuracy, Error%	[20]
6	Attacks in Cyber-Physical Systems	Random Dataset	KNN, ANN, SVM, GNB, DT	Precision, Recall, Accuracy	[21]

(Continued)

Table 2.1 Various applications in CPS using K-NN. (*Continued*)

S. No.	Application	Dataset	Method	Evaluation factor	Ref.
7	CPS in Cyber Manufacturing	Random dataset	RF, KNN	Accuracy	[22]
8	Detection of Parkinson disease	UCI-Parkinson dataset	CBR, FKNN, RF, RB, J48, SVM,	Error rate, Accuracy, Precision, Sensitivity, Specificity, F-measure	[23]
9	Medical CPS	Health care datasets	KNN, SVM, NB, DT, Fuzzy	Recall, F-Measure	[24]
10	Embedded Emotion recognition using CPS	MANHOB, DEAP	KNN	Accuracy, Sensitivity, and Specificity	[25]
11	Mobile Edge Computing	10 Datasets	NB, RF, DT, SVM, K-Means, KNN, MLP, RNN,	Accuracy	[26]
12	An energy-cyber-physical system	Real-Time dataset	DT, DA, SVM, KNN	Accuracy, Precision, Recall, F1-measure	[27]
13	Attacks in CPS	MITM, DoS	KNN, DT, RF	TP, TN, FP, FN	[28]
14	Intrusions Detection in Aerospace	UNSW-NB15, KDDCUP 99, ML-IDS	K-NN, SVM, RF, NB, MLP	Precision, Recall, Accuracy, TP Rate, FP Rate	[14]
15	Cyber-physical water supply systems	Anomalous dataset	KNN, MNB, BNB, GNB	Accuracy	[29]

2.4.2 Support Vector Machine (SVM) in CPS

SVM is a non-probabilistic binary classifier that is based on the hyperplane in feature space that will minimize the classification risk compared to optimal classification. This hyperplane is trained to differentiate between two classes and it splits the data in the best possible way. SVM is familiar with its generalizability towards solving real-life problems [14]. The main objective of SVM is to isolate from the set of classes. However, in some cases, it cannot do so because of its non-linearity, and 'Kernel' helps to obtain the intended solution. Generally used kernel functions are the sigmoid kernel, Gaussian kernel, linear kernel, and radial basis kernel, etc. [30].

Hossain *et al.* [18] used a method to verify the authenticity in CIoT. After getting the final image's feature vector, SVM helps to classify the images as authentic or forged type. To validate the performance of the model they utilized measures such as false-positive rate, true-positive rate, kappa statistics, MAE, RMSE, etc. From the experimented results it is evident that, the performance of their proposed approach is dominative over others. Table 2.2 shows different studies in CPS using SVM.

Table 2.2 Various applications in CPS using SVM.

S. No.	Application	Dataset	Method	Evalution factor	Ref.
1	Power system disturbence	15 Datasets	RF, NB, SVM, Jripper, Adaboost	Accuracy, Precision, Recall, F-Measure	[31]
2	Defending unknown attacks in CPS	VET Zoo	K-means, TF, IDF SVM	TP, FP, Accuracy, Precision, ROC	[32]
3	Attacks in CPS	SWaT	SVM, RF, DT, NN, NB	TP, FP, Precision, Recall, Accuracy, FA, TTBM	[33]
4	CPSS	Corpus	NB, KNN, DT, SVM	MAE, RMSE, RAE, RRSE, SSE, SST, D2	[17]
5	TOLA based on CPS	Random dataset	SVM, KNN, NB	Accuracy	[34]

(Continued)

Table 2.2 Various applications in CPS using SVM. (*Continued*)

S. No.	Application	Dataset	Method	Evalution factor	Ref.
6	Safety risk monitoring of CPPS	event_ warning detail	SVM, NN, MA, AR, GEP, EPABT	MAE, MAPE, MSE,	[35]
7	Cloud-based Cyber-physical intrusion detection	Random dataset	MLP, RNN-LSTM, LR, DT, RF, SVM	Accuracy	[36]
8	Estimation of a safety Critical CPS	Real Time dataset	ANN-LMBP, DT, SVM, RF	R2, RMSE, Training Time, Testing Speed	[37]
9	CPS Manufacturing	Dataset with Blackslash Issues	SVM	Accuracy	[38]
10	On-Chip LiDAR Sensors in CPS	Random dataset	MLP SVM	CCR, ECR, MAE, RMSE, RAE, RRSE	[39]
11	Automotive CPS	IMU	SVM, NN, RNN, LSTM	Confusion Matrix, Accuracy	[40]
12	Attacks in Cyber-Physical Systems	Random Dataset	KNN, ANN, SVM, GNB, DT	Precision, Recall, Accuracy	[21]
13	Cyber-Physical-Social Systems	Dataset from AMAZON	SVM, CCNN, NB	Accuracy	[41]
14	Industry 4.0	ABS, bCMS, and TCM	SVM, Naive Bayes, and J48 decision-tree	AUC	[42]
15	Detection of Parkinson disease	UCI-Parkinson dataset	CBR, FKNN, RF, RB, J48, SVM	Error rate, Accuracy, Precision, Sensitivity, Specificity, F-measure	[23]

(*Continued*)

Table 2.2 Various applications in CPS using SVM. (*Continued*)

S. No.	Application	Dataset	Method	Evalution factor	Ref.
16	Medical CPS	Health care datasets	KNN, SVM, NB, DT, Fuzzy	Recall, F-Measure	[24]
17	CPS for Thermal stress in 3D Printing	Random dataset	LR, MLP, SVM	MAE, RMSE, R2, MSE	[43]
18	Image annotation in Cyber-Physical-Social Systems	Corel-5K, IAPR TC-12	CNN, KSVM	Precision, Recall, F1 measure	[44]
19	Cyber-Physical Production Systems	Collected data from CPPS	DT, RF, ANN, SVM	Precision, Recall, Accuracy	[45]
20	CPS for Thermal stress in 3D Printing	Random Dataset	LR, MLP, SVM	MAE, RMSE, R2, MSE	[43]
21	Resistance Spot Welding (RSW)	RSW Quality	Linear Regression, SVM, MLP, RF	MSE, MAPE	[46]
22	Mobile Edge Computing	10 Datasets	NB, RF, DT, SVM,K-Means, KNN, MLP, RNN	Accuracy	[26]
23	Big Data in Agriculture CPS	IoT Dataset from Luochuan Apple	GA-SVM	MSE	[47]
24	An energy-cyber-physical system	Real Time dataser	DT, DA, SVM, KNN	Accuracy, Precision, Recall, F1-measure	[27]
25	Intrusions Detection in Aerospace	UNSW-NB15, KDDCUP 99, ML-IDS	K-NN, SVM, RF, NB, MLP	Precision, Recall, Accuracy, TP Rate, FP Rate	[14]

2.4.3 Random Forest (RF) in CPS

RF as its name implies, comprises a huge number of decision trees. Decision Trees are considered as building blocks for RF. It provides an algorithm to gauge the missing values in the RF classifier and if trees in the forest are more, then the accuracy can be accurately predicted. A RF is an ensemble approach that is operated by setting up a large number of decision trees at the time of training based on a random subgroup of training examples [33]. It is a combination of various classifiers and every classifier comes up with a vote that is the most frequent class.

Majdani et al. [20] simulated RF in the oil and gas industry especially in the area of predictive maintenance which will be used to forecast remote environmental conditions. Suppleness is achieved by combining a RF with computational intelligence. Table 2.3 represents various studies in CPS using RF.

Table 2.3 Different metrics in RF.

S. No.	Application	Dataset	Method	Evaluation factor	Ref.
1	Power system disturbance	15 Datasets	Random Forest, Naïve Bayes, SVM, Jripper, Adaboost	Accuracy, Precision, Recall, F-Measure	[31]
2	Big Data in Cloud Computing Environment	URL Reputation, YouTube Video, Bag of Words, Gas sensor arrays, Patient, Outpatient, Medicine, Cancer	Parallel Random Forest, RF, DRF, Spark-MLRF	OOB Error Rate, Accuracy	[48]
3	Attacks in CPS	SWaT	SVM, RF, DT, NN, NB	TP, FP, Precision, Recall, Accuracy, FA, TTBM	[33]

(Continued)

Table 2.3 Different metrics in RF. (*Continued*)

S. No.	Application	Dataset	Method	Evaluation factor	Ref.
4	CPS maintenance	Industrial dataset	NB, DT, RF, NN	Precision, Recall	[49]
5	Cloud-based Cyber-physical intrusion detection	Random dataset	MLP, RNN-LSTM, LR, DT, RF, SVM	Accuracy	[36]
6	Estimation of a safety Critical CPS	Real-Time dataset	ANN-LMBP, DT, SVM, RF	R2, RMSE, Training Time, Testing Speed	[37]
7	CPS in Cyber Manufacturing	Random dataset	RF, KNN	Accuracy	[22]
8	Detection of Parkinson disease	UCI-Parkinson dataset	CBR, FKNN, RF, RB, J48, SVM	Error rate, Accuracy, Precision, Sensitivity, Specificity, F-measure	[23]
9	Classification in IoT	Real-Time health care database	RF, Map Reducer	Precision, Recall, F-measure, Sensitivity, Specificity, Accuracy	[50]
10	Resistance Spot Welding (RSW)	RSW Quality	Linear Regression, SVM, MLP, RF	MSE, MAPE	[46]
11	Mobile Edge Computing	10 Datasets	NB, RF, DT, SVM,K-Means, KNN, MLP, RNN	Accuracy	[26]

(*Continued*)

Table 2.3 Different metrics in RF. (*Continued*)

S. No.	Application	Dataset	Method	Evaluation factor	Ref.
12	Bio-Modality Spoofing in Medical CPS	Face, Iris, Fingerprint by Warsaw, Replay-Attack, LiveDet 2015	RF, CNN	Accuracy, FAR, FRR	[51]
13	Intrusions Detection in Aerospace	UNSW-NB15, KDDCUP 99, ML-IDS	K-NN, SVM, RF, NB, MLP	Precision, Recall, Accuracy, TP Rate, FP Rate	[14]

2.4.4   Decision Trees (DT) in CPS

The main precedence to consider DT is its intuitive utterance of knowledge with good accuracy, and ease implementation [14]. In DT, every internal node can be considered as a test to an attribute, the branch can be represented as a result of that test, and the class label is represented by a leaf. Each record is navigated from the root node to leaf and the class label is assigned to it [33]. It uses function at every branch for the availability of the record and popularly used functions are gini index, information gain, and gain ratio. The estimated probability will be less in case the tree grows larger, which affects the number of records in the branches i.e. records will be less. Therefore, pruning is one of the important techniques that will increase the performance of the model [52]. It reduces the complexity of the final classifier, and hence it improves the accuracy by reduction of overfitting. Pruning is classified into two categories such as prepruning and post pruning. In post pruning, the tree will be built first and then branches will be reduced so that the DT level will be reduced. On the other hand, at the time of decision tree building pre pruning is helpful at overfitting.

Bezemskij *et al.* [53] have developed a method to provide security in small-remote controlled robotic vehicles which will observe the cyber-attacks against physical impact. To generate the decision rules, they used decision trees which are evaluated against DoS and command injection attacks. The impact of decision trees in CPS of various studies is illustrated in Table 2.4.

Table 2.4 Various applications in CPS using decision trees.

S. No.	Application	Dataset	Method	Evaluation factor	Ref.
1	CP Intrusion detection on a robotic vehicle	Real-Time dataset	DT C5.0	Confusion Matrix, Accuracy, FPR, FNR, AUC-ROC	[54]
2	Mobile Cyber-Physical systems	Real-Time dataset	DT C5.0	FPR, FNR, Accuracy, AUC-ROC	[55]
3	Attacks in CPS	SWaT	SVM, RF, DT, NN, NB	TP, FP, Precision, Recall, Accuracy, FA, TTBM	[33]
4	CPS maintenance	Industrial dataset	NB, DT, RF, NN	Precision, Recall	[49]
5	Cyber-Physical Social Systems	Corpus	NB, KNN, DT, SVM	MAE, RMSE, RAE, RRSE, SSE, SST, D2	[17]
6	CIoT-based cyber-physical system	CASIA, TIDE	NB, SVM, LR, J48, KNN	Accuracy, Precision, Recall, F-Measure, ROC	[18]
7	Cloud-based Cyber-physical intrusion detection	Random dataset	MLP, RNN-LSTM, LR, DT, RF, SVM	Accuracy	[36]
8	Estimation of a safety Critical CPS	Real-Time dataset	ANN-LMBP, DT, SVM, RF	R2, RMSE, Training Time, Testing Speed	[37]
9	CPS of an offshore gas turbine	PI system	MLP, DT, RF, KNN, LR, NB	MAE, RMSE, RAE, Accuracy, Error %	[20]
10	Fog-cloud based cyber-physical system	MBD	J48 DT	Accuracy, Specificity, Precision, Recall, MAE, RMSE, RRSE, RAE	[56]

(Continued)

Table 2.4 Various applications in CPS using decision trees. (*Continued*)

S. No.	Application	Dataset	Method	Evaluation factor	Ref.
11	Attacks in Cyber-Physical Systems	Random Dataset	KNN, ANN, SVM, GNB, DT	Precision, Recall, Accuracy	[21]
12	Industry 4.0	ABS, bCMS, and TCM	SVM, Naive Bayes, and J48 decision-tree	AUC	[42]
13	Medical CPS	Health care datasets	KNN, SVM, NB, DT, Fuzzy	Recall, F-Measure	[24]
14	Mobile Edge Computing	10 Datasets	NB, RF, DT, SVM, K-Means, KNN, MLP, RNN,	Accuracy	[26]
15	An energy-cyber-physical system	Real-Time dataset	DT, DA, SVM, KNN	Accuracy, Precision, Recall, F1-measure	[27]
16	CP Intrusion detection on a robotic vehicle	Real-Time dataset	DT C5.0	Confusion Matrix, Accuracy, FPR, FNR, AUC-ROC	[54]

2.4.5   Linear Regression (LR) in CPS

This is a statistical technique used to evaluate the association between the input variable and output variable i.e. it assumes the relationship among independent and dependent variables that positioned the straight line to the data [57]. The relationship is expressed as a prediction function as in Equation (2.4).

$$h(x) = w_0 + w_1 x_1 + w_2 x_2 + \cdots + w_n x_n \qquad (2.4)$$

Where $x_1, x_2, x_3, \ldots, x_n$ are features and $w_0, w_1, w_2, w_3, \ldots, w_n$ are weights.

Miao *et al.* [43] have used linear regression to adjust the settings in nozzle temperature automatically. They investigated the performance of LR, MLP, and SVM and among which, LR outperformed. From the experimental

Table 2.5 Different applications in CPS using linear regression.

S. No.	Application	Dataset	Method	Evaluation factor	Ref.
1	CIoT-based cyber physical system	CASIA, TIDE	NB, SVM, LR, J48, KNN	Accuracy, Precision, Recall, F-Measure, ROC	[18]
2	Cloud based Cyber-physical intrusion detection	Random dataset	MLP, RNN-LSTM, LR, DT, RF, SVM	Accuracy	[36]
3	CPS of an offshore gas turbine	PI system	MLP, DT, RF, KNN, LR, NB	MAE, RMSE, RAE, Accuracy, Error%	[20]
4	Resistance Spot Welding (RSW)	RSW Quality	Linear Regression, SVM, MLP, RF	MSE, MAPE	[46]

results, it is evident that the CPS reduced the distortion notably. Table 2.5 shows various studies in CPS using LR.

2.4.6   Multi-Layer Perceptron (MLP) in CPS

MLP is a broad application in ML which is an information processing model inspired by biological nervous systems like a human brain structure. It learns by itself by giving supervised training to meet the requisite complex and non-linear relations, without any pre-model. MLP is composed of several layers, every layer has neurons, which will filter the information many times. These are used to classify the data effectively [14]. Every neuron has a set of input features (x^i) and linked weights (w^i).

Majdani *et al.* [20] proposed context-aware CPS through an adaptive multi-tiered framework, which can be utilized for smart data acquisition and data processing, with minimizing the human intervention.

Table 2.6 Various applications in CPS using multi-layer perceptron.

S. No.	Application	Dataset	Method	Evaluation factor	Ref.
1	Inspecting surface mounted devices	Golden Images	ROI Algorithm, KNN, MLP	Confusion matrix, Kappa Statistics, MAE, RMSE	[15]
2	Attacks in CPS	SWaT	SVM, RF, DT, NN, NB	TP, FP, Precision, Recall, Accuracy, FA, TTBM	[33]
3	CPS maintenance	Industrial dataset	NB, DT, RF, NN	Precision, Recall	[49]
4	CP-SRS	real-life data	NN-SLM, NB-SLM	Confusion matrix	[58]
5	Image Classification for CPS	Random dataset	CNN, GA	Accuracy, Training time, Model extensibility	[59]
6	Intrusion detection using MCPS	KDD 99 Dataset	Evolving NN, DT	Performance gain, Training time comparison	[60]
7	CPS in Cyberattacks		actor-critic NN, deep reinforcement learning algorithm	–	[61]
8	Anomaly Detection in Cyber-Physical Systems	SWaT	LSTM-RNN	Accuracy	[62]

(Continued)

Table 2.6 Various applications in CPS using multi-layer perceptron. (*Continued*)

S. No.	Application	Dataset	Method	Evaluation factor	Ref.
9	Safety risk monitoring of CPPS	event_ warningdetail	SVM, NN, MA, AR, GEP, EPABT	MAE, MAPE, MSE,	[35]
10	Cloud-based Cyber-physical intrusion detection	Random dataset	MLP, RNN-LSTM, LR, DT, RF, SVM,	Accuracy	[36]
11	Estimation of a safety Critical CPS	Real-Time dataset	ANN-LMBP, DT, SVM, RF	R2, RMSE, Training Time, Testing Speed	[37]
12	CPS of an offshore gas turbine	PI system	MLP, DT, RF, KNN, LR, NB	MAE, RMSE, RAE, Accuracy, Error%	[20]
13	On-Chip LiDAR Sensors in CPS	Random dataset	MLP SVM	CCR, ECR, MAE, RMSE, RAE, RRSE	[39]
14	Automotive CPS	IMU	SVM, NN, RNN, LSTM	Confusion Matrix, Accuracy	[40]
15	Attacks in CPS	Random Dataset	KNN, ANN, SVM, GNB, DT	Precision, Recall, Accuracy	[21]
16	CPSS	Dataset from AMAZON	SVM, CCNN, NB	Accuracy	[41]

(*Continued*)

Table 2.6 Various applications in CPS using multi-layer perceptron. (*Continued*)

S. No.	Application	Dataset	Method	Evaluation factor	Ref.
17	Intrusions Detection system	–	Generative adversarial ANN, ANN	–	[63]
18	Vehicular Cyber-Physical Systems	SUMO	CNN	Delay, throughput, packet delivery ratio, and network load	[64]
19	CPS for Thermal stress in 3D Printing	Random dataset	LR, MLP, SVM	MAE, RMSE, R2, MSE	[43]
20	Image annotation in Cyber-Physical-Social Systems	Corel-5K, IAPR TC-12	CNN, KSVM	Precision, Recall, F1 measure	[44]
21	Resistance Spot Welding (RSW)	RSW Quality	LR, SVM, MLP, RF	MSE, MAPE	[46]
22	Fingerprint in smart CPS	–	KPCA, APADAE, PSO, BP, SVM	Accuracy, precision, Recall, F-Score	[65]
23	Mobile Edge Computing	10 Datasets	NB, RF, DT, SVM, K-Means, KNN, MLP, RNN,	Accuracy	[26]
24	Intrusions Detection in Aerospace	UNSW-NB15, KDDCUP 99, ML-IDS	K-NN, SVM, RF, NB, MLP	Precision, Recall, Accuracy, TP Rate, FP Rate	[14]

The developed component framework is based on MLP with error back-propagation. Compliance is accomplished through the combination of computational intelligence and ML techniques. Table 2.6 represents the studies in CPS using a MLP.

2.4.7   Naive Bayes (NB) in CPS

Bayesian networks are the probabilistic graphical analysis model giving a likelihood of events subject to certain evidence. It is equipped for utilized with discreet data in any structure. NB is considered to be the effective learning algorithm in ML which works efficiently on the principle of conditional independence assumption. Each attribute in the data set is given the same weight and they equally contribute to the outcome. These are from Bayesian inferences which will deduce the events that are evaluated previously. This assumption results in reducing the high density and considers input characteristics are independent. It can combine knowledge and past data. It is mathematically represented in Equation (2.5).

$$C^* = argmax_c\, p(c\,|\,x1,\ldots,xn) = argmax_c\, p(c)\prod_{i=1}^{n} p(x_i|c) \qquad (2.5)$$

Misra et al. [17] have proposed ML classifiers such as NB to classify learning-based prediction. Two experiments were conducted to check the destination prediction and bandwidth. Performance evaluation is increased by using ensemble techniques. Table 2.7 represents the studies in CPS using NB.

2.5   Use of IoT in CPS

Nowadays, advancements in present technologies in communication and sensor are increasing on the IoT and CPS. With the advancement in the internet, the capability of adopting CPS for the scope of the process has expanded exponentially [67]. We can define IoT as a system that has physical objects with sensors communicated through the internet via wired or wireless. Soon, IoT is going to play a major role in human's life, every device or physical object is connected via IoT [68]. The advancement of the

Table 2.7 Various applications in CPS using Naïve Bayes.

S. No.	Application	Dataset	Method	Evaluation factor	Ref.
1	Power system disturbance	15 Datasets	One R, Nnge, Random Forest, Naïve Bayes, SVM, Jripper, Adaboost	Accuracy, Precision, Recall, F-Measure	[31]
2	Attacks in CPS	SWaT	SVM, RF, DT, NN, NB	TP, FP, Precision, Recall, Accuracy, FA, TTBM	[33]
3	CPS maintenance	Industrial dataset	NB, DT, RF, NN	Precision, Recall	[49]
4	CP-SRS	real-life data	NN-SLM, NB-SLM	Confusion matrix	[58]
5	Autonomous Robotics	A dataset with physical and cyber features	Bayesian Networks	ROC, AUC	[53]
6	CIoT-based CPS	CASIA, TIDE	NB, SVM, LR, J48, KNN	Accuracy, Precision, Recall, F-Measure, ROC	[18]
7	CPS in gas turbine	PI system	MLP, DT, RF, KNN, LR, NB	MAE, RMSE, RAE, Accuracy, Error%	[20]
8	CPS in Laser Surface Heat treatment	Real-Time	Dynamic Bayesian networks	TP, FP, TN, FN, Sensitivity, Specificity	[66]
9	Cyber-Physical-Social Systems	Dataset from AMAZON	SVM, CCNN, NB	Accuracy	[41]

(Continued)

Table 2.7 Various applications in CPS using Naïve Bayes. (*Continued*)

S. No.	Application	Dataset	Method	Evaluation factor	Ref.
10	Industry 4.0	ABS, bCMS, and TCM	SVM, Naive Bayes, and J48 decision-tree	AUC	[42]
11	Medical CPS	Health care datasets	KNN, SVM, NB, DT, Fuzzy	Recall, F-Measure	[24]
12	Intrusions Detection in Aerospace	UNSW-NB15, KDDCUP 99, ML-IDS	K-NN, SVM, RF, NB, MLP	Precision, Recall, Accuracy, TP Rate, FP Rate	[14]
13	Cyber-physical water supply systems	anomalous dataset	KNN, MNB, BNB, GNB	Accuracy	[29]

CPS has great potential with IoT. Table 2.8 describes various studies and advancements in CPS related using IoT.

2.6   Use of Big Data in CPS

A variety of realities such as numbers, words, the depiction of things, or even scrutiny measurements are considered as data. In CPS, the procedure of assembling, shaping, and examining a massive amount of data for mining valuable information is termed as big data analytics. The current computing world is observing an advanced era of big data. Big data is the assortment of large-scale information or huge data such as jet engines, stock exchanges as well as social media sites and it is expanding exponentially with the period. The characteristics of big data include volume, variety, velocity, and variability [68]. Volume is associated with size which plays a crucial role in validating worth out of data. Variety is related to different behavior and resources of data. Velocity is the rate of data and variability is the irregularity that hinders the process of being competent to seize and manage the data professionally. Enhanced decision making, improved customer service, and better operational efficiency are some advantages of big data. Big data is of three types: structured, unstructured as well as semi-structured. Data that accessed effortlessly, practiced,

Table 2.8 Role of IoT in CPS.

S. No.	Application	Dataset	Method	Evaluation factor	Ref.
1	Manufacturing systems	–	UML-based approach	Min, max, avg, stddev	[69]
2	Intrusion Detection	KDD'99	MLP	Accuracy, FP Rate	[70]
3	Advanced Manufacturing and Medicine	–	GENI and FIRE	Not mentioned	[67]
4	Images Authenticity	Autonomous sources	OC-LBP	TPR, FPR, recall, Precision, F-Measure, ROC	[18]
5	Industrial	–	not mentioned	–	[71]
6	Predicting users preferences and interests	Autonomous sources	COLLABORATIVE, CONTENT BASED and HYBRID FILTERING	–	[72]
7	Mosquito-Borne Diseases	Autonomous sources	fog computing	Temporal Network Analysis	[56]
8	Industrial Manufacturing	Autonomous sources	CA-Module, A-Hub, LSP	Physical manufacturing resources	[73]
9	Misbehavior Detection	Collection of Compliance Data	SPECIFICATION-BASED rules	Lightweight Statistical Analysis	[74]
10	Mobile Edge Computing	10 Datasets	NB, RF, DT, SVM,K-Means, KNN, MLP, RNN,	Accuracy	[26]
11	Intrusions Detection in Aerospace	synthetic data, KDDCup 99	6LoWPAN	Precision, Recall, Accuracy, TP rate, FP rate	[14]

and accumulated in the stable format is known as structured data, and data with no structure is termed as unstructured data. Whereas, semi-structured data consists of both structured as well as unstructured data. These types of big data have been categorized as 1) streaming data, 2) social media data and 3) publicly available data. Where, streaming data can hold a huge amount of data and we can examine as it achieves and create outcomes on what type of information need to keep and what type of data needs to avoid. Social media data is in the form of either unstructured or semi-structured data, thus it postures a limited test at utilization and assessment. Likewise, publicly available data access huge amount of information through open databases such as the CIA World Fact book, the European Union Open Data Entry, or the US government's data. Big data can be used in many places including education, health care, banking, government, retail, manufacturing, and many more. It allows people to assess information over an existing generation of skills and architectures that maintain eminent speed, storage, detaining information, and assessment. Due to the continuing rise of collected data, large databases were built by the corporation to contribute, aggregate, and extract meaning as of individual data. As a result, overall data regarding privacy, security, intellectual property, and even liability must be recognized in a big data world [86]. Usage of big data offers industries to raise their revenue, acquire additional goals during the origin of novel applications, save money, improve efficiency, and lower the rate of existing applications. On the other hand, the data stream of traffic above the network directs to troubles of big data due to their variety, volume, and properties of speed. Also, privacy, authenticity, convenience, and discretion concerning outsourced information are the major considerations of big data from safety perception. Security has become important since the procedure of big data has amplified. Therefore, intrusion plays a vital role in the allotment of big data.

Nowadays, big data analytics for resolving the problems of the intrusion detection system has been attracting many researchers, as it supports the learning of enormous volumes of information with several formats from varied resources and detects anomalies. Generally, the assortment of systems for identifying and prohibiting the threatful attack has been categorized as antivirus, intrusion detection systems or intrusion prevention systems, etc. though the referred systems are advantageous in abundant methods, still they are incapable to evade such kind of offensive surreptitious cyber threats. The motivation behind the incompetent of these techniques is the production of a huge quantity of information that is hard and instance unmanageable to examine. So, it is unproblematic to fail to

Table 2.9 Big data in cyber-physical system.

S. No.	Application	Dataset	Method	Evaluation factor	Ref.
1	Tracking and synchronization problems	Autonomous sources	FFLM-CTSP	Lyapunov Exponent and Absolute error	[76]
2	Specification and Design Method	Autonomous sources	Architecture Analysis & Design Language	QoS	[77]
3	Big Data in Cloud Computing Environment	URL Reputation, YouTube Video, Bag of Words, Gas sensor arrays, Patient, Outpatient, Medicine, Cancer	Parallel Random Forest, RF, DRF, Spark-MLRF	OOB Error Rate, Accuracy	[48]
4	Educational	Autonomous sources	TOLA	Complexity, Efficiency, and Accuracy	[34]
5	Industrial	Smart factory features	Agent-Based Data Analysis	Corr.Coef,RAE (%)	[78]
6	Social data	Autonomous sources	Tensor Computation and Optimization Model	High-order Singular Value Decomposition	[79]
7	Socio-cyber network:human behaviors	The social network, healthcare, and intelligent transportation system	Graph-theory	Throughput	[80]
8	Industrial	Autonomous sources	Industrial cloud, the IoT, and big data methods	Not mentioned	[81]

(Continued)

Table 2.9 Big data in cyber-physical system. (*Continued*)

S. No.	Application	Dataset	Method	Evaluation factor	Ref.
9	Privacy and security	Autonomous sources	Weibull distribution	Performance, Reliability and mean time failure	[82]
10	Energy Efficient Machining	Autonomous sources	Energy efficient machining system, Fruit Fly Optimization	RMSE	[83]
11	Agricultural	Agricultural Cyber-Physical Datasets	GA-SVM	Minimum, Maximum, Mean, Standard Deviation, Skewness, Kurtosis	[47]
12	Computation	–	high-order singular value decomposition	Error Measurement, Sweep Number Comparison, Incremental tensor	[84]
13	Health Care (SARS-CoV)	Not mentioned	J48graft, RNN	Success rate, Failure rate, latency and accuracy	[70]
14	Design and development of a predictive maintenance	Autonomous sources	Offline Association Rule Algorithm and Predictive Maintenance	Support, Confidence	[85]

mark the major offensive dangerous actions. Big Data analytics (BDA) can sort through an enormous quantity of data in a fast manner and various systems can become more efficient as well as effective [75]. Authenticating the immeasurable quantity of data in contented networks can be a most important confront for the reason that there is an extremely high quantity of dissimilar kinds of origins: blogs, SNP (social networking platforms) and the contents (comments, articles as well as tweets, etc.) that contain or stored in those SNP. For that reason, there is a need for deriving trouble-free policies for authenticating those kinds of content and control content commendations from further end users. The commended end-users themselves have to be evaluated based on lying on the status and confidence criterion.

CPS has various operations include sensing data from many sensor networks. The main goal of big data in CPS is to analyze data streams that are huge, rapid, and heterogeneous. Table 2.9 represents studies in CPS in the area of Big data.

2.7 Critical Analysis

The cyber-physical system is assorted with different levels of network connectivity and abstraction, because of its current significance in industry, academia, and government. The fundamental hypothesis is that a wide scope of services can be utilized in the collaboration of networks. On the other hand, an extensive and systematic research review on CPS is not found. So, this paper leads to an in-depth literature study on CPS by inspecting existing literature from 2014 to 2020 by considering the articles from standard archives like Elsevier, Springer Link, Research gate, IEEE Explore, and peer reviewed journals. Various researches exploring techniques, algorithms, and frameworks concerning CPS are considered for this work. Especially, 75 papers studying CPS are grouped into ML, IoT, and Big data. The substance of the studies is summarized into three categorical works with year, author, and publication, area of application, dataset, the proposed method, and evaluation factors.

Based on the literature study from Tables 2.1 to 2.9, it is evident that in the year 2017 maximum number of research works was published with the k-NN, SVM, RF, DT, LR, MLP, and NB algorithm. Figure 2.3 shows the ML algorithms with CPS versus the number of publications each year. Figure 2.4 shows the number of published work of CPS with several ML methods, IoT, and Big-Data.

Figure 2.5 shows the development of CPS through various ML methods and it is evident that SVM based models are on a higher priority than other methods such as MLP, K-NN, DT, NB, RF, and LR.

Figure 2.6 concludes the number of CPS works concerning big data, ML, and IoT. The ML approaches are used in wide with 118 from our work and then with big data and IoT.

The application areas of CPS integrated with ML are briefly classified into the industry, security, medical, agriculture, research, and education

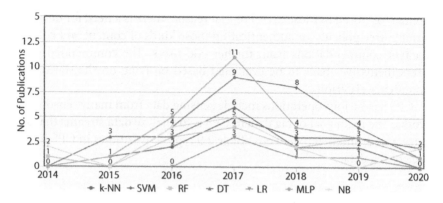

Figure 2.3 Machine learning algorithms with CPS.

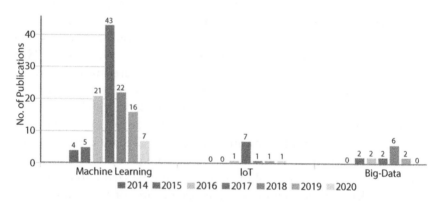

Figure 2.4 Number of publications for ML, IoT, and Big-Data with year wise.

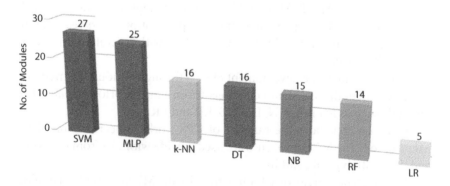

Figure 2.5 Number of machine learning algorithms proposed with CPS.

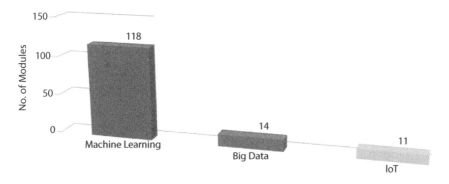

Figure 2.6 Distinguish approaches with CPS.

in our work as shown in Figure 2.7. The SVM and MLP are the most popularly used algorithms for industrial application and security. K-NN and SVM are widely used for medical applications. The DT, NB, and MLP are also widely used for research, SVM in agriculture, and no application in the area of education. Figure 2.8 elaborates on the application areas of CPS concerning ML, IoT, and big data. The ML approaches are getting largely used in industry, security-based model development, and medical domain. It's clear that IoT and big data are emerging in the fields of industry, security, medical, and research, but there is no major proposed literature studies in the application fields of agriculture and education.

The evaluation factors play a key role in identifying the effectiveness of an algorithm or framework of a developed system. Here individual study has been made for each ML model with evaluating factors. The widely used

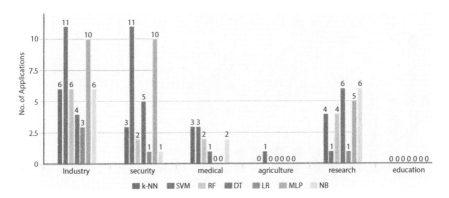

Figure 2.7 Applications of ML with CPS.

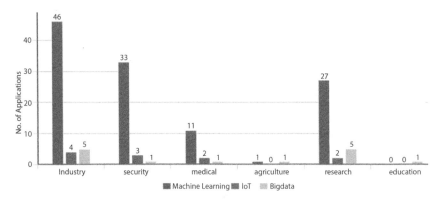

Figure 2.8 Applications of ML, IoT and Big data with CPS.

evaluation factors are accuracy, precision, recall, MAE, RMSE and other factors for the K-NN approach, as shown in Figure 2.9.

Similarly, for SVM, RF, DT, MLP, and NB approach widely used factors are accuracy, precision, recall, F-measure, and others as shown in Figures 2.10–2.14.

The LR approach widely used factors such as accuracy, RMSE, MSE, MAE, and others for performance comparison as shown in Figure 2.15.

The researcher had taken the liberty to recognize different research work through a variety of methodologies and frameworks through big data and IoT concerning CPS models. The evaluation factors that are taken into considerations for big data with CPS models accuracy, support, confidence, and other factors are shown in Figure 2.16. Similarly, for IoT with CPS models, the evaluating factors are accuracy, TPR, FPR, recall, precision, and others as shown in Figure 2.17.

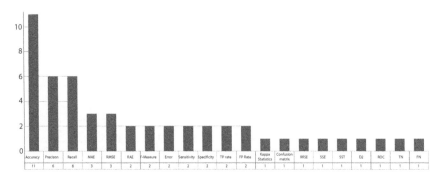

Figure 2.9 K-NN evaluation factors.

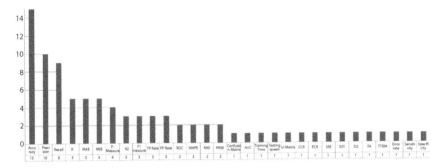

Figure 2.10 SVM evaluation factors.

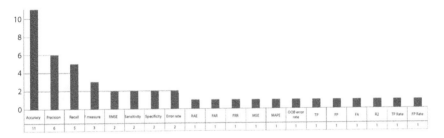

Figure 2.11 RF evaluation factors.

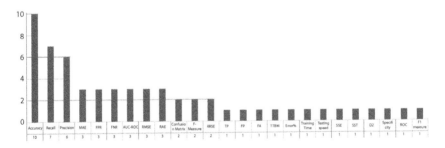

Figure 2.12 DT evaluation factors.

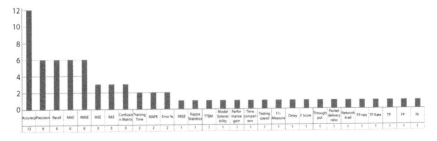

Figure 2.13 MLP evaluation factors.

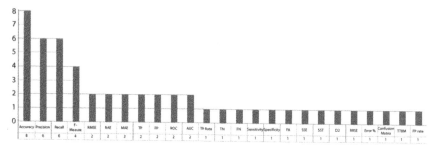

Figure 2.14 NB evaluation factors.

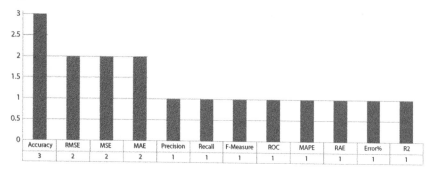

Figure 2.15 LR evaluation factors.

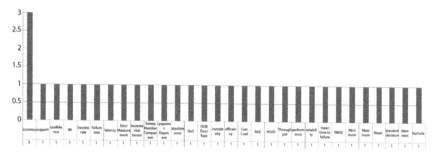

Figure 2.16 Big Data evaluation factors.

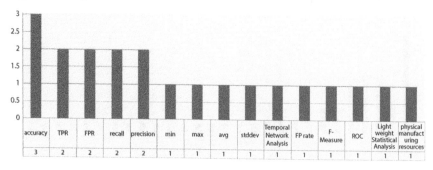

Figure 2.17 IoT evaluation factors.

The literature study shows that for CPS the most widely used datasets are UCI-Parkinson, SWaT, UNSW-NB15, KDDCUP-99, and ML-IDS. However, the rest of the dataset is the random and autonomous dataset.

2.8 Conclusion

Indeed for a secure and prosperous society, we require a great advancement in the fields of defense systems, smart infrastructure buildings and environmental control, renewable energy and smart grid, healthcare system and biomedical, cyber-security, industrial domain platforms, agriculture, education, vehicles, robotic systems, and diagnostic capabilities. The prospect is related to CPS that will lead to multifaceted systems involved by the web of associations and self-driven adaptability through complex logic. As these are perplexing versatile systems that have the developing behavior and require systems joining with other devices through engineering work in their design and operation. So, the need for developing methods, theory, and tools will help the engineers to manage the complexity in design and operations. The study emphasizes CPS and its applications with a computational algorithm, which effectively extracts the affluent statistical representations through the latest evaluation factors, technologies, and approaches in ML, IoT, and big-data framework. All these applications of the system will help us categorically, collaborate, and share assets to achieve the physical procedure. Competent ML architecture is preferred based on comparing their performance in various scenarios. The experimental results of the research community show that ML techniques give enhanced results in terms of precision, recall, and accuracy. The ML approaches demonstrate that the proposed models can be utilized in compelled environments of CPS through a model predictive control, due to their significant advancements and impressive results.

The huge data is computationally inefficient to analyze and progress in the field of CPS through ML because detecting data from numerous IoT sensor systems, handling the acquired data is a big task. This enormous amount of data is processed and extracted into valuable information systems. But the entire process is computationally inefficient due to high energy consumption overhead for the computation process and memory factors. So the mounting space between CPS with the IoT and big data analytics demands novel tools that resolve the challenges confronted by big data velocity, volume, and variety. To analyze the stream of big data, novel architecture systems with cutting edge tools are required to integrate review and decipher useful knowledge from huge streams of data with the CPS. The factors like accuracy and success rate of the big data tools are high when related to other traditional ML, for establishing a better perceptive in extracting knowledge from the data.

The scope of future work emphasis

- On various advanced ML techniques that are needed for CPS.
- The availability of a significantly fair large promissory dataset is required, but the absence of information is a considerable problem.
- The advanced IoT and big data framework architecture must come into play for extracting and sensing knowledge from the data with more scalable, efficient, robust, and secure.
- More research on CPS in the fields of agriculture and education is needed.

References

1. Rajkumar, R.R., Lee, I., Sha, L., Stankovic, J., Cyber-physical systems: The next computing revolution, in: *Proceedings of the 47th Design Automation Conference on—DAC '10*, vol. 19, no. 3, p. 731, 2010.
2. Noble, B. and Flinn, J., Wireless, self-organizing cyber-physical systems, in: *NSF Work. Cyber-Physical Syst.*, Austin, TX, pp. 1–3, 2006, [Online]. Available: http://citeseerx.ist.psu.edu/viewdoc/download?doi=10.1.1.83.9627&rep=rep1&type=pdf.
3. Zhang, Z.-K., Cho, M.C.Y., Wang, C.-W., Hsu, C.-W., Chen, C.-K., Shieh, S., IoT Security: Ongoing Challenges and Research Opportunities, in: *2014 IEEE 7th International Conference on Service-Oriented Computing and Applications*, pp. 230–234, Nov. 2014.
4. Johnson, A.P., Al-Aqrabi, H., Hill, R., Bio-Inspired Approaches to Safety and Security in IoT-Enabled Cyber-Physical Systems. *Sensors*, 20, 3, 844, Feb. 2020.
5. Sun, C., Ma, J., Yao, Q., On the architecture and development life cycle of secure cyber-physical systems. *J. Commun. Inf. Networks*, 1, 4, 1–21, Dec. 2016.
6. Sharma, V., You, I., Yim, K., Chen, I.-R., Cho, J.-H., BRIoT: Behavior Rule Specification-Based Misbehavior Detection for IoT-Embedded Cyber-Physical Systems. *IEEE Access*, 7, c, 118556–118580, 2019.
7. Kuhnle, A. and Lanza, G., *Application of Reinforcement Learning in Production Planning and Control of Cyber Physical Production Systems*, pp. 123–132, Springer Berlin Heidelberg, 2019.

8. Banerjee, S., Al-Qaheri, H., Bhatt, C., Handling uncertainty in IoT design: An approach of statistical machine learning with distributed second-order optimization, in: *Healthcare Data Analytics and Management*, pp. 227–243, Elsevier, 2019.

9. Keshk, M., Sitnikova, E., Moustafa, N., Hu, J., Khalil, I., An Integrated Framework for Privacy-Preserving based Anomaly Detection for Cyber-Physical Systems. *IEEE Trans. Sustain. Comput.*, 1–1, 2019.

10. Krismayer, T., Rabiser, R., Grünbacher, P., A constraint mining approach to support monitoring cyber-physical systems. In *International Conference on Advanced Information Systems Engineering*, Springer, Cham, pp. 659–674, June 2019.

11. Sepulveda, J., Liu, S., Bermudo Mera, J.M., Post-Quantum Enabled Cyber Physical Systems. *IEEE Embed. Syst. Lett.*, 11, 4, 106–110, Dec. 2019.

12. Genge, B., Haller, P., Duka, A.V., Engineering security-aware control applications for data authentication in smart industrial cyber–physical systems. *Future Gener. Comput. Syst.*, 91, 206–222, 2019.

13. Han, S., Xie, M., Chen, H.-H., Ling, Y., Intrusion Detection in Cyber-Physical Systems: Techniques and Challenges. *IEEE Syst. J.*, 8, 4, 1052–1062, Dec. 2014.

14. Maleh, Y., Machine Learning Techniques for IoT Intrusions Detection in Aerospace Cyber-Physical Systems, in: *Studies in Computational Intelligence*, vol. 836, pp. 205–232, Springer International Publishing, Cham, 2020.

15. de Mello, A.R. and Stemmer, M.R., Inspecting surface mounted devices using k nearest neighbor and Multilayer Perceptron, in: *2015 IEEE 24th International Symposium on Industrial Electronics (ISIE)*, vol. 2015-Septe, pp. 950–955, Jun. 2015.

16. Ide, C., Nick, M., Kaulbars, D., Wietfeld, C., Forecasting Cellular Connectivity for Cyber-Physical Systems: A Machine Learning Approach, in: *Machine Learning for Cyber Physical Systems*, O. Niggemann and J. Beyerer (Eds.), pp. 15–22, Springer Berlin Heidelberg, Berlin, Heidelberg, 2016.

17. Misra, S., Goswami, S., Taneja, C., Multivariate Data Fusion-Based Learning of Video Content and Service Distribution for Cyber Physical Social Systems. *IEEE Trans. Comput. Soc. Syst.*, 3, 1, 1–12, Mar. 2016.

18. Hossain, M.S., Muhammad, G., AL Qurishi, M., Verifying the Images Authenticity in Cognitive Internet of Things (CIoT)-Oriented Cyber Physical System. *Mob. Netw. Appl.*, 23, 2, 239–250, Apr. 2018.

19. Laghari, A., Memon, Z.A., Ullah, S., Hussain, I., Cyber Physical System for Stroke Detection. *IEEE Access*, 6, c, 37444–37453, 2018.

20. Majdani, F., Petrovski, A., Doolan, D., Evolving ANN-based sensors for a context-aware cyber physical system of an offshore gas turbine. *Evol. Syst.*, 9, 2, 119–133, Jun. 2018.

21. Wang, J., Tu, W., Hui, L.C.K., Yiu, S.M., Wang, E.K., Detecting Time Synchronization Attacks in Cyber-Physical Systems with Machine Learning

Techniques, in: *2017 IEEE 37th International Conference on Distributed Computing Systems (ICDCS)*, pp. 2246–2251, Jun. 2017.

22. Wu, M., Song, Z., Moon, Y.B., Detecting cyber-physical attacks in CyberManufacturing systems with machine learning methods. *J. Intell. Manuf.*, 30, 3, 1111–1123, Mar. 2019.

23. Devarajan, M. and Ravi, L., Intelligent cyber-physical system for an efficient detection of Parkinson disease using fog computing. *Multimed. Tools Appl.*, 78, 23, 32695–32719, Dec. 2019.

24. Li, W., Meng, W., Su, C., Kwok, L.F., Towards False Alarm Reduction Using Fuzzy If-Then Rules for Medical Cyber Physical Systems. *IEEE Access*, 6, c, 6530–6539, 2018.

25. Miranda Calero, J.A., Marino, R., Lanza-Gutierrez, J.M., Riesgo, T., Garcia-Valderas, M., Lopez-Ongil, C., Embedded Emotion Recognition within Cyber-Physical Systems using Physiological Signals, in: *2018 Conference on Design of Circuits and Integrated Systems (DCIS)*, pp. 1–6, Nov. 2018.

26. Chen, Y., Zhang, Y., Maharjan, S., Alam, M., Wu, T., Deep Learning for Secure Mobile Edge Computing in Cyber-Physical Transportation Systems. *IEEE Netw.*, 33, 4, 36–41, Jul. 2019.

27. Song, K., Anderson, K., Lee, S., An energy-cyber-physical system for personalized normative messaging interventions: Identification and classification of behavioral reference groups. *Appl. Energy*, 260, November 2019, 114237, Feb. 2020.

28. Zhang, F., Kodituwakku, H.A.D.E., Hines, J.W., Coble, J., Multilayer Data-Driven Cyber-Attack Detection System for Industrial Control Systems Based on Network, System, and Process Data. *IEEE Trans. Industr. Inform.*, 15, 7, 4362–4369, Jul. 2019.

29. Meleshko, A.V., Desnitsky, V.A., Kotenko, I.V., Machine learning based approach to detection of anomalous data from sensors in cyber-physical water supply systems. *IOP Conf. Ser. Mater. Sci. Eng.*, 709, 3, 033034, Jan. 2020.

30. Wang, Y., Amin, M.M., Fu, J., Moussa, H.B., A Novel Data Analytical Approach for False Data Injection Cyber-Physical Attack Mitigation in Smart Grids. *IEEE Access*, 5, 26022–26033, 2017.

31. Borges Hink, R.C., Beaver, J.M., Buckner, M.A., Morris, T., Adhikari, U., Pan, S., Machine learning for power system disturbance and cyber-attack discrimination, in: *2014 7th International Symposium on Resilient Control Systems (ISRCS)*, pp. 1–8, Aug. 2014.

32. Huda, S. *et al.*, Defending unknown attacks on cyber-physical systems by semi-supervised approach and available unlabeled data. *Inf. Sci. (Ny).*, 379, 211–228, Feb. 2017.

33. Junejo, K.N. and Goh, J., Behaviour-Based Attack Detection and Classification in Cyber Physical Systems Using Machine Learning, in: *Proceedings of the*

2nd ACM International Workshop on Cyber-Physical System Security—CPSS '16, no. Ml, pp. 34–43, 2016.

34. Song, J., Zhang, Y., Duan, K., Shamim Hossain, M., Rahman, S.M.M., TOLA: Topic-oriented learning assistance based on cyber-physical system and big data. *Future Gener. Comput. Syst.*, 75, 200–205, Oct. 2017.

35. Li, Q. *et al.*, Safety Risk Monitoring of Cyber-Physical Power Systems Based on Ensemble Learning Algorithm. *IEEE Access*, 7, c, 24788–24805, 2019.

36. Loukas, G., Vuong, T., Heartfield, R., Sakellari, G., Yoon, Y., Gan, D., Cloud-Based Cyber-Physical Intrusion Detection for Vehicles Using Deep Learning. *IEEE Access*, 6, 3491–3508, 2018.

37. Lv, C. *et al.*, Levenberg–Marquardt Backpropagation Training of Multilayer Neural Networks for State Estimation of a Safety-Critical Cyber-Physical System. *IEEE Trans. Industr. Inform.*, 14, 8, 3436–3446, Aug. 2018.

38. Saez, M., Maturana, F., Barton, K., Tilbury, D., Anomaly detection and productivity analysis for cyber-physical systems in manufacturing, in: *2017 13th IEEE Conference on Automation Science and Engineering (CASE)*, vol. 2017-Augus, pp. 23–29, Aug. 2017.

39. Castaño, F., Beruvides, G., Haber, R.E., Artuñedo, A., Obstacle Recognition Based on Machine Learning for On-Chip LiDAR Sensors in a Cyber-Physical System. *Sensors*, 17, 9, 2109, Sep. 2017.

40. Shin, J., Baek, Y., Eun, Y., Son, S.H., Intelligent sensor attack detection and identification for automotive cyber-physical systems, in: *2017 IEEE Symposium Series on Computational Intelligence (SSCI)*, vol. 2018-Janua, pp. 1–8, Nov. 2017.

41. Yuan, X., Sun, M., Chen, Z., Gao, J., Li, P., Semantic Clustering-Based Deep Hypergraph Model for Online Reviews Semantic Classification in Cyber-Physical-Social Systems. *IEEE Access*, 6, c, 17942–17951, 2018.

42. Alenazi, M., Niu, N., Wang, W., Savolainen, J., Using Obstacle Analysis to Support SysML-Based Model Testing for Cyber Physical Systems, in: *2018 IEEE 8th International Model-Driven Requirements Engineering Workshop (MoDRE)*, no. 1, pp. 46–55, Aug. 2018.

43. Miao, G., Hsieh, S.-J., Segura, J.A., Wang, J.-C., Cyber-physical system for thermal stress prevention in 3D printing process. *Int. J. Adv. Manuf. Technol.*, 100, 1–4, 553–567, Jan. 2019.

44. Ning, Z., Zhou, G., Chen, Z., Li, Q., Integration of Image Feature and Word Relevance: Toward Automatic Image Annotation in Cyber-Physical-Social Systems. *IEEE Access*, 6, 44190–44198, 2018.

45. Lee, J., Noh, S., Kim, H.-J., Kang, Y.-S., Implementation of Cyber-Physical Production Systems for Quality Prediction and Operation Control in Metal Casting. *Sensors*, 18, 5, 1428, May 2018.

46. Ahmed, F., Jannat, N.-E., Gavidel, S.Z., Rickli, J., Kim, K.-Y., A Conceptual Framework for Cyber-physical System in Connected RSW Weldability Certification. *Procedia Manuf.*, 38, 2019, 431–438, 2019.

47. Ruan, J., Jiang, H., Li, X., Shi, Y., Chan, F.T.S., Rao, W., A Granular GA-SVM Predictor for Big Data in Agricultural Cyber-Physical Systems. *IEEE Trans. Industr. Inform.*, 15, 12, 6510–6521, Dec. 2019.

48. Chen, J. *et al.*, A Parallel Random Forest Algorithm for Big Data in a Spark Cloud Computing Environment. *IEEE Trans. Parallel Distrib. Syst.*, 28, 4, 919–933, Apr. 2017.

49. Alexis, L. and Bueno, M.L.P., *Towards Adaptive Scheduling of Maintenance for Cyber-Physical Systems*, vol. 9952, Springer International Publishing, Cham, 2016.

50. Lakshmanaprabu, S.K., Shankar, K., Ilayaraja, M., Nasir, A.W., Vijayakumar, V., Chilamkurti, N., Random forest for big data classification in the internet of things using optimal features. *Int. J. Mach. Learn. Cybern.*, 10, 10, 2609–2618, Oct. 2019.

51. Mowla, N.I., Doh, I., Chae, K., On-Device AI-Based Cognitive Detection of Bio-Modality Spoofing in Medical Cyber Physical System. *IEEE Access*, 7, 2126–2137, 2019.

52. Da Xu, L. and Duan, L., Big data for cyber physical systems in industry 4.0: A survey. *Enterp. Inf. Syst.*, 13, 2, 148–169, Feb. 2019.

53. Bezemskij, A., Loukas, G., Gan, D., Anthony, R.J., Detecting Cyber-Physical Threats in an Autonomous Robotic Vehicle Using Bayesian Networks, in: *2017 IEEE International Conference on Internet of Things (iThings) and IEEE Green Computing and Communications (GreenCom) and IEEE Cyber, Physical and Social Computing (CPSCom) and IEEE Smart Data (SmartData)*, vol. 2018-Janua, pp. 98–103, Jun. 2017.

54. Vuong, T.P., Loukas, G., Gan, D., Performance Evaluation of Cyber-Physical Intrusion Detection on a Robotic Vehicle, in: *2015 IEEE International Conference on Computer and Information Technology; Ubiquitous Computing and Communications; Dependable, Autonomic and Secure Computing; Pervasive Intelligence and Computing*, pp. 2106–2113, Oct. 2015.

55. Vuong, T.P., Loukas, G., Gan, D., Bezemskij, A., Decision tree-based detection of denial of service and command injection attacks on robotic vehicles. *2015 IEEE Int. Work. Inf. Forensics Secur. WIFS 2015—Proc.*, no. Table I, pp. 1–6, 2015.

56. Sood, S.K. and Mahajan, I., Fog-cloud based cyber-physical system for distinguishing, detecting and preventing mosquito borne diseases. *Future Gener. Comput. Syst.*, 88, 764–775, Nov. 2018.

57. Shanthamallu, U.S., Spanias, A., Tepedelenlioglu, C., Stanley, M., A brief survey of machine learning methods and their sensor and IoT applications, in: *2017 8th International Conference on Information, Intelligence, Systems & Applications (IISA)*, vol. 2018-Janua, pp. 1–8, Aug. 2017.

58. Li, C., Rusák, Z., Horváth, I., Ji, L., Validation of the reasoning of an entry-level cyber-physical stroke rehabilitation system equipped with engagement enhancing capabilities. *Eng. Appl. Artif. Intell.*, 56, 185–199, Nov. 2016.

59. Wang, Y., Song, B., Zhang, P., Xin, N., Cao, G., A Fast Feature Fusion Algorithm in Image Classification for Cyber Physical Systems. *IEEE Access*, 5, c, 9089–9098, 2017.

60. Mowla, N., Doh, I., Chae, K., Evolving neural network intrusion detection system for MCPS, in: *2018 20th International Conference on Advanced Communication Technology (ICACT)*, vol. 6, no. 4, pp. 1040–1045, Feb. 2018.

61. Feng, M. and Xu, H., Deep reinforecement learning based optimal defense for cyber-physical system in presence of unknown cyber-attack, in: *2017 IEEE Symposium Series on Computational Intelligence (SSCI)*, vol. 2018-Janua, pp. 1–8, Nov. 2017.

62. Goh, J., Adepu, S., Tan, M., Lee, Z.S., Anomaly Detection in Cyber Physical Systems Using Recurrent Neural Networks, in: *2017 IEEE 18th International Symposium on High Assurance Systems Engineering (HASE)*, pp. 140–145, 2017.

63. Belenko, V., Chernenko, V., Kalinin, M., Krundyshev, V., Evaluation of GAN Applicability for Intrusion Detection in Self-Organizing Networks of Cyber Physical Systems, in: *2018 International Russian Automation Conference (RusAutoCon)*, pp. 1–7, Sep. 2018.

64. Jindal, A., Aujla, G.S., Kumar, N., Chaudhary, R., Obaidat, M.S., You, I., SeDaTiVe: SDN-Enabled Deep Learning Architecture for Network Traffic Control in Vehicular Cyber-Physical Systems. *IEEE Netw.*, 32, 6, 66–73, Nov. 2018.

65. Chen, Y., Du, T., Jiang, C., Sun, S., Indoor location method of interference source based on deep learning of spectrum fingerprint features in Smart Cyber-Physical systems. *EURASIP J. Wirel. Commun. Netw.*, 2019, 1, 47, Dec. 2019.

66. Ogbechie, A., Díaz-Rozo, J., Larrañaga, P., Bielza, C., Dynamic Bayesian Network-Based Anomaly Detection for In-Process Visual Inspection of Laser Surface Heat Treatment, in: *Machine Learning for Cyber Physical Systems*, J. Beyerer, O. Niggemann, C. Kühnert (Eds.), pp. 17–24, Springer Berlin Heidelberg, Berlin, Heidelberg, 2017.

67. Cecil, J., Internet of Things (IoT)-Based Cyber-Physical Frameworks for Advanced Manufacturing and Medicine, in: *Internet of Things and Data Analytics Handbook*, pp. 545–561, John Wiley & Sons, Inc., Hoboken, NJ, USA, 2016.

68. Babiceanu, R.F. and Seker, R., Big Data and virtualization for manufacturing cyber-physical systems: A survey of the current status and future outlook. *Comput. Ind.*, 81, 2015, 128–137, Sep. 2016.

69. Thramboulidis, K. and Christoulakis, F., UML4IoT—A UML-based approach to exploit IoT in cyber-physical manufacturing systems. *Comput. Ind.*, 82, 259–272, Oct. 2016.

70. Alpano, P.V.S., Pedrasa, J.R.I., Atienza, R., Multilayer perceptron with binary weights and activations for intrusion detection of Cyber-Physical systems,

in: *TENCON 2017—2017 IEEE Region 10 Conference*, vol. 2017-Decem, pp. 2825–2829, Nov. 2017.

71. Barnard, A., Frechette, S., Srinivasan, V., *Industrial Internet of Things*, Springer International Publishing, Cham, 2017.

72. Sawant, S.D., Sonawane, K.V., Jagani, T., Chaudhari, A.N., Representation of recommender system in IoT using cyber physical techniques, in: *2017 International conference of Electronics, Communication and Aerospace Technology (ICECA)*, vol. 2017-Janua, pp. 372–375, Apr. 2017.

73. Tao, F., Cheng, J., Qi, Q., IIHub: An Industrial Internet-of-Things Hub Toward Smart Manufacturing Based on Cyber-Physical System. *IEEE Trans. Industr. Inform.*, 14, 5, 2271–2280, May 2018.

74. You, I., Yim, K., Sharma, V., Choudhary, G., Chen, I.-R., Cho, J.-H., On IoT Misbehavior Detection in Cyber Physical Systems, in: *2018 IEEE 23rd Pacific Rim International Symposium on Dependable Computing (PRDC)*, vol. 2018-Decem, pp. 189–190, Dec. 2018.

75. Oseku-Afful, T., *The use of Big Data Analytics to protect Critical Information Infrastructures from Cyber-attacks, Information Security*, Univ. Technol. Dep. Comput. Sci. Electr. Sp. Eng. Master Thesis, pp. 1–64, 2016.

76. Liu, L., Zhao, S., Yu, Z., Dai, H., A big data inspired chaotic solution for fuzzy feedback linearization model in cyber-physical systems. *Ad Hoc Netw.*, 35, 97–104, Dec. 2015.

77. Selvaraj, H., Zydek, D., Chmaj, G., *Progress in Systems Engineering*, vol. 366, Springer International Publishing, Cham, 2015.

78. Queiroz, J., Leitão, P., Oliveira, E., Industrial Cyber Physical Systems Supported by Distributed Advanced Data Analytics, in: *Studies in Computational Intelligence*, vol. 694, pp. 47–59, 2017.

79. Wang, X., Yang, L.T., Chen, X., Han, J.-J., Feng, J., Tensor, A., Computation and Optimization Model for Cyber-Physical-Social Big Data. *IEEE Trans. Sustain. Comput.*, 4, 4, 326–339, 2017.

80. Ahmad, A. *et al.*, Socio-cyber network: The potential of cyber-physical system to define human behaviors using big data analytics. *Future Gener. Comput. Syst.*, 92, 868–878.

81. Cheng, B.O., Zhang, J., Hancke, G.P., Industrial Cyber-Physical Systems, in: *2019 IEEE 28th International Symposium on Industrial Electronics (ISIE)*, no. March, pp. 1620–1622, Jun. 2019.

82. Gifty, R., Bharathi, R., Krishnakumar, P., Privacy and security of big data in cyber physical systems using Weibull distribution-based intrusion detection. *Neural Comput. Appl.*, 31, S1, 23–34, Jan. 2019.

83. Liang, Y.C., Lu, X., Li, W.D., Wang, S., Cyber Physical System and Big Data enabled energy efficient machining optimisation. *J. Clean. Prod.*, 187, 46–62, Jun. 2018.

84. Wang, X., Wang, W., Yang, L.T., Liao, S., Yin, D., Deen, M.J., A Distributed HOSVD Method with Its Incremental Computation for Big Data in

Cyber-Physical-Social Systems. *IEEE Trans. Comput. Soc. Syst.*, 5, 2, 481–492, 2018.

85. Yang, F.-N. and Lin, H.-Y., Development of A Predictive Maintenance Platform for Cyber-Physical Systems, in: *2019 IEEE International Conference on Industrial Cyber Physical Systems (ICPS)*, pp. 331–335, May 2019.

86. Britel, M., Big data analytic for intrusion detection system, *2018 Int. Conf. Electron. Control. Optim. Comput. Sci.* ICECOCS 2018, no. 1, pp. 1–5, 2019.

3

HemoSmart: A Non-Invasive Device and Mobile App for Anemia Detection

J.A.D.C.A. Jayakody*, E.A.G.A. Edirisinghe[†] and S.Lokuliyana[‡]

Department of Computer Systems Engineering, Sri Lanka Institute of Information Technology, Malabe, Sri Lanka

Abstract

The Hemoglobin concentration in human blood is an important substance to health condition determination. With the results which are obtained from Hemoglobin test, a condition which is called as Anemia (a low level of Hemoglobin) can be revealed. Traditionally the Hemoglobin test is done using blood samples which are taken using needles. The non-invasive Hemoglobin level detection system, discussed in this paper, describes a better idea about the hemoglobin concentration in the human blood. The images of the fingertip of the different hemoglobin level patients which is taken using a camera is used to develop the neural network-based algorithm. The pre-mentioned algorithm is used in the developed non-invasive device to display the Hemoglobin level. Before doing the above procedure, an account is created in the mobile app and a questionnaire is given to answer by the patient. Finally, both the results which are obtained from the mobile app and the device are run through a machine learning algorithm to get the final output. According to the final result patient would be able to detect anemia at an early stage.

***Keywords*:** Hemoglobin, anemia, non-invasive, machine learning, neural network

Corresponding author: anuradha.j@sliit.lk
[†]*Corresponding author*: anu.edirisinghe77@gmail.com
[‡]*Corresponding author*: shashika.l@sliit.lk

Kolla Bhanu Prakash, G. R. Kanagachidambaresan, V. Srikanth, E. Vamsidhar (eds.) Cognitive Engineering for Next Generation Computing: A Practical Analytical Approach, (93–120) © 2021 Scrivener Publishing LLC

3.1 Introduction

This book chapter is developed by a research group of Sri Lanka Institute of Information Technology, Malabe, Sri Lanka that included "A non-invasive method to detect Anemia". The purpose of this book chapter is to present the knowledge gained from this Research.

3.1.1 Background

Anemia is a condition which happens due to the lack of red blood cells or their oxygen carrying capacity. As a result of too few or abnormal red blood cells will cause the too low hemoglobin level in one's blood level which could be described as Anemia. This is experienced when there is low iron levels in the blood which is mainly caused because of the before mentioned lack of hemoglobin condition. Hemoglobin carries oxygen and energizes cells; thus it plays a major role and symptoms like fatigue occurs when organs are not getting what they need to work appropriately. Typically, blood makes the blood red color, as hemoglobin represents the amount of red blood cells, when the blood lacks hemoglobin the bright red color of the blood decreases.

The population in both developed and developing countries affected by anemia is known as a global public health problem [1]. According to the World Health Organization (WHO), children under 5 years of age also have anemia [2] and as per the survey which was conducted by World Health Organization more than 1.62 billion people around the world are affected by anemia [2].

Same as in other countries, anemia has become the one of the most predominant neurotic conditions in Sri Lanka. According to many recent researches, more than 25% of Sri Lankans are suffering from anemia [3]. Among them, women are suffering from anemia more than the others due to their poor nutritional status, menstrual bleeding and delivering. In 2011 the World Health Organization estimated that approximately 29% Sri Lankan women were suffering from anemia during pregnancy [4]. The Sri Lanka Demographic and Health survey in 2007 found an estimated overall prevalence of anemia of 34%, 20.7% mild anemia and 13.3% moderate to severe anemia [5]. Furthermore, in 2009 a study was carried out, using a small sample of 228 pregnant women and they have estimated the percentage of anemia during pregnancy to be approximately 17% in Sri Lanka, 29% in Colombo and 7% in Kurunegala [5].

The causative factors for anemia can be listed as follows.

- Due to blood loss
- Due to faulty or lack of red blood cells production
- Due to lack of folate, vitamin B12 and A [2]
- Due to the failure of bone marrow [6].

Certain forms of anemia are caused due to different reasons and in different ages. Similarly, pregnant women face to iron-deficiency weakness on account of the blood misfortune from monthly cycle and expanded blood flexibly request during pregnancy [6]. Because of the medical problems and poor diet, older adults can also have a big risk of suffering from anemia [6]. Kids and grown-ups with iron-deficiency anemia have helpless memory or poor intellectual aptitudes bringing about lackluster showing in school, work exercises [6]. Children who were born from mothers who has anemia regularly have low birth weight and face a higher danger of dying in the earliest stage of life. According to many annual surveys more than 300,000 babies are born with anemia every year [7]. Normally healthy red blood cells function for 90–120 days, anemia effected blood cells only function for 10–20 days [7].

Although many people are suffering from anemia, there isn't any specified method to test anemia. In most cases, anemia is identified accidently in situation where the patient is asked to test his/her blood to diagnose any other disease. The conventional process of assessing blood to check the Hemoglobin level takes much more time and effort. Normally it is done using a blood sample of the patient and it is observed over a glass slide under microscope and counts each type of distorted cell separately [7]. Hence it takes a lot of time and requires highly trained medical practitioners and equipment. Further this technique brings pain to the patient and people become cautious to get their blood tested regularly to check the hemoglobin level. Although the blood testing environment should be a clean and safe one, developing and poor countries often do those tests in relatively unclean environments thereby making a huge risk of infection. Previously mentioned processes are expensive for both hospitals and patients [8].

Thus, it is necessary to develop a non-invasive method to measure the hemoglobin level of a person. It creates a more attractive, real time and infection free, painless method. This research paper aims to develop a non-invasive smart device to detect hemoglobin level of a patient without withdrawing blood.

3.1.2 Research Objectives

This paper discusses the literature surrounding Anemia (Low Hemoglobin level), Existing Anemia detection methods, most accurate detection method, its principles, mechanism and areas of future research.

Objective 1: Develop a non-invasive device to detect Anemia.

- The overall objective of this project is to develop a non-invasive device to detect Anemia. Any person would be able to test their Hemoglobin level easily without going for any harmful, time wasting and invasive blood testing method. Outcomes of this project would help to detect anemic patients easily and create healthier people by curing them at the earliest possible stage.

Objective 2: Create an infection free and painless operation for the patients by developing a non-invasive device.

- The main problem for people to get cautious about checking their Hemoglobin level is the pain which causes during the blood withdrawing process. The blood withdrawing environment and medical equipment should be clean and safe. Otherwise it could lead to infectious diseases. But many poor countries don't do it safely. Not only poor countries, many people don't concern about cleanliness during the blood withdrawing process. Therefore, by developing an infection-free and painless method many people will be encouraged to test their Hemoglobin level. Especially children would do it. Furthermore, pregnant women and old people could do the testing without fearing about any infection.

Objective 3: Detect anemia and cure at the earliest possible stage.

- Although Anemia is a considerable disease, many people don't get it serious. There isn't any specified method to test Anemia. Therefore many people don't even know about Anemia and some don't know actually there is a disease called Anemia. Whether people know about Anemia or not, it could bring death to people. By developing the non-invasive Anemia detection device people would be able to detect anemia easily, because it gives real time results. Hence people would be able to do treatments for anemia at the earliest possible stage.

Objective 4: To derive an algorithm to detect hemoglobin levels with the inclusion of neural network techniques.

- The Anemia detection device should be error free for any kind of person. Both females and males could be able to test their hemoglobin level without any error. In this world, there are different skin colored people and the device should give the correct hemoglobin value for those people. Also there could be people with skin diseases and different types of skin (rough, soft, etc.). But the anemia detection device should output the error free value for every person. Therefore, Neural Network techniques lead the device to that error-free environment. It helps the device to make a platform for all kind of skin types.

Objective 5: To develop a mobile application for information exchange and distribution.

- User would be able to get a good understanding about the device and its process through the mobile application. And also he/she can get a better idea about the disease and its symptoms. The mobile application consists of a questionnaire related to the anemia. It helps the device to output the most accurate value by using both mobile application information and neural network-based device result.

3.1.3   Research Approach

The research team followed a six-phase plan with the targets to build up an itemized research plan during phase 1; develop a suitable prototype in phase 2; collect data to develop the algorithm in phase 3; implement the neural network based algorithm throughout the whole phase 4; develop the mobile application as the phase 5; and, finally, complete the whole circuit of the device and the final output device in phase 6.

During phase 1, the research team conducted a literature review of Anemia and developed a point by point research plan. A better understanding about anemia, its symptoms and existing anemia detection devices and used techniques was gained during the phase 1. The result of this initial phase was a specialized update including detailed data on the approach for collecting and analyzing data or information.

During phase 2, a prototype of the device was designed. The main objective of developing this prototype is to collect data to develop the neural network based algorithm. First the prototype was designed by minimizing the errors of existing anemia detection devices. The required lighting system, camera, an electronic circuit to power up the lighting system were included in the prototype.

Phase 3 included collecting data from different kind of people to develop the algorithm. First of all, it was required to get permission from Health Ministry and other relevant sectors to collect data from hospitals. 5 hospitals were selected as data gathering centers. The required documents filled and the permission from relevant sectors was granted. Throughout the 3rd phase the data was gathered from all kinds of people using the developed prototype.

In phase 4, the research team started the implementation of Neural Network-based algorithm. The selection of suitable microcontroller was also included in this phase.

During phase 5, the Research Team developed an android mobile application, then connected it to the device.

As the final phase, in phase 6, the Research Team designed the whole device by including the lighting system, an electronic circuit, the camera, the microcontroller with the implemented algorithm and the mobile application. In the beginning of the 6th phase the whole device was designed using solid works software and then the completed device was developed. As the end of the final phase and the end of the entire project, the documentation and report making were done.

3.1.4   Limitations

This project has been developed for smart health efforts between both medical sectors and patients. To develop the algorithm a large amount of data was needed. But the health ministry only allowed the research team to collect data from limited hospitals. The implementation process incorporates steps to gain from botches and alter the process to the particular setting.

3.2   Literature Review

In the past researches have invested in several new technologies that make it possible to determine an individual's hemoglobin level without withdrawing blood. Akansha Aggrawal and his team in 2015 introduced 'Cyte' which is a public blood test service for everyone who needs to get their blood analyzed [1]. Using this device individuals can get their blood analyzed with its result being sent to their mobile phones. Cyte uses occlusion spectroscopy where the optical microscope shines light through the skin so it can analyze the blood flowing through the capillaries. The global market for non-invasive monitoring devices is growing at a moderate pace. This market is expected to grow up to USD 21,586.18 million by 2023. Thus it is understood that there would be an increased demand for non-invasive devices in the near future.

Lewis *et al.* used "NIR spectroscopy and photoplethysmography (PPG)" for the measurement of blood components [2]. During different wavelengths, the absorption-coefficient of blood is differed. This fact was used to compute the optical absorbability characteristics of blood which is yielding data about blood parts like hemoglobin (Hb) and blood vessel oxygen immersion (SpO2) [2]. To calculate the before mentioned parameters, the ratio between the peak to peak pulse amplitudes and the measured PPG time signal were used. The developed optical sensor systems were used in between 600 and 1,400 nm for a measurement of the oxygen saturation, hemoglobin concentration and pulse by using five wavelengths. Prototype-devices with LED were used and they were based on radiation of monochromatic light emitted by laser diodes.

The rapid and non-invasive measurement of hemoglobin and the availability of continuous hemoglobin information can possibly be massively helpful in clinical practice in an assortment of circumstances [3, 4]. The results from evaluations of SpHb with pulse CO-Oximetry indicate that SpHb measurements seem to have comparative precision as capillary hemoglobin assurance when contrasted with research facility investigation. Nevertheless, there is opportunity to get better of the innovation (which is on-going), for educating clinician on the best utilization of the innovation and adjusting clinical pathways to exploit this new innovation. The convenience of these devices takes into consideration the widespread screening of all introducing patients for anemia which could demonstrate mysterious bleeding or other disease measures requiring intercession.

Edward Jay Wang, William Li and their team have developed a device called "HemaApp", a smartphone application which noninvasively monitors blood hemoglobin concentration using the smart phone's camera and different lighting sources [5]. HemaApp measures hemoglobin concentrations by using the absorption properties of hemoglobin and blood plasma at multiple wavelengths of light. To achieve this, the user's fingertip with the RGB camera with different light sources illuminating was used. As well as hemoglobin, the other contents of blood may also absorb some colors. Therefore the white LED was selected for our project lighting source. According to their past researches a smart phone has become a standard equipment and a smart phone based solution helps to decrease the weight on these workers and lessens the expense of hardware. Therefore the concept of developing a mobile app became a useful idea for our project.

According to the research which was done by Dr. Raid Saleem Al-Baradie and Anandh Sam Chandra Bose *et al.* explained "a portable smart non-invasive hemoglobin measurement system" and, they have described advantages of non-invasive hemoglobin measurement system [6]. Furthermore, their research gives a point by point thought regarding the hemoglobin concentration in the blood.

Putut Dewantoro and the team have developed another "smartphone based non-invasive hemoglobin measurement system" [7]. They have mentioned the challenges of transforming the instrument with invasive methods into non-invasive. They solved this problem using PPG signals recorded from the patient's finger using their developed method [7]. The hemoglobin level can be measured using calculation which is done by using AC and DC components and Bluetooth was used to connect the device with a smartphone.

Pavithra, Anitha Mary and their group members have developed a low cost non-invasive device for measuring hemoglobin [8]. As in the previous mentioned research, they have also used PPG signals to measure hemoglobin level. They have used two different light wavelengths to measure the exact difference between hemoglobin and deoxyhemoglobin.

Syafeeza and his group members have developed "a design of finger vein capturing device with quality assessment using arduino microcontroller" [9]. Their device captures human finger vein image and be controlled by arduino microcontroller. It uses the concept of near-infrared (NIR) emitted by a bank of NIR Light Emitting Diodes (LED). Whether it is low cost, using a normal camera will be more protective than NIR and we finalized with using a camera to develop our non-invasive device.

Kusuma and Divya Udayan have done a better research about machine learning and deep learning methods in heart disease [10]. Their research has conducted an efficient audit of the uses of machine learning, deep learning procedures and apparatuses in the field of heart illness research regarding heart disease compilations, predictions and diagnosis [10].

Akmal Hafeel, M. Pravienth, N. Kayanthan, H.S.M.H. Fernando, Shashika Lokuliyana, Anuradha Jayakody *et al.* have done a project called "IoT Device to Detect Anemia: A Non-Invasive Approach with Multiple Inputs". This project is an extension of the above mentioned project and the main aim is to improve this project with minimal errors and more efficiently.

3.3   Methodology

The main research problem can be described as "How to detect anemia (lack of Hemoglobin in blood of an individual) without conventional blood tests".

Traditionally the Hemoglobin test is done using blood samples which are taken using needles. Normally it is done using those blood samples of the patient and it is observed over a glass slide under microscope and counts each type of distorted cell separately. Hence it takes a lot of time and requires highly trained medical practitioners and equipment. Further this technique brings pain to the patient and people cautious to get their blood tested regularly to check the hemoglobin level. Although the blood testing environment should be a clean and safe one, developing and poor countries often do those tests relatively in unclean environments thereby making a huge risk of infection. Previously mentioned processes are expensive for both hospitals and patients.

Thus, it is necessary to develop a non-invasive method to measure the hemoglobin level of a person. It creates a more attractive, real time and infection free, painless method. This research aims to develop a non-invasive smart device to detect hemoglobin level of a patient without withdrawing blood. Outcomes of this project would help to detect anemic patients easily and create more healthy people by curing them at the earliest possible stage.

3.3.1   Methodological Approach

Anemia happens when the healthy number of red blood cells is decreased. Red blood cells convey oxygen to the entirety of the body's tissues, so a low red blood cell tally shows that the measure of oxygen in your blood is lower than it ought to be. A considerable lot of the symptoms of anemia are brought about by diminished oxygen conveyance to the body's indispensable tissues and organs. Anemia is identified by the value of hemoglobin which is the protein inside red blood cells that conveys oxygen from lungs to body's tissues [2].

Normally blood shows red color and if we take a picture of blood, it still shows red color. The brightness of blood could vary due to many reasons. Normally a healthy person's blood shows dark red color. Hemoglobin is the main component in blood which brings red color to blood. Therefore an Anemic person's blood shows light red color (a color near to orange color) than the healthy person's.

After many experiments, the Research Team came up with the idea that the color difference of blood which causes due to the variation of Hemoglobin level can be used as the main feature to develop the "non-invasive anemia detection device".

3.3.1.1 Select an Appropriate Camera

The next question was to find a non-invasive way to capture blood color of a person. Various kinds of experiments were done to choose the most accurate way to capture a clear picture of blood without using any painful or harmful method. Hence, thumb tip of a person was selected as the picture capturing area. Because it is easy to capture an image using a thumb tip and after giving it a suitable lighting system it gives a clear image of blood. First the research team tested the view of the thumb tip using a mobile phone flasher and a mobile phone camera. The mobile phone flasher was used as the lighting system and mobile phone camera was used to capture the image. Thus it gave a nice image and helped a lot to continue the research.

Then the research team wanted to find a better camera to capture the clearest and the most accurate image of blood that flows through thumb tip. Many experiments were done using different cameras to find the better one.

All of the available cameras were used to capture images and at the end, the best camera was selected by comparing each of the image. First the mobile phone camera was used. Then an IR camera, Raspberry Pi camera, a microscope, USB endoscope and a web camera were used to capture images of the thumb tip. According to outcomes, web camera was selected as the camera which is used to develop the Anemia detection device.

3.3.1.2 Design the Lighting System

Then, as mentioned before, to get an accurate picture of blood flowing through thumb tip, there should be a sharp and bright lighting system. The lighting system should be able to make blood flow visible to the camera. The next task was to design the perfect lighting system for the device.

Before design the lighting system, there were some factors to be concerned.

1. Brightness of the light
2. Color of the light
3. Which kind of a bulb/light to be used
4. Distance between lighting system and finger
5. Angle between lighting system and finger.

To capture a clear image brightness of the light should be high. Because the light should be able to go through skin and supply enough brightness to capture an accurate picture of blood that runs through a vein.

Hemoglobin Blood includes a variety of components like: Platelets, Red blood cells, and White blood cells [2].

Before finalize the lighting system, another small research was done to find whether any of the content which is in blood absorbs any color or not. According to the research, it was found that Hemoglobin and some other contents that are in blood absorb colors too. But more than the other contents Hemoglobin absorbs colors. Due to the many researches, the research team has found that Hemoglobin absorbs blue, green colors and it reflects red and orange colors. Therefore white color lighting system was finalized.

The main objective of this research is to develop a non-invasive device. Hence the light should be safe and harmless. Hence it is not safe to use Infrared or any other wave as the lighting system. Therefore a white color LED was used to develop the device.

To capture the best image, there should be an appropriate distance between the finger and the light. Many experiments were done to find the most suitable distance.

The angle between the finger and light was also an important factor to be concerned about. After a number of experiments, the most accurate angle was selected.

Finally, according to the all above mentioned factors, "A super bright white color LED" was selected to develop the device. It was developed as shown in Figure 3.1.

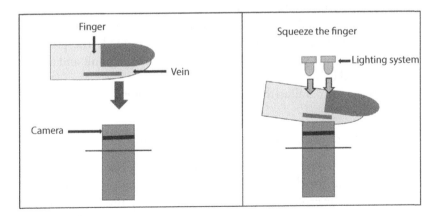

Figure 3.1 Conceptual Design of lighting system and camera position.

The lighting system that should be included above the finger and camera should be near the lower part of the thumb tip, because the blood vein is in the lower part of the thumb. The light flow should supply directly to the skin of thumb rather than supply it directly to nail of thumb. Otherwise, light flow would not flow through the nail easily. Hence it would not give a good image.

Thumb tip should be near to the camera to capture a clear image. As we all know, blood flows continuously through veins. To capture a good image, blood should be stopped flowing for a second. Therefore, the person should squeeze his/her finger a bit to stop the blood flow. After squeezing the image should be captured under enough light supply.

3.3.1.3   Design the Electronic Circuit

To power up the lighting system, there should be an electronic circuit. According to the requirements of super bright LED, a suitable circuit was designed. Three Lithium Polymer batteries were used as the power source. One of the objectives of the research was to design a rechargeable device. Therefore Li-Po batteries were used due to its rechargeable ability. In parallel to the circuit, a charging unit for batteries was also implemented. A switch was used to operate the light.

Then the lighting system, camera and the circuit were combined together.

3.3.1.4   Design the Prototype

To collect data, there should be a prototype device. So, the previously mentioned device parts should be combined together. Hence a suitable design was drawn using solid works and 3D printed the design. Before get the final output many experimented designs were designed. The prototype device was included with a case for circuit and charging unit and also for the camera and lighting system.

Figures 3.2 and 3.3 illustrate the developed prototype.

3.3.1.5   Collect Data and Develop the Algorithm

The next step is to collect data from individuals to develop the algorithm. The main reason for choosing Neural Network to develop the algorithm is to minimize the error of final outcome. To develop the Neural Network based algorithm a large number of data set was needed. Therefore, first, five

Figure 3.2 Thumb tip inserting part.

Figure 3.3 Completed prototype.

hospitals were selected to collect data, then gained required permission from Health Ministry and other required Health Sectors.

After collecting data from all kind of people, the algorithm was developed using Neural Network. A table was created with captured images and their hemoglobin values. Then a Neural Network based platform was developed to identify any input image and to give its hemoglobin value. Tensorflow was used to develop the algorithm. The algorithm was implemented by comparing each and every image with its hemoglobin value.

3.3.1.6 Develop the Prototype

The developed prototype was big in size and was hard to connect to the patient. Therefore the prototype was developed into a small clipping device. Therefore, the team has decided in using a Raspberry Pi to configure the device. The camera module was designed as a clipping device, which can be clipped on to the patient's hand and an image of the squeezed finger was taken. In order to take that the camera should be configured so that it is able to take the photos in a more engaged way so the level of recognizable proof is high. Finally, those pictures were sent to the Raspberry Pi to run through the algorithm.

3.3.1.7 Mobile Application Development

The mobile app was designed so that there is a user login so that the user has to register before logging into the system. The user has to enter some information to register to the system. Then according to the database, the system is designed so that users can use their usernames and passwords to access the accounts. Using the proper credentials the user is granted access to two platforms, wherein the user has to answer the questions that are designed in a questionnaire based according to the symptoms of the disease which would be:

- General Fatigue
- Dizziness
- Pale Skin
- Difficulty in concentration
- Leg cramps
- Insomnia
- Shortness in breathing and headache, when exercising
- Unusually rapid heartbeat
- Cold feet and hands
- Tongue swelling or soreness
- Feeling faintish and blackout [5].

The design of the questions mainly address the above-mentioned symptoms and it was designed in a way that each symptom would indicate the severity level of anemia the patient is diagnosed with. This would be the main factor in determining the amount severity of anemia of the patient.

3.3.1.8   Completed Device

In configuring the connection between the server and the device should be established. In order to achieve this, the team needs a WIFI-module or a module that would connect with the internet for transferring data to the server. In order to do that the team used the node ESP8266 for the purpose. The device was connected to the WIFI by configuring the module using AT commands this would establish the connection between the server and device via API key that is given for each. The server provides two keys for the communication purpose, to send in data as well as send the data out. The two API keys that are provided by the server are the read API and the write API key. This should configure the device to establish the connection to transfer the details from the device to the server. The server which is the AWS server which is used also needs to be configured to receive data and those can be analyzed in a manner so that it can be subjected to machine learning after the input from the app is also taken into the device. This would make it possible for the device to transfer the required data to the server whenever an input is taken and after image was run through the algorithm.

After the device is configured with server the app should also be connected to the server and for that configuration too the team shall be using the keys that are given by the server to transfer the details accordingly. In order to do that the team has to configure the app to a certain socket so that whenever the data is input into the app the details would be transferred to the app. The transfer of information is vital because it is required so that communication channel between the server, device and app generate more accurate and relevant output.

The next main part of the app is the part where the result of the entire process can be seen. As shown in Figure 3.4, in order to achieve a successful output, the team used an algorithm in the server so that both the input from the server and the input from the client are processed and the result is achieved. Then the output was sent to the app where the user would be able to see the results. That would make the user to simply store the output and get them for later medical purposes. This is the main task that shall be performed by the app. The app will also be designed with a good User Interface where the user would also be able to arrange the data that the user gets when testing. Then the proper ordering of the results would also be done in the app.

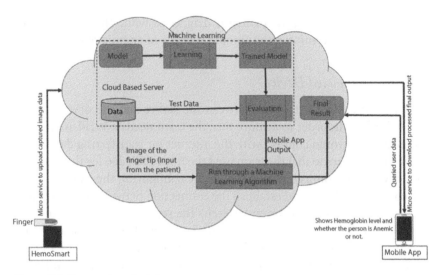

Figure 3.4 Proposed methodology.

Based on both inputs that are given by the app and the device, first, the device guides input to the server and the app was also configured with the server in order to fulfil the required changes that were committed as input for the server. The server at that point measures the data that is taken from two sources of info. In order to fulfill this, the team implemented supervised machine learning. In this step the team used a methodology where a set of training data was used to achieve this. This training data was taken as a constant data set to be collected and run in these algorithms. In these algorithms the server would assume a significant job so the sources of info taken would be from information that has just been gathered from patients determined to have anemia just as a test from a healthy individual, so the preparing machine learning algorithm can be trained to every informational index, which would grow the odds of getting more precise outcomes are high. This would help in identification of the disease at an early stage.

In supervised machine learning initially the output is fed into the algorithm through the system. This would mean that the machine knows what the output would already be depending on the criteria that were used to run in the algorithm [12]. Although the system doesn't know what the ultimate result is, it would know how to achieve to desired output. This design was implemented in the project. The output was fed with relevant data sets so that the algorithm is trained so that it is able to decide what the possible outcomes from the inputs that are fed. This is running in the server

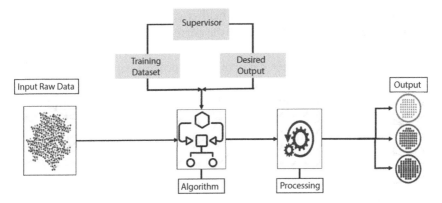

Figure 3.5 Procedure of supervised machine learning.

fulfilling the requirements and coming up with the final output as shown in Figure 3.4.

Figure 3.5 illustrates the flow chart of supervised machine learning.

3.3.1.9   Methods of Data Collection

There are two methods that anyone can use to collect and analyze data [21]:

1. Quantitative Research
2. Qualitative Research

In this research, during the data collection stage, it was needed to capture images of fingertips to compare images and also the hemoglobin levels of each image were needed. So, it can be categorized under both quantitative and qualitative research. It can be called as the mixed methods approach. Here both the numbers and pictures were used as data.

3.3.2   Methods of Analysis

First, a preparatory work was needed to ready the collected data for analysis. All the collected data were explored to see what was in there. An Excel table was made by including all the captured images of finger tips according to their hemoglobin values. By doing so, all the collected data were managed and sorted. As per the Hemoglobin value shows a low value, the brightness of red color of the captured images was also decreased. After, the captured images were used to develop the algorithm.

When a patient uses the device, his/her captured fingertip image goes through the same algorithm to give the correct hemoglobin value according to the algorithm.

Other than that, another data collection process happens through the mobile application as well. Through the mobile app questionnaire, some of the anemia-related questions were asked from every patient. According to the answers he/she gives, an output will be given.

Finally both the outputs run through a machine learning algorithm to give the most accurate final outcome.

3.4 Results

3.4.1 Impact of Project Outcomes

The finger-prick method is widely used to determine the Hemoglobin concentration given its speed, simplicity, transportability, reproducibility and cheapness. However, the method has its own drawbacks such as: invasiveness and risk of infections and complications from the finger prick. In addition, pressing the finger may cause a shift in fluids at the moment of drawing the sample. Thus, pressure on the fingertip to extract enough capillary blood may increase the plasma concentration and falsify the reading. However the use of the device in the research is ease of use, no calibration required, a reusable, no trauma to the donor/patient, no risk of infection, no danger of contact with contaminated biological matter, and less scope for human error which the finger prick entails. Further it reduces pain for the donor and the risk of wound complications.

In most cases, Anemia is diagnosed as an accidental finding in situations where the patient had been asked to get a full blood count in order to diagnose some other disease. The process of assessing blood to check the hemoglobin levels is a time-consuming process that requires trained medical practitioners and equipment to withdraw blood from the patients. Further this technique brings pain to the patient which may be a reason why many individuals are reluctant to get their blood tested to check the hemoglobin levels. Similarly, in rural areas of developing countries extracting blood is often done in relatively unclean environments thereby presenting a greater risk of infection.

Also specially trained medical personnel are needed to extract blood and then perform the necessary tests. Therefore this research aims to design a non-invasive device that works together with the input from a mobile application to detect anemia without extracting blood. The use of this device also leads to a reduction the number of specially trained medical personnel needed to perform anemia detection tests while simultaneously reducing the amount and the complexity of the training required by those personnel.

Furthermore, the use of this device would encourage women of all ages to get their blood screened often so that anemia can be detected and cured at the earliest possible stage. This would benefit the world as a whole in trying to eradicate the problem of anemia thus improving the quality of life of the people living in developing countries.

The ultimate outcome of the research is the smart non-invasive anemia detection device together with the mobile application that is capable of determining a change in the physical symptoms of the person using a pre-defined questionnaire. This device would be capable of identifying patients with anemia at the earliest stage possible. The target markets for this device were hospitals, medical clinics, large pharmaceutical corporations and individual patients who would prefer to get their blood screened often. The technologies used in the research project were Neural Network, Machine learning, Android mobile app Development and Wireless networks.

Another deliverable of the research was a mobile application that would be used to monitor the physical symptoms of the user via a pre-defined questionnaire. The outputs of both the mobile app and the sensor device are used to predict whether the user is suffering from anemia or not. Through this app the user would be able to monitor his/her hemoglobin levels over a period of time and take necessary actions accordingly.

3.4.2 Results Obtained During the Methodology

3.4.2.1 Select an Appropriate Camera

Many cameras were used as experiments to find the most suitable camera for the device.

1. Mobile phone Camera

This was the first camera which was used to capture a fingertip image. Though it gave clear images, the research team wanted clearer images.

2. InfraRed Camera

This experiment gave black and white images as the output. Therefore it was rejected.

3. Raspberry Pi Camera

The Raspberry Pi Camera is a fixed focus module, so that anything from about 0.5 m to infinity is acceptably sharp. Although there are some strengths, there are some weaknesses like, hard to film or photograph anything in between 50 and 75 cm (it will be out of focus). Therefore it was hard to include to the device design. Then it was also rejected.

4. Microscope Model Camera

This camera gave clear images of skin of a person. But the objective of the research is to capture an internal image which is the blood content in a vein. Rather than giving internal images this input external clear images. Then this was also rejected.

5. Web Camera

Finally this was selected as the most suitable one to develop the device with. It gave clearer colored images without any fixed distance to focus.

3.4.2.2   Design the Lighting System

The main objective was to design a non-invasive device. Therefore, the design should not include any harmful or painful lights. Hence, when selecting the most accurate lighting system, the first thing to be concern about was which kind of a light would be used. According to every fact, A Super Bright White LED was selected.

During selection one of the main factors to be concerned about was the color of that LED. Therefore, different experiments were done using different color of LEDs. The gained results of those experiments are shown below from Figures 3.5 to 3.10. Figure 3.11 shows the gained result from the experiment which was done using Super bright white LED.

3.5   Discussion

Overall objective of the research is to develop a non-invasive method to detect Anemia which is known as lack of Hemoglobin in blood.

The developed non-invasive device was designed as a clipping device and it was a covered device. There were many reasons to select a covered design.

1. Light should be flow directly to the fingertip. If there isn't a covered device, the light flow spread out of the finger.

Figure 3.6 With a green LED.

Figure 3.7 With a yellow LED.

Figure 3.8 With an orange LED.

Figure 3.9 With a blue LED.

Figure 3.10 With a red LED.

Figure 3.11 With a white super bright LED.

2. Hence, it could lead to a higher background noise when developing the neural network-based algorithm.

First the Research Team was planning to use Image Processing instead of Neural Network to develop the algorithm. But, after considering the following facts, neural network was selected.

Fact 1: Neural network is more efficient than Image Processing.

Fact 2: The main objective is to develop a device which can use any person. Therefore Neural Network made that objective a possible one. There were many skin colored people with different ages. There were some people with skin diseases as well. Using neural Network helped to address those problems in developing the algorithm, because Neural Network creates a platform with regard to the all given inputs.

Fact 3: The main feature which used to develop the algorithm was the color difference of captured images. If there was another difference rather than color, Neural Network identifies it and creates a new platform by itself. However, image processing doesn't do that.

The research team used convolutional neural network (CNN) instead of feed-forward network. CNNs extract many abstract features at each layer and scan the image with learnable "filters". Filters which are in early layers are used to detect edges or color gradients and then complex shapes are registered by layers. Convolutional Neural Network shares parameters. The convolutional operation is usually done on images to get their features.

Image Processing can be named as one of the Convolutional Neural Network's applications. Therefore researchers say, Neural Network is taking over the place which had for OpenCV in the field of computer vision. We first were going to use image processing to develop the algorithm and as mentioned before selecting convolutional neural network led the whole project to the success. Computer vision techniques show a better accuracy in image classification. Therefore they are dominated by convolutional neural networks.

Then Neural Network—Keras was used to develop the algorithm as shown in Figure 3.12. Keras which is capable of running on top of TensorFlow is an open-source neural-network library written in Python.

Data scientists utilize different sorts of machine learning algorithms to find patterns in large data that lead to significant instincts. Neural Network is a subset of Machine Learning. Neural network structures algorithms in

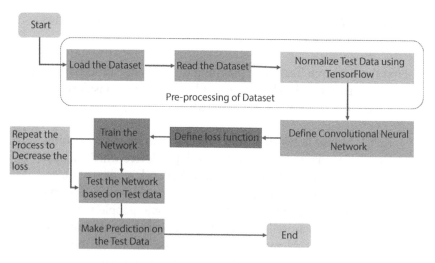

Figure 3.12 Flow chart of convolutional neural network.

layers of design can learn and settle on keen choices all alone, whereas Machine learning make decisions based on what it has learned only. Hence Neural Network was chosen over Machine Learning for the algorithm development of this project.

As shown in Figure 3.12, collected data set of thumb tip images was used to train the Convolutional Neural Network. Then, Test data was used to test the Network. Figure 3.12 illustrates the whole process of Convolutional Neural Network which was used to derive the final result from HemoSmart.

3.6   Originality and Innovativeness of the Research

- A non-invasive method is used
- Faster
- Low cost
- More efficient
- Real time
- Time saving.

According to past researches the technology that has been used to detect anemia was time wasting and complex. The proposed method is more efficient and easier than the existing methods.

3.6.1   Validation and Quality Control of Methods

- There is no needle to puncture and withdraw blood because the system will be painless.
- Infection free operation because of the non-needle method.
- No harmful rays will be used.
- Any person who is in any age or any gender can use the device.
- Some of the normal blood test results will be compared with our device outcome and the error will be measured.
- Obtain the expert input from a clinician preferably from a Consultant Physician for the whole project from development of the conceptual framework onwards.

3.6.2   Cost-Effectiveness of the Research

According to the comparison the non-invasive method is low cost than the conventional blood testing method.

3.7   Conclusion

Anemia is a widespread disease that affects millions of people worldwide every year. Doctors have said that anemia has a risk of leading it to cancers. Nowadays, due to highest rate of people suffering from Anemia particularly in poor and developing countries, some researches are implementing new strategies to detect anemia at the earliest possible stage. Therefore the developed non-invasive anemia detection device would help people to detect anemia easily and cure it before it gets worse.

References

1. Santos, C.F.C., *Haemoglobin screening using noninvasive methods*, Medical Laboratory Observer, Nelson Publishing, Inc., 2015.
2. Kraitl, J., Timm, U., Ewald, H., Lewis, E., Non-invasive sensor for an *in vivo* haemoglobin measurement. *Sensors*, 2011, IEEE, Limerick, pp. 276–279, 2011.
3. Lacroix, J. and Tucci, M., Noninvasive or invasive haemoglobin measurement? *Crit. Care Med.*, 40, 2715–2716, 2012. [PubMed].

4. O'Reilly, M., Understanding noninvasive and continuous haemoglobin monitoring. *Crit. Care Med.*, 41, 5, e52, 2013. [PubMed].

5. Wang, E.J. *et al.*, HemaApp: Noninvasive blood screening of hemoglobin using smartphone cameras. *Proceedings of the 2016 ACM International Joint Conference on Pervasive and Ubiquitous Computing ACM*, 2016.

6. Al-Baradie, R.S. and Bose, A.S.C., Portable smart non-invasive hemoglobin measurement system, 10th International Multi-Conference on Systems, Signals & Devices, 2013.

7. Dewantoro, P., Gandana, C.E., Zakaria, R.O.R.H., Irawan, Y.S., Development of smartphone-based non-invasive hemoglobin measurement. International Symposium on Electronics and Smart Devices (ISESD), 2018.

8. Pavithra, K.S., Mary, X.A., Rajasekaran, K., Jegan, R., Low Cost Non-Invasive Medical Device for Measuring Hemoglobin. *ICIEEIMT 17*.

9. Syafeeza, A.R., Faiz, K., Syazana-Itqan, K., Wong, Y.C., Noh, Z.M., Ibrahim, M.M., Mahmod, N.M., Design of Finger vein Capture Device with Quality Assessment using Arduino Microcontroller. *Journal of Telecommunication, Electronic and Computer Engineering*, 9, 1, 55–60.

10. Kusuma, S. and Divya Udayan, J., Machine Learning and Deep Learning Methods in Heart Disease (HD) Research. International Conference on Machine Intelligence and Signal Processing. 1483–1496, 441–451, 2018.

11. Mao, K.Z., Zhao, P., Tan, P.H., Supervised learning-based cell image segmentation for p53 immunohistochemistry, IEEE Transactions on Biomedical Engineering, 2006 Jun; 53, 6, 1153–63, 2006.

12. He, K., Ren, S., Sun, J., Zhang, X., Deep Residual Learning for Image Recognition, CoRR, IEEE Conference on Computer Vision and Pattern Recognition (CVPR), 2016.

13. Batista, J., Caseiro, R., Henriques, J.F., Martins, P., High-Speed Tracking with Kernelized Correlation Filters, IEEE Transactions on Pattern Analysis And Machine Intelligence, 2015.

14. Amorim, D.G., Barro, S., Cernadas, E., Delgado, M.F., Do we need hundreds of classifiers to solve real world classification problems. *J. Mach. Learn. Res.*, 15, 90, 3133–3181, 2014.

15. Chandrashekar, G. and Sahin, F., A survey on feature selection methods. *Int. J. Comput. Electr. Eng.*, 40, 1, 16–28, 2014.

16. Campbell, K., Anemia—causes and treatment. *Nurs. Times*, 99, 43, 30, 2003.

17. Charles, C.V., Summerlee, A.J., Dewey, C.E., Anemia in Cambodia: Prevalence, etiology and research needs. *Asia Pac. J. Clin. Nutr.*, 21, 2, 171–181, 2012.

18. Jayathissa, R., National Food Security Survey (NFSS), Current Nutritional status of children in Sri Lanka. *Sri Lanka Nutr. Bull.*, 1, 5, 2009.

19. Department of Census and Statistics Sri Lanka, Prevalence of Anaemia among Children and Women, *Demographic and Health Survey 2006/7*, Health Sector Development Project, Ministry of Healthcare and Nutrition, Colombo, 2009.

20. Weinstein, A., Herzentein, O., Gabis, E., Korenberg, A., Screening of anaemia using occlusion spectroscopy Transfusion. Blood Reviews, 50, 91A–92A, 2010.
21. Palinkas, L.A., Horwitz, S.M., Green, C.A., Wisdom, J.P., Purposeful sampling for qualitative data collection and analysis in mixed method implementation research, *Administration and Policy in Mental Health and Mental Health Services Research*, 42, 533–544, 2015.
22. Padma, T. and Jinavah., P., Non-Invasive Haemoglobin Estimation through Embedded Technology on mobile application. *Int. J. Appl. Eng. Res.*, 13, 10, 7853–7856, 2018.
23. Aldrich, T.K., Moosikasuwan, M., Shah, S.D., Deshpande, K.S., Length-normalized pulsephotoplethysmography:a noninvasive method to measure blood haemoglobin. *Ann. Biomed. Eng.*, 30, 1291–8, 2002.
24. Jeon, K.J., Kim, S.J., Park, K.K., Kim, J.W., Yoon, G., Noninvasive total hemoglobin measurement. *J. Biomed. Opt.*, 7, 45–50, 2002.
25. Kraitl, J., Timm, U., Ewald, H., Lewis, E., Non-invasive sensor for an *in vivo* haemoglobin measurement. *Sensors*, 2011, IEEE, Limerick, pp. 276–279, 2011.

4

Advanced Cognitive Models and Algorithms

J. Ramkumar*, M. Baskar and B. Amutha

Department of Computer Science and Engineering, SRM Institute of Science and Technology, Chennai, India

Abstract

With the demand of users getting enormous nowadays, the utilization of high-end resources, paves the way for the exploration of advanced technologies/mechanisms to meet the user's requirements. IoT technology plays an intermediary role between the users and devices, which connects to it. While considering the development of smart cities, IoT sensors play a significant role in their growth, and those devices are deployed and connected. IoT connectivity helps the humans to use for their utility with one another, and individual needs as we know IoT devices utilization keeps on increasing enormously. Cognitive offer effective communication and smart thinking of ability by training the learning datasets available so far. The intelligent is materialized through learning human activities, i.e., voice, social media, etc. along with IoT sensors. The cognitive approach with IoT provides connectivity to everyone and everything as we know IoT connected devices keeps increasing rapidly. When IoT gets integrated with cognitive technology, performance is improved, and smart intelligence is obtained. Different types of datasets with structured content are discussed based on cognitive systems. IoT gathers the information from the real-time datasets through the internet, where IoT network connects with the multiple numbers of devices.

Keywords: Cognitive, communication, datasets, learning, Internet of Things, artificial intelligence

*Corresponding author: ram.kumar537@gmail.com

Kolla Bhanu Prakash, G. R. Kanagachidambaresan, V. Srikanth, E. Vamsidhar (eds.) Cognitive Engineering for Next Generation Computing: A Practical Analytical Approach, (121–140) © 2021 Scrivener Publishing LLC

4.1   Introduction

In recent days, the cognitive technology plays a vital role in the field of computer science in terms of intelligent human simulation based on data mining, i.e., dataset processing and analyzing, recognizing the data pattern and language processing and analyzing [1]. Thus, cognitive technology will play a significant role in the interaction between humans and technology and it arises in the field of Artificial Intelligence, Machine Learning, Automation, etc. As artificial intelligence refers to the intelligence simulation among humans in which humans are automated and make them simulate based on the actions they perform. It helps to automate learning and solve problems when humans are associated with the machine. Now, there is a better relationship between artificial intelligence and cognitive technology and artificial intelligence is a subset of cognitive technology [2]. So far it is proved that IBM Watson supercomputer and Microsoft Azure are embedded with cognitive technology as it is having the processing rate of 80 teraflops and makes it to communicate/think as same as human [3].

As cognitive computes the system to learn automatically, there is the fundamental reason behind the interaction of humans with the machine [4]. It is even programmed to make the system more continent. They can also be analyzed and processed to make reason, how it can able to interact with humans and experience the activities.

4.2   Microsoft Azure Cognitive Model

Generally, Microsoft provides services with built-in protocols/algorithms based on Artificial Intelligence and also relevant API (Application Programming Interface). API helps to develop agents, webpages and Applications based on Artificial Intelligence and functionalities by the developer as there is a lack of appropriate AI research employees who can do those jobs to provide cognitive services in the enterprise sector [5]. Enterprise needs to provide infrastructure and select the AI tools based on their budget and needs. In this case, the user has an option to choose and integrate Microsoft AI protocols based on the selection of a functional library to provide cognitive services on the Azure platform and cloud computing platform [6].

As there are many cloud-based service platforms, AI services provide the Microsoft cloud provider [7]. For many AI functionalities, cognitive functions are provided based on the purpose of deep learning, machine vision and evaluating sentimental analysis. Based on the above discussion, Microsoft is more compatible with cognitive services along with the natural language to understand the chatbot functionalities of AI, which is offered by Azure bot service [8]. This Microsoft azure bot services helps to position the chatbot tool to provide services based on recipient call interaction and discussion based on forum and websites related to chatbot diagnosis [9].

The services provided by cognitive computing helps to enhance the functionalities of agents who support the increasing growth in scaling the services. To make the services as a quick reference, to perform translation services based on language and to recognize users and other identification based on image and reasonable information, i.e., machine vision. AI provides service with various functionalities that impact with different enterprises which able to create services for their own. By delivering automation to the machine, which can work as a human in the enterprise to reduce cost and despite human workers, these services are posturing threats to them.

From Figure 4.1, the Cognitive model gets categorized into four services, namely, machine vision, natural language, speech and web knowledge based on Microsoft Azure. This Microsoft Azure helps in building business services with reduced cost by built-in application, storing data and creating services in the cloud platform [10]. SNP technologies provide AI-based cognitive services by adding machine learning intelligence as humans, giving automation by programming and search functionalities and capabilities to their applications. By adding above the features to the application interface, learning algorithms based on machine and real-time

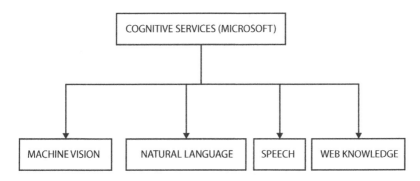

Figure 4.1 AI services-based Microsoft Interface.

computing applications help SNP technologies to build improved intelligence into the claims [11]. This enhanced intelligence application helps to activate services in the background and regular basis with certain functionalities like recognizing facial and speech context, detecting the human emotional intelligence and understanding the language and content readability.

From the cognitive model, there are four service helps to enhance the growth of business and are discussed below.

1. Machine Vision:

This category helps to construct a user-defined classifier among image information based on the cognitive service of Microsoft azure. This user-defined machine vision helps to build these cognitive services faster and easier deploy these services to enhance the classification of images based on artificial intelligence and machine learning [10]. These cognitive services based on machine vision helps to facilitate features like analysis of facial recognition, analysis of handwritten recognition, attention of character optically, which gets varies from images to all the real-time videos, etc. [11].

2. Speech Context:

By using Microsoft Azure of cognitive services, the cognitive interface helps to integrate speech processing functionalities, which transforms into several applications and services [12, 13]. By using the speech processing interface, it helps to function based on speech styles where users are used to recognizing the speech texture and convert those text based on their needs.

3. Natural Language:

Context-based learning helps to provide communication, where language plays a significant element in these services [14]. By developing cognitive services based on these language interfaces, they can able to understand the various text to communicate.

4. Web Knowledge:

These cognitive services help to provide complete database creation and web-based tools to acquire knowledge based on the availability of these tools. This knowledge can be obtained based on a specific application interface by integrating the created resource with various functionalities to construct several applications and services [15]. The multiple information, different text and context knowledge are extracted, scanned and derived by the cognitive services offered by Microsoft Azure.

Other than these four elements, cognitive services further categorized into Web search as discussed below:

1. Web Search:
This web search helps to find the information that needs for the extraction of various web pages, video streaming, news web search, and images, etc. These services influence, which makes cognitive integrates with different AI algorithms, which are powerful to provide various capabilities for searching relevant information, extracting to compare those results to analyze and summarize and from that, the corresponding data are taken into consideration.

From the above applications, Microsoft Azure plays a vital role in the integration of AI services to provide various needs to offer.

4.2.1   AI Services Broaden in Microsoft Azure

In recent days, Microsoft makes more effort to make artificial intelligence dominating in services. For that, Microsoft is enhancing its services by incorporating various collections by establishing cloud-based services based on a machine learning platform, which is nothing Microsoft cognitive services. Other than the cognitive functions, anomaly detector and machine vision services are the two services offered based on intelligence [16]. Anomaly detector aims to include the unusual activity based on lots of data transactions and machine vision helps to facilities AI models by training and deploying based on detecting objects.

There are several steps to incorporating AI services into Microsoft Azure are represented in Figure 4.2.

Microsoft Azure helps the applications to add more functionalities of intelligence based on various circumstances and those circumstances include recognizing speech, translating text and converting text into speech based on image and detecting objects. From the previous discussion, mainly, the anomaly detector helps to identify a pattern that represents irregular forms/shapes that allows us to be figurate out the problem in those aspects as it is available based on the application interface [17]. Microsoft Azure with AI-based machine vision helps to train and classify their objects and export those objects into various devices like Android,

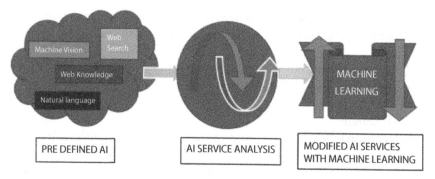

Figure 4.2 Incorporating AI services into Microsoft Azure.

edge-based devices, etc. When some of the significant features are added into AI service, it helps to optimize the issues of datasets extraction and classification of well-defined objects.

4.3 IBM Watson Cognitive Analytics

4.3.1 Cognitive Computing

IBM Watson plays a significant role and an essential part of cognitive computing and its revolution. Concerning IBM Watson, cognitive is nothing but the human behavior or thoughts that differ in several aspects such as analytical, evaluation, learning, observation and logical thinking. Based on the above behavioral issues, inner human cognition is understood based on physiological/neurological ideas. With this social ideology, cognitive computing helps to processes information functionalities [18]. The artificial intelligence has a tremendous development, which mainly depends on the architecture of the system and IBM made the machine as the thinker to be the axiom for the future information technology enterprise. From the derived term of cognitive computing, Watson, who is the founder of IBM, made IBM Watson which is the super thinking machine with the context of big data. This IBM Watson incorporated several technologies such as NLP (Natural Language Processing), Machine Learning, Cloud Computing, web semantic and integrating and optimizing the data as represented in Figure 4.3. The Watson technology is moving with the integration of cloud platforms, which provides solutions in the field

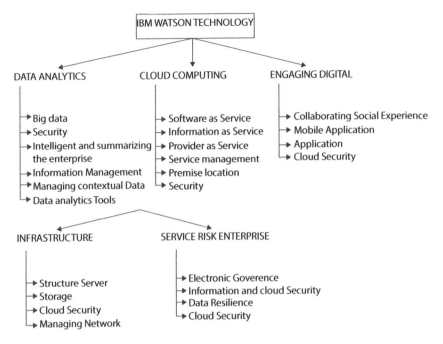

Figure 4.3 IBM Watson technology.

of healthcare, finance, etc. [19]. So far, we have discussed how now the Watson technology started balancing with cognitive computing with other technologies to be incorporated as represented in Figure 4.4 [20].

4.3.2   Defining Cognitive Computing via IBM Watson Interface

This cognitive computing provides technology that integrates artificial intelligence and processing the data. Apart from AI, the cognitive include machine learning, data reasoning, NLP (Natural language Processing, machine vision and HCI (Human–Computer Interaction). It is a simulation of human intervention that computerizes thoughts and logical thinking. Cognitive uses are mining the data with recognized patterns and NLP, which will simulate human intellect. The objective of cognitive technology is to develop an automated system that will solve various problems with the assist of the system.

When cognitive systems use various algorithms based on machine learning helps to acquire knowledge/data based on the process of mining when

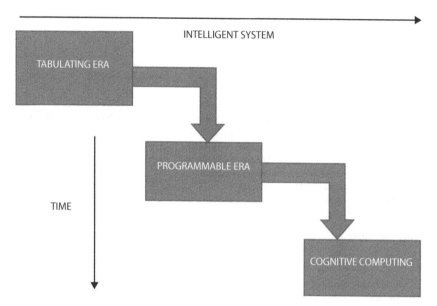

Figure 4.4 Evolution of computing towards cognitive.

the system acquires a certain amount of information. Then the refined data forms a pattern and then processes the data to solve various problems based on modeling. Then artificial intelligence is integrated with cognitive computing and additional concepts of NLP, neural networks and virtual/ augmented reality, etc., and this cognitive help to develop IBM Watson technologies. Generally, cognitive technology helps to scale the knowledge level and corporation between machines and human and it learns the cognition of the human. This cognitive is not a programmed machine but learns the thought and behavior of the human, learns and processes the data for their needs. For cognitive computing, the supercomputer is implemented by IBM as IBM Watson, which is built and constructed based on the cognitive paradigm.

4.3.2.1 Evolution of Systems Towards Cognitive Computing

At the beginning of system evolution, there is a tabulating system gets emerged, which is an electro mechanical machine used to summarize the data stored in the form of punched cards. Especially for collecting the sensor data concerning population and other categories, by using the tabulating system, it is difficult to take and collect such type of information.

So, they have moved from the tabulated system to programmed systems, which is infinitely better to perform for such information processing. Then again, IBM has announced IBM Watson based on cognitive computing, which will process more and more with better accuracy. This IBM Watson will integrate both humans and machines to perform a particular work, but it won't replace humans with the machine [21]. As human is well implemented in some thinking and other capabilities, the machine will perform well and save time for certain things. This substitution work will build some effort between the human and machine in terms of IBM Watson technology. While comparing the device, the human will be more boosted in terms of sensing, summarizing data, abstracting, generalization, moral thoughts, etc. and the machine will boost in terms of identifying patterns, knowledge location, NLP, machine learning and capacity. So based on this, there is a platform build between the human and machine.

4.3.2.2   Main Aspects of IBM Watson

There are several aspects of IBM Watson's cognitive system, which will helps to understand, learning and reasoning. Those aspects are discussed below:

a. Understanding:
The cognitive technology will think and perform as human through NLP or another writing type. The cognitive systems able to differentiate and understand language like English, French, etc. other than C, C++, Java programming. As the text is feed into the system through email and then audio is feed into the system through Alexa and Google now, etc. and finally, IBM has fed the video to learn and provide watching ability.

b. Reasoning:
After understanding the data with specific ideas and thoughts, reasoning can take more advancement. In this way, the cognitive system takes a tremendous amount of information and that can be understood and to be processed to answer specific questions/queries.

c. Learning:
Learning gets continued based on technology concerning time and make it more expertise. The cognitive system learns to obtain better knowledge as

a probabilistic approach and gets expertise based on the existing information. It provides more accurate/better information as a result. For example, for weather prediction, if more information is gathered, the resultant will be more accurately predicted and provided.

4.3.2.3 Key Areas of IBM Watson

Based on Watson on cognitive systems, there are certain areas which are essential and they are working on it:

A. IBM Watson is working on detecting cancer among health organizations to provide some free equipment to patients with less cost will save from life risk.
B. IBM Watson is developing robots based on embodied robots, which will be more useful in certain places like hotels and banks.
C. Using IBM Watson, we can teach more languages and maintain some optimized speed as SyNAPSE, which is so much familiar and close as humans.

4.3.3 IBM Watson Analytics

In this cognitive system, we able to build a visualization of data and analytical prediction and able to analyze the data without transferring the data for processing. The analytics are predicted based on cognitive capabilities through data pattern identification, understanding the data through automation with less time and more accuracy and make the user utilize server/workstation to provide some run-up processor.

Generally, IBM Watson acts as a smart data analytics, which will visualize the data by pattern identification and understanding of the data. To understand and acquire results/answers for the data interaction, this IBM Watson will direct to perform data identification, predicting the data through automation and more cognitive functionalities [22]. The results are visualized by making Watson analytics can be spotted and viewed. Then IBM Watson can perform analytics, especially for social media, which will visualize the data through automation with specific data identification through the platform of the cloud. By identifying the data, we can gather some familiar content and find their relationship and pattern visualization.

4.3.3.1   IBM Watson Features

A. Smart Data Identification:
First, identify the relevant pattern of specific data, which will process some functionalities of the cognitive system and offer some information and process to obtain results and familiar to them.

B. Analysis Simplification:
After obtaining the data, make it understand and define how it will be based on automation without spending more time and cost. So that more identification and patterns obtain, which will be a new derivation for the enterprise.

C. Advance Analytics Accessibility:
Analytics accessibility can connect the data and process without taking a complex process of refining and preparing the data. Advanced analysis won't take much time and cost to process the information for specific results.

D. Dashboard Self-Service:
Maintain the identification in the typical panel so that it is easy for us to construct the data visualization and save time to identify the data.

4.3.3.2   IBM Watson DashDB

Through IBM Watson, we can configure the next generation to optimize the process through transactional DB/Data Warehouse. This DashDB will optimize the database through IBM Watson, which will deliver the user needs either through transaction (or) workload analytics [23, 24]. Through the configuration of adding new containers, IBM has added software-defined scenarios like a public cloud, which will manage fully with specific cloud platforms [25]. To process this IBM with software-defined, we need specific features such as,

A. Data to be Focused:
To optimize the workload by running, implementing and use it by choosing the configured DashDB.

B. Variation in Price and Growth:
There is a different size plan available based on transaction and analytical systems and need to select the size based on the increase in the database size in the future.

C. Technology Base:
Based on database, SQL used as a typical DB for all the technologies, which makes to move the workload easier and it has multiple functionalities among various vendors and provides a solution.

D. Providing High Value:
As DashDB has availability and security, which is having higher priority and it's not having a single point of failure.

4.4   Natural Language Modeling

4.4.1   NLP Mainstream

Mainly NLP is used to manipulate the text and strings to acquire some knowledge using some statistical techniques based on some comments to process the learning concept. This NLP is very much useful in achieving some results in specific applications like extracting the data, questionnaire and answering section, translating the language from one to another through the machine. This NLP gets processed by significant data methods to implement and solve based on the above application. This knowledge-based concept has some issues to overcome the computation and store the NLP as significant [26]. Natural language has both NLU (Natural Language Understanding) and NLP (Natural Language Processing), which are two concepts, plays a vital role in the field of science and technology as represented in Figure 4.5.

This NLU is somewhat familiar to NLP and it is the subset of the NLP field of science and technology. In robotics, NLU possesses some services and tasks performs for a particular area based on the representative who is having some knowledge and functionalities as required earlier. As robotics is very much praises as it is specific to NL understanding. Instead of applying NLP into the system, NLU is creating some knowledge deeper and make the system to be fit for all the scenarios.

NLP is more significant when the system is finding the appropriate NLP, which is to be configured and implemented through NL understanding

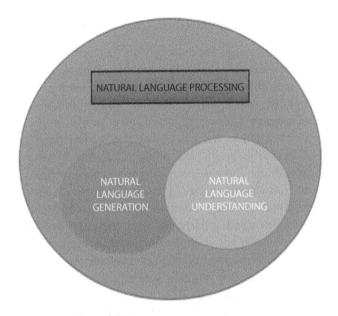

Figure 4.5 NLG/NLU subset of NLP.

[27]. When considering the Questionnaire/Answering scheme, which can access some critical content to be processed, when it has indication and formulation, then the answer is required based on the clear understanding, analysis, and reasoning. All the applications offered by the NLP will provide the same task simplification to fulfill the task performed. When NLP has certain visual content and other punctuations in the text need some more effort to understand the NLU as represented in Figure 4.6.

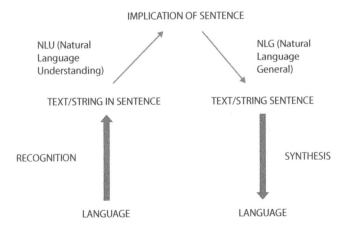

Figure 4.6 Natural language processing.

4.4.2 Natural Language Based on Cognitive Computation

Generally, natural Language Processing helps to configure and implement based on the knowledge extracted and reasoning with assumptions and now it is integrated with the cognitive system model. By using natural language processing, applications will develop with useful significance along with the component of memory and perception of the cognitive model. By using a high degree of assumption, there is no need to use any other natural language to be added to the system [28]. While processing the natural language in the cognitive model, there is some hidden language to be added. While configuring and implementing the cognitive model, there is a preassembling of symbolic/notation language added along with the constraints/rules that are applied. When processing particular data, there is a need for symbolic language to be processed based on memory. Mainly in robotics, these symbolic language is used to perform certain events to be completed.

The natural language used symbolic language which uses some language formally uses some sorting methods as it is not having any complexity in symbolic language when included in the cognitive model. In the earlier days, this cognitive model uses artificial intelligence and as nowadays, the cognitive model used natural language processing into specified applications. The cognitive model uses specific application development used on artificial intelligence, which uses certain constraints like language approach based on semantics. Here we have considered Tala language, which uses symbolic includes data and set of procedures. It has data structures represented into symbolic forms that have syntax and semantics of information [29]. While considering the data and system, the cognitive model uses pattern matching method to perform a specific process and attain some achieve at human-based artificial intelligence, which denotes as Tele Agent.

From the above statements, we infer that the cognitive model adds some set of rules and protocols like the consensus of AI, which will hide the representation in specific applications based on inference and semantics. This consensus of standards and protocols will help the cognitive model to achieve human-based AI based on Tele Agents. There are significant issues that arise in terms of cognitive computing, which is nothing but the complete implementation of human-based AI through the cognitive model.

4.5 Representation of Knowledge Models

Knowledge representation is nothing but understanding the certainty, judge value, and purpose, which is represented in the form of symbolic notations to make intelligent systems through automation. When making the objective of the knowledge model, it can be made up by achieving the scope of the data, correctness, inference effectiveness, creation, and data robustness. Here we have applied a knowledge model to make useful computational events based o text and cognitive technology [30]. Now machine learning methods are used to provide automation through the knowledge base and representation is not much easy but is can be achieved with great success.

The knowledge method with artificial intelligence is a significant element of AI and provides intelligent based on the knowledge base. We have several knowledgebases which represented as symbolic notations such as certainty, judge value and purpose to make modifications. Through the knowledge representation, we can construct the knowledge base and using that we can connect with the outside world [31]. We can identify and find the substructure of knowledge base and it can be specific to certain functionalities as a certainty, judge value and purpose.

For example, we consider "Some cat is a pet." Then we represent those sentence as predicate calculus formula,

$$\exists \, x \, Cat \, (x) \, \wedge \, Pet \, (x)$$

Here '∃' refer as there exist and 'x' as variable and '∧' as and.

To create an AI-based intelligent system, which is a significant objective to achieve a specific task to be defined. Based on the problem of knowledge representation, the data structure set has identified the information for a particular application [32, 33]. When considering the programmed system, there is an integration of data structure and data needed for a specific event. By using AI, we can learn the task but not easy to automate, which is nothing but decoding the data structure. This knowledge representation classified into,

A. Architecture:
While creating the knowledge representation architect, schema and procedure are needed.

B. Content:
Features of knowledge representation are represented based on communication, time and cost.

C. Implementation:
Knowledge representation is configured based on data structure and process of reasoning.

D. Interface:
In the knowledge representation, the creation of a knowledge base which connects with the external world.

E. Learning:
After constructing the knowledge base, we can analyze the data automatically.

From the Figure 4.7, we have knowledge representation with several other elements to make the system more intelligent.

A. Perception:
Using perception, we can obtain data from the external source and identify the noise noticed through which AI is spoiled. If the perception has acquired any noise (or) any other, it has to determine how to respond to it.

B. Learning:
Learning component learns the obtained data by the perception and their motivation is to make the system to learn to it and not to make it by the

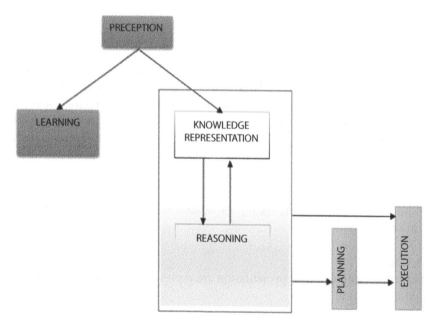

Figure 4.7 Knowledge representation design.

program. The learning process is self-motivation and can improve on their own. If the order is learning different things, it requires knowledge and heuristics attainment, inference, searching, etc.

C. Knowledge Representation and Reasoning:
Knowledge base makes the system think as human to act intelligently. This knowledge representation makes the system work intelligently from a top-down approach instead of the bottom down where intelligence will behave based on the agent. Then reasoning makes the system to automate based on a certain procedure and obtain knowledge whenever needed.

D. Planning and Execution:
Based on the study of knowledge representation and reasoning, planning makes to achieve a particular goal based on the initial state, conditions followed and sequence of actions. After the planning process completed, then execution process executes the complete process.

4.6 Conclusion

As cognitive technology is providing intelligence to the system as humans, there is a specific process like collection, processing, analyzing and recognizing are needed. Initially, we have discussed how cognitive plays a significant role in artificial intelligence by referring to the simulation process of making the system automated through the process of simulated actions. Cognitive has discussed two main technology processing tools, like Microsoft Azure and IBM Watson's cognitive models. In Microsoft Azure, there are several cognitive services offered, namely, machine vision, natural language, speech and web knowledge. Then we discussed how Microsoft Azure provides AI services through cognition. Another cognitive model as IBM Watson, which provides cognitive services based on human behavior and thoughts through evaluation, analysis, observation and logical thinking. IBM Watson is broadly categorized and its evolution of the system to cognitive computing discussed. Cognitive computing key role with natural language processing in which the natural language understanding and natural language generation are the two subsets. Finally, we have addressed the knowledge representation through cognitive computing and their design process.

References

1. Franklin, S., Madl, T., D' Mello, S., Snaider, J., LIDA: A systems-level architecture for cognition, emotion, and learning. *IEEE Trans. Auton. Ment. Dev.*, 6, 19–41, 2014.
2. Chen, M., Miao, Y., Hao, Y., Hwang, K., Narrowband internet of things. *IEEE Access*, 5, 20557–20577, 2017.
3. Chen, M., Herrera, F., Hwang, K., Cognitive computing: Architecture, technologies, and intelligent applications. *IEEE Access*, 6, 19774–19783, 2018.
4. Alhussein, M., Muhammad, G., Hossain, M.S., Amin, S.U., Cognitive IoT-cloud integration for smart healthcare: A case study for epileptic seizure detection and monitoring. *Mobile Netw. Appl.*, Springer Publications, 23, 6, 1624–1635, 2018.
5. Salvaris, M., Dean, D., Tok, W.H., *Microsoft AI Platform: Deep Learning with Azure*, pp. 79–98, Apress, Berkeley, CA, 2018.
6. Shaikh, K., Eagle-Eye View of Azure Cognitive Services, in: *Developing Bots with QnA Maker Service*, pp. 1–29, Apress, Berkeley, CA, 2018.
7. Wu, S.-H., Chao, H.-L., Ko, C.-H., Mo, S.-R., Jiang, C.-T., Li, T.-L., Cheng, C.-C.C., Liang, C.-F., A cloud model and concept prototype for cognitive radio networks. *IEEE Wireless Commun.*, 19, 4, 49–58, 2012.
8. Yan, M., Castro, P., Cheng, P., Ishakian, V., Building a Chatbot with Serverless Computing, in: *Proc. Of 1st International Workshop on Mashups of Things and APIs*, Article No. 5, pp. 1–4, 2016.
9. Ruane, E., Young, R., Ventresque, A., Training a Chatbot with Microsoft LUIS: Effect of Intent Imbalance on Prediction Accuracy, in: *Proc. of 25th International Conference on Intelligent User Interfaces Companion*, pp. 63–64, 2020.
10. Del Sole, A., *Introducing Microsoft Cognitive Services. In: Microsoft Computer Vision APIs Distilled*, pp. 1–4, Apress, Berkeley, CA, 2017.
11. Machiraju, S. and Modi, R., Azure Cognitive Services, in: *Developing Bots with Microsoft Bots Framework*, pp. 233–260, Apress, Berkeley, CA, 2018.
12. Tajane, K., Dave, S., Jahagirdar, P., Ghadge, A., Musale, A., AI Based Chat-Bot Using Azure Cognitive Services, in: *Proc. of Fourth International Conference on Computing Communication Control and Automation (ICCUBEA)*, Pune, India, 2018.
13. Reis, A., Paulino, D., Filipe, V., Barroso, J., Using Online Artificial Vision Services to Assist the Blind—An Assessment of Microsoft Cognitive Services and Google Cloud Vision, in: *Proc. of Trends and Advances in Information Systems and Technologies, WorldCIST'18*, pp. 174–184, 2018.
14. Quarteroni, S., Natural Language Processing for Industry. *Informatik Spektrum*, 41, 105–112, 2018.
15. Iyengar, A., Supporting Data Analytics Applications Which Utilize Cognitive Services, in: *Proc. of IEEE 37th International Conference on Distributed Computing Systems (ICDCS)*, Atlanta, GA, USA, 2017.

16. Srivastava, Y., Khanna, P., Kumar, S., Estimation of Gestational Diabetes Mellitus using Azure AI Services, in: *Proc. Of Amity International Conference on Artificial Intelligence (AICAI)*, Dubai, United Arab Emirates, 2019.

17. Lee, K.Y. and Ha, N., AI platform to accelerate API economy and ecosystem, in: *Proc. of International Conference on Information Networking (ICOIN)*, Chiang Mai, Thailand, 2018.

18. Chen PhD, Y., Elenee Argentinis, J.D., Weber, G., IBM Watson: How Cognitive Computing Can Be Applied to Big Data Challenges in Life Sciences Research. *Clin. Ther.*, Elsevier Publications, 38, 4, 688–701, 2016.

19. Ahmed, M.N., Toor, A.S., O'Neil, K., Friedland, D., Cognitive Computing and the Future of Health Care Cognitive Computing and the Future of Healthcare: The Cognitive Power of IBM Watson Has the Potential to Transform Global Personalized Medicine. *IEEE Pulse*, 8, 8, 4–9, 2017.

20. Memeti, S. and Pllana, S., PAPA: A parallel programming assistant powered by IBM Watson cognitive computing technology. *J. Comput. Sci.*, Elsevier Publications, 26, 275–284, 2018.

21. Sudarsan, S., Evolving to a new computing ERA: Cognitive computing with Watson. *J. Comput. Sci. Coll.*, 29, 4, 4, 2014.

22. Earley, S., Cognitive Computing, Analytics, and Personalization. *IT Prof.*, 17, 4, 12–18, 2015.

23. França, M. and Werner, C., Perspectives for Selecting Cloud Microservices, in: *Proc. of IEEE International Conference on Software Architecture Companion (ICSA-C)*, Seattle, WA, USA, 2018.

24. Kollia, I. and Siolas, G., Using the IBM Watson cognitive system in educational contexts, in: *Proc. Of IEEE Symposium Series on Computational Intelligence (SSCI)*, Athens, Greece, 2016.

25. Almutairi, A.A. and El Rahman, S.A., The impact of IBM cloud solutions on students in Saudi Arabia, in: *Proc. of the impact of IBM cloud solutions on students in Saudi Arabia*, Cairo, Egypt, 2016.

26. Wang, Y. and Berwick, R.C., Formal Relational Rules of English Syntax for Cognitive Linguistics, Machine Learning, and Cognitive Computing. *J. Adv. Math. Appl.*, 2, 2, 182–195, 2013.

27. Kacprzyk, J. and Zadrozny, S., Computing With Words Is an Implementable Paradigm: Fuzzy Queries, Linguistic Data Summaries, and Natural-Language Generation. *IEEE Trans. Fuzzy Syst.*, 18, 3, 461–472, 2010.

28. Dale, R., Scott, D.R., Di Eugenio, B.D., Introduction to the special issue on natural language generation. *J. Comput. Linguist.*, 24, 3, 345–353, 1998.

29. Nirenburg, S. and McShane, M., The Interplay of Language Processing, Reasoning and Decision-Making in Cognitive Computing, Natural Language Processing and Information Systems. *NLDB 2015, Lecture Notes in Computer Science*, vol. 9103, 2015.

30. Kaltenrieder, P., Portmann, E., Myrach, T., Fuzzy knowledge representation in cognitive cities, in: *Proc. of IEEE International Conference on Fuzzy Systems (FUZZ-IEEE)*, Istanbul, Turkey, 2015.

31. Brasila, L.M., Azevedo, F.M., Barretoc, J.M., Hybrid expert system for decision supporting in the medical area: Complexity and cognitive computing. *Int. J. Med. Inf.*, 63, 1–2, 19–30, 2001.
32. Tian, Y., Wang, Y., Gavrilova, M.L., Ruhe, G., A formal knowledge representation system for the cognitive learning engine, in: *Proc. of 10th International Conference on Cognitive Informatics and Cognitive Computing (ICCI-CC'11)*, Banff, AB, Canada, 2011.
33. Bobrow, D.G. and Winograd, T., Multi-disciplinary. *J. Cogn. Sci.*, 1, 1, 3–46, 1977.

5

iParking—Smart Way to Automate the Management of the Parking System for a Smart City

J.A.D.C.A. Jayakody[1]*, E.A.G.A. Edirisinghe[1], S.A.H.M. Karunanayaka[2], E.M.C.S. Ekanayake[2], H.K.T.M. Dikkumbura[2] and L.A.I.M. Bandara[2]

[1]Department of Computer Systems Engineering, Sri Lanka Institute of Information Technology, Malabe, Sri Lanka
[2]Department of Information Technology, Sri Lanka Institute of Information Technology, Malabe, Sri Lanka

Abstract

Due to the highest usage of vehicles which occurs with developing economy and the improved city modernization level, traffic congestion and parking have become one of the main social problems. Despite the progress, there is still a need for an enhanced and distributed solution that can exploit data and provide an appropriate and real-time method on parking systems. This paper describes the design and implementation of a smart parking management system (SPMS) which can solve the previously mentioned parking problem. Huge traffic causes a considerable deal of damage, like the increment of accidents, the air pollution caused by a substantial amount of $CO2$ released by vehicles, and the unnecessary stress on drivers who must drive in often narrow and very busy roads and time wastage to find a free spot to park. Thus, to take care of the parking issue, present day advances have been made to furnish vehicle parks with smart devices that help street clients to identify the nearest available car park. In this paper, the development of the new fully automated parking system which is called iParking is presented. IParking is a design and a development of a smart parking system that will ensure the implementation of the outdoor parking system for the Smart City concept by using image processing (IP) and machine learning (ML). With connected to smart parking, a mobile app alerts the user about available spaces and

Corresponding author: anuradha.j@sliit.lk

Kolla Bhanu Prakash, G. R. Kanagachidambaresan, V. Srikanth, E. Vamsidhar (eds.) Cognitive Engineering for Next Generation Computing: A Practical Analytical Approach, (141–166) © 2021 Scrivener Publishing LLC

guide user to the exact location with accuracy. IParking system aims to take the driver's stress out while finding a parking space in city centers where all cars in the city are looking for parking slots in the same time.

Keywords: Smart parking, machine learning, internet of things, convolutional neural networks, artificial neural networks, short message services

5.1   Introduction

Nowadays the vehicle usage has increased and vehicle parking has become one of the serious issues in urban zones of both developed and developing countries. Today in the world 55% of the people live in urban areas and the proportion that we can expect it to increase is 68% by the end of 2049 [1], which will at last lead to expanded blockage and interest for a huge upgrade of smart traffic management. People spend more than 7 min in searching for a parking spot. This helps like 30% of the traffic flows in cities [1] and contributes to traffic congestion during peak hours.

Finding an available parking space is a basic issue in most present day urban areas, especially the shortage of available vehicle spaces is clear in numerous open spots such as universities, hotels, market areas, hospitals, shopping malls, and airports. Moreover, many outdoor vehicle parks create a traffic jam which happens while searching for a parking place. Smart cities especially have gotten to be one of the key reasons for the city gridlock, air pollution and driver frustration. Thus, there is a huge need for a real time, secure, intelligent, efficient and reliable parking system. Furthermore it should be used for looking through the vacant parking slots, direction towards the parking process, negotiation of the parking fee, along with the proper management [17] through the whole parking process.

Through this research a smart parking system which is known as iParking, allows drivers to access parking information through their smartphones. In this research, a smart parking system that allows drivers to effectively find the available parking places with accurate root guidance and automated payment facility was designed and implemented. An effective solution to this system can be provided by various new technologies. In this paper, firstly an overview of the concept of the iParking system, their categories, and different functionalities are given. This research describes the technologies around parking availability monitoring, accurate root guidance to the available parking lot, parking reservation and pricing according to the vehicle type and time.

iParking includes the development of an android mobile application to book the parking area. There is no manual process, the whole parking system is automated and it helps to save time. The mobile application is developed with a registration page. First of all, in this registration step the car number will be checked automatically when the car enters [14, 15]. Then the vehicle can be parked according to their booking. The main goal is to provide a time-saving parking system that prevents traffic and confusion while parking. The iParking system results in time-saving parking through the booking facility for parking through an android application and the automated car recognition and parking slot status. Outdoor advertising, it exhibits huge advertisements to passing drivers. It exhibits huge advertisements to passing pedestrians and drivers. These types of advertisements are intended to catch the attention of the target audience in a blink of an eye and thus have a lasting impact on the mind of the reader.

Smart Parking systems typically gather information about available parking spaces in a particular geographical area and the process is real-time to place vehicles according to the available positions. It involves real-time data collection, low-cost sensors, getting GPS correct location details and mobile-phone-enabled automated payment system that allow people to find parking in advance or very accurately anticipate where they will probably discover a spot. When deployed as a system, iParking thus reduces car emissions in urban centers by reducing unnecessary city blocks which happens while searching for a parking space. It also permits people and cities to carefully manage their parking facility. According to Figure 5.1,

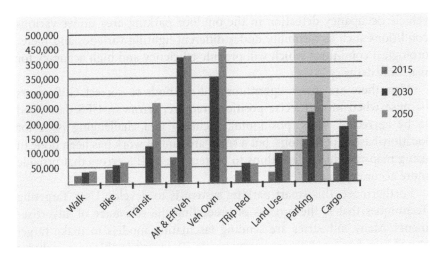

Figure 5.1 Analyzing efficiency in parking [16].

iParking could help in 220,000 gallons of fuel savings till 2030 and approx. 300,000 gallons of fuels saved by end of 2049 [16].

5.2 Background & Literature Review

5.2.1 Background

A lot of cities worldwide are working to become smart. One of the most popular applications in smart cities is the smart parking system, as they help people to save time, reduce fuel consumption, and decrease carbon dioxide emissions. Smart parking systems have a defined architecture with specified components. Although there are many kinds of research done, still a small amount of work has been done for the concept of outdoor smart parking systems in Sri Lanka.

Furthermore, most of these parking systems do not cover the following areas: real time availability of slots in different weather conditions, navigating user to the available slot by showing the position with great accuracy and the facility of the fully automated parking payment system by detecting vehicle number plate in any condition and by providing payment patterns. Most importantly a lot of systems do not have a unique market value because most parking systems only provide the parking facility and do not focus on providing some benefits for the users who come to the parking area, like digital targeted advertising.

Many researchers have successfully implemented many algorithms to detect objects. But a small amount of work has been done to identify vehicle occupancy detection in the outdoor parking area under various conditions such as flexibility under different lighting varieties and meteorological conditions which will provide efficiency and high accuracy for real-time delivery.

Also, there are many algorithms and methods to correct GPS errors because when more precise positions require, errors in GPS data need to be corrected. Thus, positioning accuracy is a challenging issue for location-based applications, but a small amount of work has been done in using map-matching algorithms to correct these GPS errors that provide more accurate results.

Furthermore, this smart parking system is to develop User Targeting Techniques that is the process of predicting the relevance of advertisements. Many industries are sending fascinating models to make target crowd bunches for different commercials. The work in this area includes

Analysis using Machine Learning and it is capable of identifying and displaying the relevant content of a particular object.

Image processing is used to recognize vehicles by identifying license plates. It is basically used for parking access control and security purposes. First, the vehicle comes near the entrance gate and a signal is sent to the camera. Then the camera is activated and takes a snapshot.

The system applies certain algorithms to analyze the vehicle image. Next, the image is enhanced, the vehicle plate is placed, and the character is extracted from the vehicle plate. The system attempts to coordinate the perceived vehicle plate number to the vehicle license plate database. If "Allow", the gate will open, then vehicles will be allowed through.

Recognition of vehicle license plates also has the advantage of storing images of vehicles that can be used to fight crime. Vehicle speed, weather conditions, vehicle type, distance between vehicle license plate and camera, plate type (rectangle, bent type), orientation of vehicle license plate, vehicle font character type, efficiency, and accuracy are variables that affect the recognition system [19].

License plates usually have a rectangular shape with a known aspect ratio, so they can be extracted by finding all possible rectangles in the image [18]. To find these rectangles, an edge detection method is commonly used.

Hence, a literature review is carried out based on every sub topic.

5.2.2 Review of Literature

"Smart parking reservation system using short message services (SMS)" by Hanif, Badiozaman and Daud [5] have presented a smart parking system which reduces the time wastage during finding a parking spot in commercial car park areas [5]. This parking reservation framework is inherent such a way that clients can book their parking spots via a SMS. The system has developed as a fully automated system by using a Peripheral Interface Controller (PIC). This microcontroller is able to store data about available parking spaces, include passwords and permit or deny access to the parking area. A prototype of a car park system was designed to show the potential of the proposed work. The demonstration has shown the system's ability to reserve the car park, gain entry to the parking area and thus remove the hassle of looking for empty parking lots. There are many advantages in this system. Such as; enhance security with password requirements and with the ease of use, the system can be used and applied anywhere. And there are some disadvantages either, like; High installation cost, GSM function

creates a bottleneck and the microcontroller needs to put a lot of lads that can disturb the system.

Yang, Portilla, and Riesgo *et al.* stated that *"Smart Parking Service based on Wireless Sensor Networks"* [6] and, the authors have presented the design and implementation of a Smart Parking Services prototype system based on Wireless Sensor Networks (WSNs) that allows drivers to effectively locate the available parking spaces [6]. This system consists of wireless sensor networks, embedded web server, central web server, and mobile phone applications. In the system, low-cost wireless sensor network modules are installed in each parking slot equipped with one sensor node within the device. The parking space status is detected by the sensor node and is periodically reported to the embedded web server via the wireless sensor networks that are deployed. Using Wi-Fi networks in real time, this information is sent to the central web server and the vehicle driver can locate empty parking lots using regular mobile devices too. The android app is easy to use and with a great interface, GPS helps cover the maximum area available and it displays various options for parking can be listed as advantages of this project, while the user cannot use the reservation function, unavailability of multi-layer parking in infrastructure can be listed as disadvantages.

Shih and Tsai *et al.* stated that *"A Convenient Vision Based System for Automatic Detection of Parking Spaces in Indoor Parking Lots Using Wide-Angle Cameras"* [7]. They have proposed an indoor vision-based parking system. The wide-angle fisheye-lens or cat dioptric cameras which are easy to set up by a user with no technical background were proposed in this research. Easiness of the framework arrangement mostly originates from the utilization of another camera model that can be aligned utilizing just one space line without knowing its position and heading. Also the camera allows convenient changes in detected parking space boundaries. A genuine vision-based parking area has been built up and important examinations directed. The accuracy, practicality, and strength of the proposed techniques were showed by experimental results. Although it has disadvantages like; No mean is provided to address weather conditions that may affect visibility and Reservations. General users can easily set up the system without any technical background and wide angle camera is used to cover the entire territory of the parking area can be categorized under advantages [7].

"Automated Parking System with Bluetooth access" by Singh, Anand, and Sharma [8] have developed a fully automated parking system for both two wheelers and cars. This described system extemporizes upon the current parking framework by improving its security includes and mechanizing

the parking process accordingly wiping out the requirement for manual mediation. The system has an inbuilt Bluetooth reader to authenticate and identify the owner. This kills the utilization of tokens or paper bills. Space the executives and mechanization are performed with the assistance of an ARM microcontroller which controls the mechanical engines to leave the vehicle at a fitting parking area [8].

"*Car Park Management with Networked Wireless Sensors and Active RFID*" by El Mouatezbillah, Djenouri, Boulkaboul and Bagula [9] have proposed an automatic car park management. Integration of networked sensor/actuator and radio frequency identification (RFID) technologies was used and the emerging internet of things (IoT) context was used as service provider. In view of this combination, they have proposed a scalable and low-cost car parking framework (CPF). A fundamental model usage and experimentation of certain modules of the proposed CPF has been performed. Trial results exhibit extensive decrease in cost and energy consumption [9].

"*Automatic Parking Management System and Parking Fee Collection Based on Number Plate Recognition*" by Rashid and Musa [10] have talked about an automatic parking system and electronic parking fee collection method based on vehicle number plate recognition. The objective of this system was to create and execute an automatic parking system that would increase the effficiency and security of the public parking lot as well as collecting parking fees without using a magnetic card. This system is developed with less human interaction. Hence it was a big help to develop the iParking system which is a fully automated smart parking system. iParking system contains fully automated parking guidance system as in this research. In this research they have used image processing in parking operation and payment procedure, and in iParking system machine learning will be used to minimize the errors of image processing [10].

"*New Smart Parking System Based on Resource Allocation and Reservations*" by Geng and Cassandras [11] have suggested a new method of "smart parking" for a city environment. The system allots and saves an ideal parking space dependent on the cost capacity of the driver joining the vicinity to the objective and the expense of parking. The system approach solves the problem of mixed-integer linear programming (MILP) at every point of the decision specified in a time-driven sequence. Based on simulation results, compared with uncontrolled parking processes, this system reduces the time wastage on finding a parking space, whereas the overall parking capacity is more efficiently deployed. They have also described full execution in a carport to test this system, where another light system conspires is proposed to ensure client reservations [11].

"An Accurate GPS-IMU/DR Data Fusion Method for Driverless Car Based on a Set of Predictive Models and Grid Constraints" by Wang, Deng and Yin [12] have proposed an accurate GPS–inertial measurement unit, data fusion method in view of a lot of prescient models and inhabitance framework requirements.

In this paper, the system proposes a novel data fusion method for precise localization problems of driverless cars using a set of ARMA predictive models and occupancy grid constraints. It is only based on on-board GPS–IMU and DR navigation data [12].

Study on *"Differential GPS Positioning Methods"* by Shao and Sui [21] have presented about the three typical methods for differential GPS according to the different type of information sent by the base station, they are differential position; differential pseudo-range; differential carrier phase [21].

From this research the main idea about GPS positioning was gained [21].

"Automatic parking space detection system" by Bibi and Nadeem [3] have presented a vision based smart parking framework to assist the drivers to find an appropriate parking space and book it efficiently. In here they have used image processing and though this research image processing procedure can be understood. When the car enters or exits the parking lot, its presence and details like size of the vehicle take into an account and those information will be used in further process [3].

"Parking spaces modeling for inter spaces occlusion handling" by Masmoudi and Wali [2] suggested an idea to provide smart parking performance and to solve the problem which caused due to the lack of space in parking areas and also between two vehicles. They used an event-based detection approach to detect objects and tracked them using a Kalman filter. The goal of this paper is to introduce a new approach to provide parking vacancies with reliable results and to address the problem of interplace occlusion [2]. This research paper is proposing a new approach for the parking architecture extraction in view of the on-road surfaces, as it is the less impeded model.

Then arrangement of the cars in the parking area, mentioned parking spaces on street surfaces shown in Figure 5.2 with red area, will reflect the parking model with the less occlusion possible and provide good performance for the detection of parking events [2].

Fabian *et al.* stated that *"An algorithm for parking lot occupation detection"* [4], and he has proposed an unsupervised vision based system for parking space detection. But they have used image processing to work under many

Figure 5.2 Different parking models presentation [2].

different conditions. This system claims that the major problem in images detection is the occlusions and shadows using recognition algorithms [4].

"Parking lots space detection" by Wu and Zhang [13] have proposed a parking detection system which has the following steps:

1. pre-processing
2. extraction of model features
3. multi-class SVM (Support Vector Machines) recognition
4. MRF (Markov random field)-based verification [13].

Initially, the input video outlines are turned to uniform axes and portioned into little fixes containing 3 parking spaces such as Figure 5.3. This paper presented a novel method via using only a few frames which are captured by a single camera for unsupervised parking lot space detection [13].

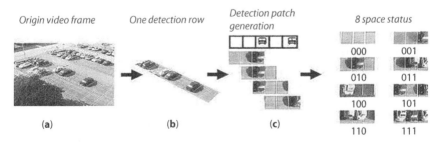

Figure 5.3 Preprocess the input frame and generate detecting patches [13].

"Parking space classification using convolutional neural networks" by Cazamias and Marek [18] have described a parking occupancy classifier. In this research they have used convolutional neural network (CNN) as a classifier. The workhorse of this algorithm is a Convolutional Neural Network (CNN), a deep learning data structure that works especially well for computer vision tasks [18].

"Networked Wireless Sensors, Active RFID, and Handheld Devices for Modern Car Park Management" by Djenouri, Karbab, Boulkaboul and Bagula [19] have implemented a Car Parking Framework (CPF) which can manage a smart parking system that combines sensors (detection of parking spaces), RFID tags, and readers [19]. This system uses serial cable communication.

Sharma, Kulkarni, Kalbande, Dholay *et al.* stated that *"Cost Optimized Hybrid System in Digital Advertising using Machine Learning"* [20], but they have suggested an Audience Targeting Strategies method of predicting the importance of ads to individuals. Machine learning algorithms analyze the personal data of individuals that they share with companies on a voluntary basis. The results are promising for targeting the audience [20, 21]. The authors have suggested many deep neural network techniques.

Audience Expansion: Audience Targeting Techniques is the method of assessing the importance of ads to individuals. Several industry giants, such as Facebook and LinkedIn, are introducing innovative models to build target audience audiences for different advertising. Research in this area includes Advertisement Analysis using Machine Learning, Audience Expansion for Online Social Network Advertising [20].

"AI-Based Targeted Advertising System" by Yu, Lee, Lim, and Razak [20] have proposed an intelligent targeted advertising system with following functionalities,

1. Gender and age identification using facial recognition
2. Vehicle recognition
3. Multiple object detection.

Facial recognition is applied to recognize gender and age on the basis of facial characteristics. Various item acknowledgment innovation is utilized for vehicle types and for various classes of article acknowledgment dependent on their novel attributes [20].

In this research machine learning techniques have used same as iParking to improve the effectiveness. Machine learning algorithms are implemented for higher acknowledgment exactness and subsequently accomplished better focused on publicizing impacts [20].

The models used in the recognition framework are pre-prepared with the idea of machine learning for exceptionally precise outcomes and improved execution. With the system's ability to display targeted advertising content, advertisers benefit as they could significantly reduce their promotional costs due to the effectiveness of targeted advertising. As for the viewer, they will be introduced to material that is more important to them and will be given the products and services that they may need [20].

5.3 Research Gap

The following features have been discussed.

- Accuracy: The percentage of accuracy of the model

High: more than or equal 80%
Medium: more than or equal 50% less than 80%

- Efficiency: Effectiveness of anticipating/identifying results considering the time it takes to foresee
- Proper system/visualization: Intelligent dashboard that is fit for giving clear visuals and the framework interface application.
- Scalability: These systems can further modify in future.
- Weather conditions: Work properly under certain weather conditions (sunny/rainy/cloudy and shade)
- Lighting conditions: Work properly under any lighting conditions
- Security: Security of the system
- Cost: Maintenance cost, Implementation cost, Device cost
- GPS location error analysis—Displaying corrected GPS position accuracy
- Marketing value: Providing Digital Promotions/Advertisements for a target audience

5.4 Research Problem

Some identified parking systems don't provide navigation for the parking lot, thus users will have to search manually to find a parking lot. But unfortunately, if the parking area does not have enough space to park the vehicle, they will have to go through the same procedure again and look for parking space, which will contribute most to time loss and traffic congestion.

In terms of GPS precision in an outdoor environment, there has been little improvement in the last few years. Outside, the GPS range of the phone is about five meters, but it's been steady for a while. For example, GPS-enabled smartphones are usually accurate within a 4.9 m radius of the open sky.

GPS satellites distribute their signals in space with some accuracy, but what users receive depends on additional factors, such as; bridges and trees, including satellite structure, signals from buildings or walls, signal blockage due to structures and atmospheric conditions.

If the system is not maintaining in real time, users will have to drive through all parking divisions just to find an available parking slot.

The images of the vehicle license plate which is taken by using the optical character reader technology may get blurred and it may cause to less accuracy in the smart parking system.

Some of the most existing systems used sensors for lot occupancy detection by using sensors for checking the availability. It will lead to many issues like, it will need a large number of sensors because a lot of sensors are required corresponding to each parking slot, electrical power supply required (possibly using rechargeable batteries), maintenance activities raise the huge cost when considering its use for a whole outdoor parking area, also the complexity of installation (in-road implantation), and some sensors may not work properly under certain weather conditions.

Some cameras of existing systems are not in the correct position. Therefore, it can't see all the slots, because it might be obstructed by any object. Though some existing systems are using more cameras to cover all the slots in the parking area, it is only capable of covering some small areas, so it is a huge waste of cost.

Parking assumes a significant function in a client's choice of where to shop. Along these lines, publicizing is a sort of Out-Of-Home publicizing that snatches the odds of outside advancement which regularly accomplishes alluring outcomes. However, in the cutting edge occupied world, individuals need more an ideal opportunity to watch papers or customary commercials and rather than conventional announcements with static messages, advanced boards with greater adaptability and cutting-edge messages are taking their method of supplanting them. Traditional advertising is not capable of targeting a certain audience and display relevant advertisements for better attention. Also, there are some other relevant issues occur like, inadmissible promotions are shown to the crowd, unfit to target open air crowd, restricted functionalities. These issues bring about wastage of assets, significant expenses in publicizing, and inadequate promoting.

Advertising can be achieved by daily newspapers and television in many ways. But in the competitive world, people are very busy. Usually people go for their daily work early in the morning, and we come back in the evening. They don't have much time to look at the newspaper or television.

A driver who comes from a distance may not be aware of the shops around the parking area. Normally people go to the park to buy something, sometimes it takes too long for people to identify the stores. Often shops that have what they want can be found near the parking area.

Discounts are sometimes depending on the divisions. Assume, Keells supermarket, in Keells branch near the parking area, they offer some discount. In other branches, however, it does not give. If the user just wants to take it in the branch which is near the parking area, it's safe for the money.

Traffic may increase when finding parking areas as well as air pollution and road accidents may increase. When having early reserved parking slot user saves their time.

5.5   Objectives

The main objective of the research is, constantly, accurately, efficiently and in real time monitoring a series of parking lots to determine the availability and occupancy using a fixed camera under certain weather conditions (sunny/rainy/cloudy and shade) and lighting variations of the outdoor parking area in the smart city.

Other objectives of the research can be listed as below.

- The Global Positioning System corrects certain effects, but there are still residual errors that are not corrected. Fixing these errors is a major challenge for improving the GPS position. Therefore, develop and apply a proper model for the effective correction of Global Positioning System (GPS) errors using mapping algorithms can be named as another objective. This framework is utilized to furnish parking reservations with lower evaluating and scanning time for clients and asset use for the parking cycle.
- LPR (license plate recognition) system uses to identify registered vehicles, check the user authentication and store the entrance time and vehicle details into the database. Payment will automatically be calculated by detecting the vehicle

according to vehicle type and the entry, exit time of the vehicle and implement the payment process on the desktop application and send a notification to the user about the payment details using the mobile application.

- Explore the behavior pattern and its predictability of the occupancy of the vehicle parking zone and parking period. Rather than analyzing the overall available areas of a car parking zone, the system digs into the parking behavior styles in finer granularity. Recollect the differential parking behaviors among special sorts of customer satisfaction. After prediction identify what are the rush hours.

- In the current busy world, people won't find enough time watching traditional advertisement methods but by using digital advertising in an outdoor parking system, users can save some time watch the promotions/advertisements of shops/ items while using the parking facility. It benefits the publicists as they could altogether decrease their limited time costs because of the adequacy of focused promoting. Concerning the crowd, they will be presented to content that is more applicable to them and is offered items and administrations that they may require. So that, analyze customer detail patterns (gender, age, and job, etc.) and segment the targeted audience, this will enhance the market value of the proposed system.

- Filtering user's job role and marital status and display advertisements according to the users.

- Develop a Mobile app for parking slot reservation.

5.6 Methodology

There were five (5) main sub sections in the methodology. Figure 5.4 illustrates the whole system diagram.

5.6.1 Lot Availability and Occupancy Detection

Firstly, the video image of the parking area was acquired by a fixed camera, and then the pre-processing of each frame image was carried out, including image color conversion, image de-noising, and image morphological transformation [4]. The processing of the image was divided into system initialization, image acquisition, image segmentation, image enhancement, and image detection. The thresholding method was used to get a free image

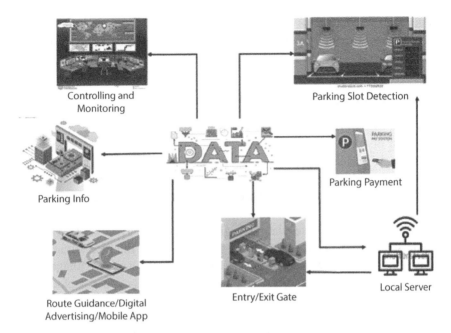

Figure 5.4 System diagram.

of darkness and the Canny Edge detection algorithm was suitable for edge detection to separate the shadow and the object. There were some identified filters to solve these various detection issues under certain weather conditions and lightning varieties, such as HOG (Histogram of Oriented Gradients), SIFT (Scale-invariant feature transform) and color Spaces (YUV, HSV, and YCrCb). After the image processing stage, the occupancy detection classifier status was given using CNNs (Convolutional Neural Networks) and a binary SVM (Support Vector Machine).

5.6.2   Error Analysis for GPS (Global Positioning System)

The accurate path to the available slot was calculated by using the Global Positioning System. Thus, this system used a method to enhance the position accuracy of a GPS receiver which has used map data rather than any additional sensors. A Map-Matching (MM) algorithm was used to position data from a navigation system with spatial road network data. The points extracted from the roads prior to operating the algorithm were utilized as map data. A MM algorithm uses a range of positioning and navigation data, including position, distance, speed, and road network topology, to identify the correct road segment on which the vehicle is traveling and the location of the vehicle on that road segment. The key task of the MM algorithm was to identify the correct road segment from a pool of candidate road segments. The method matched the disparity between the trajectory of the GPS and the digital map information.

5.6.3 Vehicle License Plate Detection System

The first step in the license plate recognition system (LPR) was to find the position of the plate from the vehicle image. The system also recognizes the vehicle license plate at the entrance gate and can take action to enter or leave the vehicle. A typical PC-based system with a PIC microcontroller and a video camera catches and processes video frames containing a visible car license plate.

An automatic license plate recognition technology consists of three basic steps. They are recognition of the position of the plate attached to the vehicle, text image segmentation and convert character images into beautiful identifiable images. The plating area usually consists of a white background and black text. Therefore, the transition between black and white is very intensive in this area. Finding the area that contains most of the transition points is enough to find the plate area. For this purpose, this system applied a canny edge detection operator to the vehicle image to obtain transition points.

In this process, the blob (Binary Large Object) coloring algorithm has a powerful architecture for determining closed non-contact areas in binary images. In this task, the System applied a 4-way blob coloring algorithm to a binary-coded license plate image to retrieve characters. After implementation, the segmented characters were obtained from an image of the license plate area. This system also suggested ANN (artificial neural network) for OCR (Optical Character Recognition). ANN is a statistical model of a real-world system. Simplify the code and improve the quality of the image recognition process.

The system uses ultrasonic sensors to confirm the parking or leaving of the vehicle. Then the payment will be automatically calculated according to the vehicle type and the time period it stayed in the park and parking fees will also be applied according to usage at peak times.

5.6.4 Analyze Differential Parking Behaviors and Pricing

Discovered the pattern of behavior and its predictability of parking lot occupancy/reserved and parking time period. K-means cluster algorithm was used to partition the vehicles in a specific time, after this system calculates the features for each vehicle to the parking lot. According to the other periodicity, identify what are the peak hours and then we identify the main frequencies and used these main frequencies to recreate the time domain sequence and forecast the future value. According to the above predictions rating was changing with the time periods. If it was peak hour, parking rate was getting high. If it was normal hours, parking rate was not changing and if many parking slots were free, the parking rate was getting low. Likewise, parking rates will be changed.

5.6.5 Targeted Digital Advertising

Machine learning algorithms can be utilized from numerous points of view to accomplish amazing customized experience. The three most famous ways are prescient investigation, cost advancing and crowd focusing on. Advanced Advertising has caught wide consideration from the market. It is an integral asset to contact right individuals at the right time. Additionally, it lessens the expense of broadcasting ads as the ad is shown uniquely to individuals who may be keen on the substance. The interest prediction for audience targeting provides accuracy using the Naive Bayes classifier. The process started with data collection. After a period of time, the system collected data for each advertisement. Audience categorization was then carried out to classify users in categories then customize the ad for that class is shown to specific users. This was filtered by users Gender, Age, Job, etc.

Using a Bayesian algorithm, it then compared the information of users with that of the advertising database, figured out the most suitable ads and compared the results, and showed the ad to the user.

5.6.6 Used Technologies

The following set of technology domains were used in this module for implementation of the system.

- ❖ Computer Vision
  - Vacant parking lots detection

- ❖ Machine Learning
  - To train a dataset of parking slots in order to recognize them and for classification of parking availability and occupancy based on visual features extracted through Computer Vision.

- Position accuracy improvement of GPS.
- Improve Audience categorization for digital targeted advertising.

❖ Deep Learning
  - A branch of Deep Learning, which is Convolutional Neural Networks (CNN), will be used to preprocess images and achieve performance.
  - Artificial Neural Networking (ANN), will be used to character segmentation of vehicle license plate.

5.6.7   Specific Tools and Libraries

The following list provides the specific tools and libraries that were employed in the system module.

❖ Android Studio
  Frontend web framework in designing the UI for the module

❖ OpenCV
  Programming function Library which is mainly used in real-time computer vision.

❖ MATLAB
  Use to process images one generally writes function files, or script files to perform the operations

Use for GPS position correction

  ❖ Java—Create Admin console
  ❖ React—Development of mobile application
  ❖ Pdfkit
    Python library for generating PDF documents
  ❖ Tensorflow
    TensorFlow is a free and open-source programming library for dataflow and differentiable programming over a scope of assignments. It is a representative numerical library and is utilized for AI applications, for example neural systems.

Table 5.1 Used tools.

Area	Fields	Tools
Data Science	Model Building	Python
Machine Learning	Classifiers	Gaussian Mixture Model (GMM) K-nearest neighbor (kNN) Support vector machine (SVM) Naive Bayes
Mobile Application Developing	Application	Android Studio
Database Management	Database	Firebase
Image Processing	Dataset	Images
Data Analytics	Image Process	MATLAB

Table 5.1 shows the tools that used in the research according to the fields and the particular areas.

5.7   Testing and Evaluation

Step 1: Functional Testing

Functional testing is a method of quality assuring (QA) and also known as a black-box testing method, which bases its test cases on the software product requirements under study. Functions are evaluated by feeding them input and analyzing performance, and the internal structure of the system is rarely considered (unlike white box testing).

Source code is the place where the whole system is tested against specifications and functional requirements. The functional testing step occurs in the source code.

Actual system use is simulated during the functional testing. The aim is to get as close to real system use as possible and establish test conditions that are relevant to user requirements.

Step 2: Usability Testing

Usability goes beyond functionality testing and combines testing for functionality and for the entire user experience. This should be possible inside or by getting outer analyzers that fit potential client base.

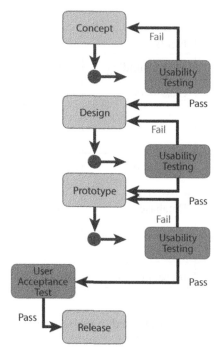

Figure 5.5 Steps of usability testing.

As shown in Figure 5.5, the usability testing involves the following steps:

1. Develop a testing strategy that ensures all functions of your application will be examined. These include navigation and content.
2. Recruit test participants, either internally or externally.
3. Run the test under the observation of experts.
4. Analyze the results and improve this proposed system accordingly.

Step 3: Interface Testing
This testing ensures smooth operation of all connections between the Web server and the application server interfaces. This involves testing the systems of communication and ensuring that error messages are shown correctly. Additional issues to check are that both the user and the server are managing the interruptions correctly.

Step 4: Testing of Compatibility
Ensuring your application is compatible with all browsers and devices is a key step in web application testing.

Step 5: Performance Testing
In the wake of guaranteeing this framework application's usefulness is working appropriately and responsively on all programs and gadgets, the time has come to investigate how it performs under substantial burden. This incorporates testing the application under various web speeds and how it carries on under ordinary and pinnacle loads (load testing). To decide the limit of this application, it is put under expanding measures of worry until it stops to work (stress testing).

Testing for flexibility is a pivotal movement to discover how this application carries on under worry before your clients do. Ensure, test the usefulness under various situations and equipment designs, and this application recoups from crashes in the most ideal manner conceivable.

Step 6: Testing of Security
The last step of this system testing makes sure this system is protected against unauthorized access and harmful actions through viruses or other malicious software. Such a checklist should include tasks in the following areas:

- Error Handling
- Denial of Service
- Authorization
- Session Management
- Data Validation
- Secure Transmission
- Authentication
- Specific Functionality Tests
- Cryptography.

5.8   Results

The research work described in this chapter is vision-based and it utilizes a web camera for both license plate recognition and a coordinate-based methodology for slot detection.

In the vehicle registration plate recognition process first the number plate was extracted using the Haar classifier and then converted it to text using Tesseract OCR. This was tested over 40 vehicles using the videos

Table 5.2 Test results for parking space detection.

Number of the trial	Number of vehicles	Correct reading	False reading
1	5	5	0
2	2	2	0
3	8	7	1
4	1	1	0
5	4	4	0

obtained through internet resources. The extraction of the license plate was successful for 38 vehicles and text conversion of the license plate was successful for 28 vehicles over there.

The system contains a success rate of 95% for license plate extraction and rate of 82.35% text conversion. Text conversion shows less accuracy than plate extraction mainly due to the less accuracy in the text conversion in double line license plates in Sri Lanka. In the slot detection process, first we identify the parking coordinates through image processing techniques and then the parking boundaries are drawn according to the recognized coordinates. Finally the free and occupied slots are differentiated with vision based techniques.

The accuracy of slot detection is tested with several input videos obtained at a vehicle park with 13 parking slots as shown in Table 5.2.

5.9 Discussion

For the parking slot detection process, accuracy at trials 1, 2, 3, 4 and 5 respectively are 100, 100, 87.5, 100 and 100% while the rate of false reading at the above trials respectively are 0, 0, 12.5, 0 and 0%. Accuracy variations occur, when increasing the number of vehicles is due to the camera quality and the location of the camera that we used in testing. The web camera that we used in the testing process had a less resolution and less lightning correction.

One of the principle parts of the stopping the executives framework is the accessibility and inhabitance location. For a huge scope execution, the framework necessities will be simple, snappy, and inside financial plan. The target of the current arrangement is to be precise and effective, as it is commonly utilized with regards to paid-for parking garages. Subsequently, by far most of the current arrangements are sensor-based gadgets (e.g., proximity sensors) related with each accessible parking spot. The huge number of sensors required with the related system framework (conceivably remote), the electrical force flexibly required (potentially utilizing battery-powered batteries), and the unpredictability of establishment (in-street implantation), along with the related upkeep exercises raises the expense of such an answer, making it restrictive while thinking about its utilization for an entire open air stopping territory or a broad zone.

This technique is for recognizing parking spots inhabitance and accessibility utilizing a fixed camera. This sort of approach includes handling pictures and perceiving the nearness of vehicles by utilizing PC vision techniques. The strategy accompanies critical advantages over the exemplary recognition techniques: altogether lower costs related with the underlying execution, negligible expenses related with scaling, simple reconfiguration of a current parking garage, and the likelihood to likewise utilize and record the pictures and video takes care of for reconnaissance and security purposes.

This system attempts on the Image Processing Technique through the MATLAB as a Software platform. Since it is difficult to set the camera opposite to the parking areas, it is trying for space identification affected by light assortment, diverse climate conditions, vehicles' shadow, and impediment. To obtain high detection accuracy under these critical conditions, this system train and recognize from the image frame by the machine learning algorithm, Support Vector Machines (SVM), convolutional neural networks (CNN) architecture instead of segmenting them directly to find out the available space.

One of the main objectives of the research was to develop and apply a proper model for the effective correction of GPS errors using mapping algorithms. This task was accomplished by determining the exact latitude and longitude of users by collecting a range of information from satellite modules. The statistical accuracy of the user's position was directly related to the statistical accuracy of the distance measurement. This framework was utilized to furnish parking reservations with the lower evaluating and scanning time for clients and asset use for parking measure. Accordingly, this framework has a few commitments as expanding use of parking areas and improving experience of parking measure for clients by more powerful time utilizing.

This system used Machine learning algorithms that can analyze customer detail patterns (gender, age, job, etc.) and segment the targeted audience, this would enhance the market value of the proposed system. Because in the current busy world people won't find enough time watch traditional advertisement methods but by using digital advertising in an outdoor parking system, users can save some time watch the promotions/

advertisements of shops/items while using the parking facility. It benefits the publicists as they could fundamentally lessen their limited time costs because of the viability of focused promoting. Concerning the crowd, they will be presented to content that are more pertinent to them, and be offered items and administrations that they may require. LPR system used to identify registered vehicles, check the user authentication and store the entrance time and vehicle details into the database. The parked vehicle comes to the exit gate then again identify the vehicle and store the exit time and calculate payment details. After calculating the payment it sends a notification to the users.

Over time, smart parking solutions can generate data that reveals user-lot correlations and trends. These patterns end up being priceless to part proprietors regarding how to make changes and upgrades to drivers.

Furthermore, returning clients can supplant day by day manual money installments with telephone account charging and application installments. This additionally empowers client devotion projects and significant client input.

And this software improves the performance of cognitive systems and provides a cheaper and faster way to make decisions. The system generates a report on the vehicle number for which the plate was captured. When the vehicle license plate is captured, the characters are recognized and displayed on the screen. Apart from this, the system also works for security purposes, so you can find stolen or stolen vehicles [19].

Therefore, increasing accuracy and efficiency requires addressing various constraints and concentrating on designing algorithms to extract vehicle license plates.

5.10 Conclusion

Our objective was to fabricate a profoundly exact programmed recognition framework that is steady and financial for industry applications. A fruitful usage of the framework would bring about less traffic and decrease swarmed lines for parking spots like shopping centers and business structures where numerous individuals share a stopping zone. This paper enhances the system's performance which is based on a real time process being user friendly, time saving, reducing the fuel wastage and maintaining the traffic congestion under control. The efforts made in this research work are intended to improve the current parking infrastructure of the urban areas and thereby aiming to make the lives of people easier. For those reasons, the booking framework that works continuously to catch data and communicate data with respect to free parking spots to the clients. We accept that this framework would consistently propose the best stopping to the client, so the client would not need to worry about the stopping, the headings and so on.

References

1. Arnott, R. and Inci, E., An integrated model of downtown parking and traffic congestion. *J. Urban Econ.*, 60, 3, 418–442 2006.
2. Masmoudi, I., Wali, A., Alimi, A.M., Parking spaces modelling for inter spaces occlusion handling, in: *Proceedings of the 22nd International Conference in Central Europe on Computer Graphics Visualization and Computer Vision*, Plzen, Czech Republic, June 2014.
3. Bibi, N., Majid, M.N., Dawood, H., Guo, P., Automatic parking space detection system, in: *2017 2nd International Conference on Multimedia and Image Processing (ICMIP)*, Wuhan, China, March 2017.
4. Fabian, T., An Algorithm for Parking Lot Occupation Detection, *Conference on Computer Information Systems and Industrial Management Applications*, 2008.
5. Hanif, N.H.H.M., Badiozaman, M.H., Daud, H., Smart parking reservation system using short message services (SMS), *International Conference on Intelligent and Advanced Systems*, IEEE, 2010.
6. Yang, J., Portilla, J., Riesgo, T., Smart Parking Service based on Wireless Sensor Networks, *IECON - 38th Annual Conference on IEEE Industrial Electronics Society*, IEEE, Montreal, QC, Canada, 2012.
7. Shih, S.-E. and Tsai, W.-H., Senior Member, IEEE, A Convenient Vision-Based System for Automatic Detection of Parking Spaces in Indoor Parking Lots Using WideAngle Cameras. *IEEE Trans. Veh. Technol.*, 63, 6, 2521–2532 July 2014.
8. Singh, H., Anand, C., Kumar, V., Sharma, A., Automated Parking System With Bluetooth Access. *Int. J. Eng. Comput. Sci.*, 3, 5, 5773–5775, May 2014.
9. El Mouatezbillah, K., Djenouri, D., Boulkaboul, S., Bagula, A., Car Park Management with Networked Wireless Sensors and Active RFID, CERIST Research Center, Algiers, Algeria University of the Western Cape, Cape town, South Africa, 978-1-4799-9802-0/15© IEEE, 2015.
10. Rashid, M.M., Musa, A., AtaurRahman, M., Farahana, N., Farhana, A., Automatic Parking Management System and Parking Fee Collection Based on Number Plate Recognition. *Int. J. Mach. Learn. Comput.*, 2, 2, 93–98, April 2012, Published 2014.
11. Geng, Y. and Cassandras, C., New "Smart Parking" System Based on Resource Allocation and Reservations. *IEEE Transactions On Intelligent Transportation Systems*, 14, 3, 2013.

12. Wang, S., Deng, Z., Yin, G., An Accurate GPS-IMU/DR Data Fusion Method for Driverless Car Based on a Set of Predictive Models and Grid Constraints, Engineering, Medicine, Computer Science Sensors (Basel, Switzerland), 2013.

13. Wu, Q. and Zhang, Y., Parking lots space detection corpus, 2006.

14. Faradji, F., Rezaie, A.H., Ziaratban, M., A morphological-based license plate location. *IEEE International Conference of Image Processing*, vol. 1, pp. 57–61, IEEE, San Antonio, Texas, USA, Sep.–Oct. 2007.

15. Tiwari, B., Sharma, A., Rathi, B., Singh, M., Automatic Vehicle Number Plate Recognition System using Matlab. *IOSR-JECE*, 11, 4, Ver. II 10–16, Jul.-Aug. 2016.

16. Jordan, C. and Marek, M., *Parking Space Classification using Convoluional Neural Networks*, Stanford University: Stanford, CA USA, 2016.

17. Djenouri, D., El Mouatezbillah, K., Boulkaboul, S., Bagula, A., Networked Wireless Sensors, Active RFID, and Handheld Devices for Modern Car Park Management. *IJHCR*, 6, 3, 33–45, July-September 2015.

18. Sharma, A., Kulkarni, S.V., Dhanajay, Cost Optimized Hybrid System in Digital Advertising using Machine Learning. *IJITEE*, 8, 8S2, June 2019.

19. Perlich, C., Dalessandro, B., Stitelman, O., Machine Learning for Targeted Display Advertising: Transfer Learning in Action. *Machine Learning*, 95, 1, 103–127, 2014.

20. Yu, T.J., Lee, C.P., Lim, K.M., Fa, S., AI-Based Targeted Advertising System. *Indones. J. Electr. Eng. Comput. Sci.*, 13, 787–793, 2019.

21. Shao, M. and Sui, X. Study on Differential GPS Positioning Methods, *International Conference on Computer Science and Mechanical Automation (CSMA)*, 2015.

6

Cognitive Cyber-Physical System Applications

John A.[1][*], Senthilkumar Mohan[2] and D. Maria Manuel Vianny[3]

[1]School of Computer Science, Galgotias University, Greater Noida, India
[2]School of Information Technology and Engineering,
Vellore Institute of Technology, Vellore, India
[3]Department of Computer Science and Engineering, Chitkara University,
Punjab, India

Abstract

The cognitive Engineering is commonly used in the analysis, design, decision making and socio-technical system. The applications of cognitive physical system are human-robot interactions, transport management, industrial automation, healthcare, agriculture etc. The main core components of cognitive system are control system, networking, IoT, data analysis, security, and information management system etc. The main properties of cognitive cyber physical system are pervasive computing, huge networking, reorganizing, degree of automation, interactions of with and without supervision. The implementation of cognitive cyber physical system having three levels such as computational model, algorithm or architecture and implementations. All the applications of cognitive physical system having these three levels for observation and communications.

In this chapter gives the brief information about various applications of cognitive cyber physical system applications and working of each application. The human and robot interaction applications applied into different fields such as industry, various automations and healthcare etc. These applications are involved in supervised mode and semi-supervised mode. In this chapter gives the supervised and unsupervised applications. The chapter consists of representation about the components, properties of cognitive cyber physical system, general working model of human robot, various applications related to cognitive cyber physical system, future direct direction and conclusion.

---

[*]Corresponding author: johnmtech@gmail.com

Kolla Bhanu Prakash, G. R. Kanagachidambaresan, V. Srikanth, E. Vamsidhar (eds.) Cognitive Engineering for Next Generation Computing: A Practical Analytical Approach, (167–188) © 2021 Scrivener Publishing LLC

Keywords: Cognitive cyber-physical system, various applications, issues

6.1   Introduction

Cyber-physical system (CPS) is the combination of analog, digital, physical and human integrated using logical and physical systems. The term cyber-physical system was introduced by Lee [1]. The system provides infrastructure to provide smart services in real life environments. The CPS assembles the various phases of components in different application fields. Therefore, CPS assembly should get priority to enhance the performance of system. The traditional assembling and automatic assembling are expensive and inflexible. In this situation there is a need for more attention to flexible physical system assembly. Human–robot collaboration (HRC) is an important method to be flexible for physical assembly. In assembling, different HRCs are used in the different aspects. The HRC is a method that is not important in various assembling systems and is not a priority. The HRC with cyber-physical system has various benefits in different areas such as industrial manufacturing, healthcare, transport, etc. For example, the cyber-physical system is used to help in the design, modeling, maintenance and development of human–robot collaboration system. In the computation for HRC, an appropriate model is very important and the model is easily determined by CPS. Using the CPS, the control system of physical devices and communication system are easily made. Another form of CPS is mobile CPS, which is the system under mobility. It is the important subcategory of CPS. An example of mobile cyber-physical systems is a robotic, transport system controlled by animals or other devices [2]. The smart hand-held system is also an example of CPS. The number of reasons that supports mobile cyber-physical system is also considered as CPS. Some of the reasons are as follows:

i.   The computational and processing resources are having local storage.
ii. Multiple input and output, touch screens, CPS, light sensors are used for controlling.
iii. Different communication mechanisms also used such as WiFi, Bluetooth and connecting devices, etc.

iv. Java, C# and Java script are some of the high-level programming languages used.

v. End user having recharge of battery and maintenance.

The implementation of mobile CPS utilizes mobile network connectivity to cloud environments or server. Examples for Mobile CPS are analyses and track CO_2, traffic predictions measure traffic, and monitors cardiac patients. This chapter presents properties, components, collaboration with Human–Robot Collaborative Manufacturing, along with various applications such as transport, industry automation, healthcare and finally research direction of Cognitive cyber-Physical System and conclusion.

6.2 Properties of Cognitive Cyber-Physical System

Some of the main properties of CPS systems are as follows:

- Each component in the CPMS is an independent organization with cognitive skills such as perception, decision-making, communication and collaboration. Each CPS has the capacity to make decisions independently;
- Improved component and system performance in the FMS's current intelligence and independence;
- CPMS has the capability to adapt to production changes in short and fast times
- The portability, local and central storages are the important essential services.
- Touch screen, GPS, Speakers, sensors, microphone, camera are the various input and output devices used.
- WiFi, Edge computing, 4G are the some of the devices used to communicate one device to another device.
- Various Advanced high-level programming languages are used to enable the faster development of the system such as C++, Java, C#, etc.
- Easily distributes the accessible app, such as Apple App and Google Play Store.
- Connects the multiple discrete devices into one system.
- Regular battery charging, data storage of user.

6.3   Components of Cognitive Cyber-Physical System

Different components are used in CPS. The components differ based on the different applications [3]. For example, generally the cyber-physical system has the following components such as smart grid, autonomous system, monitoring system, control system, automatic pilot system, etc. The above-mentioned components vary based on each and every application. Physical system combines the concepts of mechatronics, cybernetics, process and design. The Process control of physical system is often called built-in or embedded systems. In embedded systems, the emphasis is often on things that are designed to be minimized, and limited to the greater interaction between physical and computer components. The CPS design and communication is also similar to the Internet of Things (IoT), which shares the same IoT basic principle. However, CPS produces high-level combinations and interactions between physical and computational components. For example, are various components connected in the smart factory as shown in Figure 6.1. The various components such as handheld device, WiFi, connecting devices, RFID reader and Tag, Web and cloud storage are interconnected together.

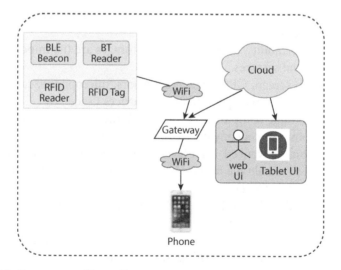

Figure 6.1 Components of Smart Factory.

6.4   Relationship Between Cyber-Physical System for Human–Robot

Human–robot interaction (HRC) combines human activity with the help of robots [4]. The machine does not use a person, but instead combines its skills and helps it in performing difficult tasks or job. This is a main task in the manufacturing and production industry. In factories, there is no distinction between the automated and written workspaces. The humans and robots work well together, without being isolated without a safety fence.

The sophisticated industrial robot combines different precise components such as: active action object, a CPU to control, store, execute the system, and the various power sources. With the new technological advancements and industry to evolve, robotic control systems are now entering the paradigm such as Cyber-Physical Systems. The CPS compared to traditional systems such as Programmable Logic Controllers improves the use of interactive systems with one another to gain readiness, robustness, and synergy in robotic systems. HRC are applied in many fields, such as surgeons, manufacturing, elder care, rehabilitation, etc. The HRC is

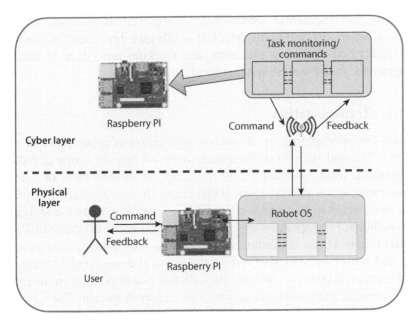

Figure 6.2 Relationship between cyber and physical layer integration.

often applied in the execution of household and sorting tasks or used to use information provided by physical touch between a robot and or robot and a human device. Techniques for differentiating HRC include interim and intergovernmental relations with robots, agency autonomy and leader–leader relationships. Figure 6.2 shows the relationship between cyber and physical layer integration. In Figure 6.2 cyber layer components are used to take the decision and controlling purpose. The physical layer is used to interact with the real environments. The cyber layer consists of control system, task monitoring, human side control algorithm and task commands algorithms. The physical layer consists of human integration part, human robot collaboration part and robot operating system or real time controlling operating system, etc. The combining physical and cyber layer, different collaboration protocols are used. In Figure 6.2 Message Queuing Telemetry Transport (MQTT) protocol is used to collaborate both physical and cyber layers.

6.5 Applications of Cognitive Cyber-Physical System

The Cognitive Cyber-Physical System is applied into different areas such as Smart manufacturing, Agriculture, Education, Energy management, Security, Environmental monitoring, Transportation systems, Process control, Smart city and home, Medical health care device, etc. In this section described various applications and working procedure of various Cognitive Cyber-Physical Systems are shown below.

6.5.1 Transportation

Smart Transportation is an important application of cyber-physical systems (CPS) and the aim of the system is addressing the scope of reduce congestion, traffic accidents, fuel consumption, reduce time of vehicle movement, and traffic safety on traffic jams. Therefore, smart transport's role is expected to be a major contributor in the development and design of intelligence transport systems using CPS. The entire process of CPS in smart transport has communication, wireless sensor, embedded processor and sensor network that reduce the physical component activities in real traditional transport system. The CPS and its components in the cyber world reduce the traditional activities of transport system. The CPS has many physical components in transport system such as vehicles, human drivers, machinery and sensors, road side unit, transmitter and receiver and infrastructure. Some of the main features of CPS for intelligence Transport system are as follows:

- Transport CPS topology is constantly changing due to fast movement of vehicles.
- The CPS topology transportation the humans and drivers can exit or join at any place and time because of tracking and sensing of locations and services.
- The density of vehicles movements predictions depends are various situations such as rural and urban areas.
- The most previous wireless technologies are not accessed the faster movement of vehicles but using the CPS can predict and trace the faster movement of vehicles.
- Smart transport can manage the unlimited power virtually, storage, computing capabilities, manage the automotive network and wireless network movement etc.
- The CPS security applications timely forward the message in emergency situations from one node of communication to another node.
- Generally, the multimedia messages have high bandwidth compared to the normal message, but the CPS applications transfer the data easily in dynamic bandwidth.

The standard transport system that use road sides equipment model also use the CPS components as shown in Figure 6.3. The model includes three variants elements such as cars, roadside services equipment, and central locations Server. Each car has its own unique ID, Identification Number, GPS and transmitter, road side equipments (RSEs) and receiver. The RSE is also a unique identification number and the both vehicle and RSEs communicate using single on chips and wireless communication module. The moving vehicles internally communicate with RSE and make a connection with short interval of time. RSEs are connected to cloud or central server via wires or wireless transmission mode. The road side unit also collects information periodically and moves it to a central server.

6.5.2   Industrial Automation

The industrial revolution is becoming insufficient to accommodate the existing methodology and business required for more adequate technology and new business methods. The flexible, complex industries operate

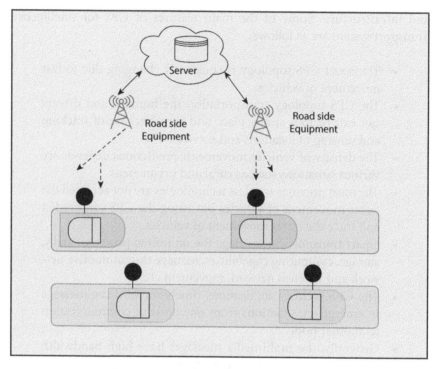

Figure 6.3 Transport system using CPS components.

their business. The business people are facing different pressure related to quantity, quality, cost, customization of products and they need an effective production system. Due to these reasons they evaluate new flexible, cost effective and effective systems in real time productions and planning. The introduced new "automated collaboration" model is a main industry-backed platform and purpose is to design, operate, and develop tools and methods for detecting flexibility, flexibility, deception, network interactions enabled by the interface between new embedded devices and built-in systems. This movement coincided with the emergence of computational technology, that is, information and data processing in mechatronics, gradually changing the traditional local store into an industrial ecosystem, where the connected network systems are integrated with multiple devices and systems are rooted, as well as business partners and customers, in business processes and value interact with the physical and the logical environment. So, these physical, logical, interconnected and sensed areas are fully connected with the help of CPS.

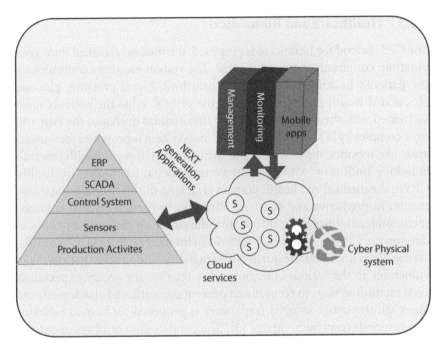

Figure 6.4 CPS Industrial interface.

For example, IMCAESOP [5] project is considered as the future generation industrial CPS methods to build modern technologies, where building
is integrated into the service-oriented applications and cloud to increase
the operational capabilities. The future generation CPS system integrates
all the virtual components, such as hardware, connecting devices and software components. In this project both virtual components and software
components are integrated together. But the service related the service in
physical devices on CPS, service in network on CPS, other services such
as outside of the cloud and storage in CPS are all separated layer wise.
These three combinations of application program interface enable CPS to
change its abilities and both provide third parties and use services that
represent their virtual environment. Such flexibility serves as the enabler
of the most flexible and complex CPS in various industrial applications.
The various parts of CPS in industries are shown in Figure 6.4. In Figure
6.4 three layers are interfaced together as physical parts such as sensors
and control system, the storages part in cloud and interaction part such as
mobile applications, monitoring and management. With the help of these
three CPS interface easily manages the business.

6.5.3 Healthcare and Biomedical

The CPS method for healthcare is proposed, the method classified into computation, communication and control. The system monitors continuously the patient's health attributes like a heartbeat, blood pressure, glucose, etc., and if health parameter reaches the critical value the patients must be treated with the remedial measure. This method decreases the cost and time complexity [1]. CPS with a closed-loop system is proposed for various areas like robotics, flight system and many more. However, health research is lacking until now, with dynamic computational techniques for health. CPS in the medical and health domain is lacking the high-resolution information in predictive and outcome attributes in the real natural environment. mHealth (mobile health) is introduced for an emerging opening to develop the CPS for mobile [2]. CPS–IoT (Internet of Things) with healthcare services improves the quality of human life. The attacker tries to make vulnerable in the various emerging cyber-attacks. The security specialists keep on finding ways to recover and prevent sophisticated attack methods. The cognitive cyber-security framework is proposed for human behavior and responds to privacy threats [3]. The combination of physical entities and computational elements interact with humans during many modalities. The various security attacks like forest, along with featured selection introduced the feature augmentation technique. The privacy-preserving of the raw information, the FA-RF approach, significantly minimizes the communication delay forced on the network as computation and communication of the cloud is removed [6].

The telemonitoring issue with high-risk pregnancy women's in the home is proposed, with few design problems during the monitoring being listed out. The MCPS technique is considered for various issues like support for caretakers' easy maintenance, smart altering, automation of medical workflow, plug &play model, medical devices interoperability, etc. The telecare method consists of two networks namely BAN (BODY Area Network) and PAN (Personal Area Network). The telemedical system becomes dependable during the deployment, which provides huge community value to high-risk pregnant women, particularly those living the dispersed rural areas [8]. Stroke is affecting the brain and results in death within a few hours. Stroke is one of the dangerous and fatal diseases, which can be avoided by finding the stoke nature and react promptly by using the intelligent health system. CPS is used to find out the presence of stroke in the patients, the person having the stroke with high risk or low risk with survival rate. The data from CPS communicates to the doctor and alerts the

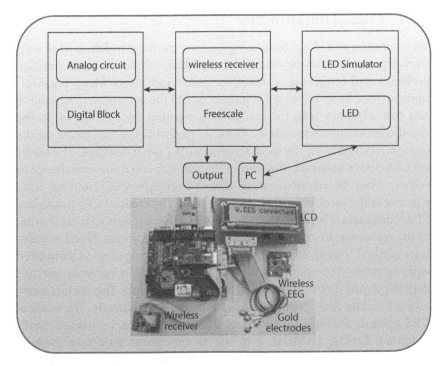

Figure 6.5 ECG Connection Interface using CPS.

current patient situation. The system works and entirely depends on data acquired from the sensor of electroencephalography from the patient's brain [9]. The general ECG connection using CPS is shown in Figure 6.5. This interface has analog circuit, digital block, wireless receiver and LED simulator as shown in Figure 6.5.

The major challenge in the biomedical CPS is combining the physical system with neuroscience and assisting with human disabilities. EEG (Electroencephalography) is the non-invasive technique to provide the assistive method by brain electrical signals. The unique prototype of hybrid BCI (brain–computer interface) is proposed, the combination of mental task classification and SSVEP (steady-state visual evoked potential) used to detect with EEG channels. The microcontroller with the sensor of wireless EEG combined enhances the convenience, portability, effectiveness of the cost. The results compared with normal humans with tetraplegia patients, the neural network classification with BCI accuracy of 74% and data transfer rate 27 bits per minute [7].

6.5.4   Clinical Infrastructure

Virtualization and cloud computing become the most widely used in software deployment, storing various types of data, computations on complex problems and streaming of real-time audio and video. Many organizations migrate to server-based solutions due to the advantage of scalability and cost-efficiency with the applications running from the server in the cloud computing environment. The CPS performs the task based on the request received from the local actuator with a given deadline. The medical CPS device keeps on monitoring the patient's condition and chance to recover from the erroneous state, effective utilization of resources, cost-effective is the most ultimate plan to perform the medical CPS healthcare IT environment. Cloud service with private service results to fairly sharing of the resources, to execute the medical CPS applications. Novel middleware method with an effective virtual resource sharing method stimulated with autonomic computing [10]. The medical domain becomes effective digitally day by day, improves effectively and efficiently. The doctors easily access the data and give their suggestions most expediently. The medical CPS towards the new technologies like, eye trackers, networked head-mounted displays (HMDs), give rise to new communication medium chances [11]. The MCPS which enables the future generation of eHealth systems is planned to interoperate safely, efficiently and secured way. The safety-critical devices interconnected perform the analysis of the patient's health information, with the treatment procedure to be followed by medical staff and doctors cost-effectively. The integrated clinical environment is a trivial solution towards promoting medical devices in a heterogeneous environment. The novel architecture ICE ++ is proposed along with mobile edge computing which combines NFV and SDN methods to make automatic and more effective [12].

CPS deployed in various industries based on considerable success stories. The implementation of CPS in the limited hospital feature is due to various reasons. Clinical operation and patient safety are the most critical considerations in health outcomes. CPS with Houston Methodist Hospital discusses various challenges and difficulties during success. The agile development of CPS interacts with computational scientists and clinicians [13]. Hospital-acquired infections (HAI) are the various infections effects from healthcare staff, patients, doctors and many more in the environment. HAI is the major problem that results in increasing the mortality rate and the economic condition of the hospital becomes more burdensome. The software perspective of the innovations for business with CPS is implemented

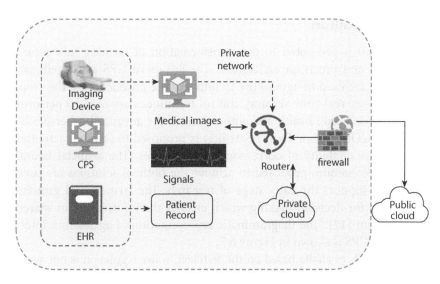

Figure 6.6 Clinical infrastructure using CPS.

in the European Union research funded research project. The major aim is to make automation of the monitoring activities and clinical workflows combined, which results in more than 90% of infections in the hospitals [14]. The structure of clinical infrastructure is shown in Figure 6.6. All the components of clinical infrastructure are interconnected using CPS.

The CyPhyS+ introduced low-cost and standard CPS for old age homes which used remote health monitoring. 6LoWPAN is the end-to-end healthcare system, which is more secure and reliable during the data acquisition process. The method is designed to work on low energy operations and resource restriction environments. The results ensured that CyPhyS+ is more robust and has minimal energy usage and SNMP based monitoring performance. The proposed method incorporated with CBC-MAC,128 bit AES based on security encryption authentication schemes used [15]. In the last couple of years, medical specialists have been working towards the improvement of the treatment technique to increase the speed and reduce the treatment activities of the pain. CPS plays a potential role in monitoring and improves the quality of patients' life. Automation of the process and continuously monitoring of the patient's condition is based on that treatment required to perform automation various medical devices required. The proposed system finds out the root cause of the disease, researches on new disease nd existing disease treatment procedure and available information in the centralized CPS [16].

6.5.5   Agriculture

Industry 4.0 is promoted to the transformation of farming into future generation and precision agriculture. The advanced CPS and intelligent inventions are used in agriculture to improve the production of the crop. Optimization, real-time sensing, control techniques are used to perform testing the soil crop health and automation of the advanced cyber-physical tools. SeDS (Sensor-Drone-Satellite) is proposed to farming activities and the sustainability of corresponding objectives. The artificial neural networks techniques proposed to achieve the optimal solutions are used effectively support the early stage of research. The farmers and growers used SeDS for decision making which enables the information in shared environment [17]. The diagrammatic representation of agriculture interface using CPS is shown in Figure 6.7.

The growth of alfalfa based on the fertilizer, water regulation is not accurate based on the conditions which fail to track the growth. The precision regulation based on ACPS is proposed, for fertilization, water irrigation to the alfalfa, namely (PRMWFA-ACPS). The proposed model includes the biophysical sub-model, where the computation used checks the condition of the plant. The simulations carried out depend on the PRMWFA-ACPS with Ptolemy [18]. The CPS-based framework and workflow of the greenhouse with agriculture proposed, is named MDR (Monitoring detecting responding). MDR-CPS is designed for various activities like monitoring, responding, detecting based on the different types of stress. Collaborative control theory with MDR-CPS to deploy is based on the collaborative

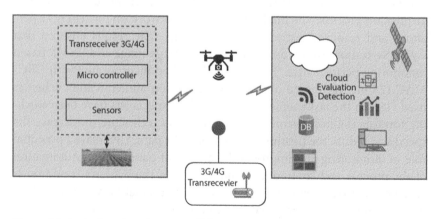

Figure 6.7 Agriculture interface using CPS.

requirement planning to address the errors with CPS [19]. The novel method for climate-smart agriculture for CPS (ACPS) is introduced with farming precision. The main objective is to find out the fault location and tracking the field by applying multivariate data. The classification method combines location with classifiers of the node, novel hybrid classification is proposed. The proposed system detects the irrigation, soil conditions, and nutrients by using the sensor data along with location prediction [22].

ACPS is introduced for the management of various activities and services in agriculture precision. The new method SPVWS (solar photovoltaic water system) is proposed for remote management of irrigation. The ACPS is designed to the extent and adopts the solar irrigation feature typically. The client–server architecture distributed in fashion by the vertex becomes a more active platform that guarantees the communication between the supervisory level in the cloud, the operational level with greenhouse deployment. The cloud environment incorporates various microservices performing the analysis with data mining to support the control tasks remotely [20]. The CCP-CPS (Collaborative Control Protocol for Robotic and Cyber-Physical System) is proposed for smart and agriculture precision which monitors and finds the stresses in the crop present in the greenhouses. Collaborative Control Theory is used in two ways, agent and protocol levels. The simulation results identify the location of crops with the highest number in the greenhouse, effective utilization resources and finally, stress situation quick and capability of the tolerance level. The human integration with the cyber augmented system greenhouse is used for monitoring systems [21].

6.6   Case Study: Road Management System Using CPS

The CPS is the combination of different technologies such Information and Communication Technology (ICT), Internet of Things (IoT), Industrial Internet and Networked Control Systems (NCS). Let us discuss the case study on smart accident management system in the traffic full road and home automation with smart home device management system. Technically speaking, CPS is the best implementation environment and widely used since it has rich application interface and easy management design for any automation applications such as road accident management, home device automaton, border security system, video surveillance system, etc.

6.6.1 Smart Accident Response System for Indian City

In view with road accident in India, there are countless accidents that have been happening nowadays as population are increasing in metro capital cities like Delhi, Mumbai, Chennai, Calcutta and Bangalore. The World Health Organization (WHO) report of 2018 says that almost 1.35 million people have died in road accidents and in India more than 150,000 people have died and it will increased if precaution is not proposed by means of awareness about accident with general public and smart automation remedies by quick arrival of ambulance and other medical remedies at places where the incidents happened. Adopting the smart accident response system is inevitable which is also a quick remedial action now and for the future. The smart city's IoT-based applications has been discussed.

Technical Terminologies for Smart Road Accident Response System

Technically discussing, the CPS components can be adopted in Indian traffic with Radio Frequency Identification (RFID) [12] and Zigbee-oriented Bluetooth technology for smart personal Area Network to serve quickly with error-free communication. The applications of RFID have been discussed with Ref. [13] for various smart automation applications and technical overcomes and challenges. RFID is the most suitable tag that can fit in each vehicle and can be easily categorized according to vehicle type. Later categories of vehicles will be prioritized to sort the vehicle for situation response. For example, suppose an accident happened at particular place and traffic is more on the road. The smart system accident response system insists the on-road traffic to identity and keeps the path for ambulance. This way it highly keeps way to ambulance and also it helps the ambulance to reach the hospital on time.

The Zigbee is the highly preferable technology for short distance communication among VANET Networks which could be adopted to create smart accident response system. The communication sectors include nearby traffic police, ambulance services and emergency medicine service. The Zigbee technology is working with delivering 256 Kbps data transfer and it is widely adopted for VANET. The IoT technology has been adopted in applications like smart ambulance service, sensitive information management system, and smart road traffic management system and so on. The various components of CPS are interconnected as shown in Figure 6.8. In Figure 6.8 internet, infrastructure, mobility, vehicles are fully interconnected together.

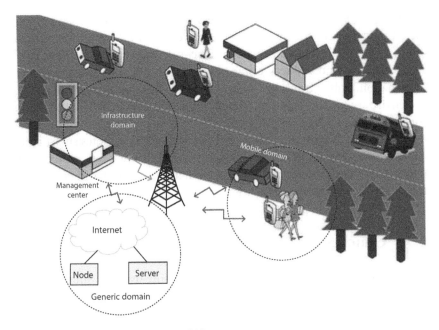

Figure 6.8 Road management using CPS.

Road Side Unit (RSU), Vehicle to Vehicle communication and vehicle to RSU communication. The factor influencing energy efficient communications are on board sensors, power and storage availability, dynamic topology, intermittent connectivity, mobility pattern.

In CPS on board sensors are the major sensitive components which are able to communicate with neighbor vehicle's board sensors. It transmits necessary data information over wireless communication. Since the nodes are dynamic with respect to other nodes, the data transmission might be having distance issue and which leads to more power consumption. On other hand the amount of data is transmitted and receiving is highly unpredictable. In that case dynamic nodes should have consistence power and storage. The major challenge in managing the CPS is the dynamism of nodes. Vehicles are moving with respect to destination based on the other nodes (vehicles) movement. The dynamism of network is there frequently. Managing network topology is a challengeable one. Intermittent connectivity is the movement of nodes and its data transmission are unpredictable, and at times sudden disconnection are possible even frequently. Again, disconnected data transmission must be resumed necessarily then and there. Mobility pattern, the mobility nodes and its speed can be predicted with respect to road type, size of vehicle, road condition and so on. IoT with CPS in Intelligence road network improves traffic flow, road safety security and reduces crime response time to incidents, traveler's information, public transport, improves traffic flow, accurately improving the environment and information sharing from vehicle. IoT with CPS in Intelligence in VANET improves accident prediction, future data prediction, Vehicle collusion prediction, etc. IoT with CPS promotes smart cities energy management, parking management and future data prediction in parking management, service management, information sharing from customer to customer through vehicle.

6.7   Conclusion

The cognitive cyber-physical system is commonly used in different applications. The core components of CPS layers are used in different purposes. Generally, the layers are used in analysis, design, decision making and sociotechnical system. The applications of cognitive physical system are human–robot interactions, transport management, industrial automation, healthcare, agriculture, etc. In all the applications human individual interactions and group behavior are important. The main core components of cognitive system are control system, networking, IoT, data analysis, security, information management system, etc. The main properties of cognitive cyber physical system are pervasive computing, huge networking, reorganizing, degree of automation, interactions of with and without supervision. The implementation of cognitive cyber-physical system has three levels such as computational model, algorithm or architecture and implementations. Each application of CPS has different challenges and design issues. This challenge differs based on the different applications. Each application of physical and cyber components have different design issues. The various design challenges across all the abstraction, layers and architecture. Some of the design and operation challenges are energy management, fault detection, resource management, human interaction, etc. The implementation side of the CPS cost is also one of the main issues in real environments. The future work, plans for cost analysis and develops a system for performing multiple operating modes for different applications.

References

1. Lee, E.A., Cyber-Physical System: Design Challenges. *2008 11th IEEE International Symposium on Object and Component-Oriented Real-Time Distributed Computing (ISORC)*, Orlando, FL, pp. 363–369, 2008.

2. Marwedel, P. and Engel, M., Efficient computing in cyber-physical systems. *2012 International Conference on Embedded Computer Systems (SAMOS)*, Samos, pp. 328–332, 2012.

3. Guan, X., Yang, B., Chen, C., Dai, W., Wang, Y., A comprehensive overview of cyber-physical systems: from perspective of feedback system. *IEEE/CAA J. Autom. Sin.*, 3, 1, 1–14, 2016.

4. Minartz, T., Ludwig, T., Knobloch, M., Mohr, B., Managing hardware power saving modes for high performance computing. *2011 International Green Computing Conference and Workshops*, Orlando, FL, pp. 1–8, 2011.

5. Colombo, A.W. and Bangemann, T., IMC-AESOP outcomes: Paving the way to collaborative manufacturing systems. *12th IEEE International Conference on Industrial Informatics (INDIN)*, 2014.

6. Monisha, K. and Rajasekhara, B.M., A Novel Framework for Healthcare Monitoring System Through Cyber-Physical System, in: *Internet of Things and Personalized Healthcare Systems*, SpringerBriefs in Applied Sciences and Technology, Springer, Singapore, 2019.

7. Nilsen, W. *et al.*, Modeling Opportunities in mHealth Cyber-Physical Systems, in: *Mobile Health*, J. Rehg, S. Murphy, S. Kumar (Eds.), Springer, Cham, 2017.

8. Abie, H., Cognitive Cybersecurity for CPS-IoT Enabled Healthcare Ecosystems. *2019 13th International Symposium on Medical Information and Communication Technology (ISMICT)*, Oslo, Norway, pp. 1–6, 2019.

9. Reddy, Y.B., Cloud-Based Cyber Physical Systems: Design Challenges and Security Needs. *2014 10th International Conference on Mobile Ad-hoc and Sensor Networks*, Maui, HI, pp. 315–322, 2014.

10. Gu, L., Zeng, D., Guo, S., Barnawi, A., Xiang, Y., Cost Efficient Resource Management in Fog Computing Supported Medical Cyber-Physical System. *IEEE Trans. Emerging Top. Comput.*, 5, 1, 108–119, Jan.–March 2017.

11. Mowla, N.I., Doh, I., Chae, K., On-Device AI-Based Cognitive Detection of Bio-Modality Spoofing in Medical Cyber Physical System. *IEEE Access*, 7, 2126–2137, 2019.

12. Chai, R., Naik, G.R., Ling, S.H. *et al.*, Hybrid brain–computer interface for biomedical cyber-physical system application using wireless embedded EEG systems. *BioMed Eng. OnLine*, 16, 5, 2017.

13. Jezewski, J., Pawlak, A., Horoba, K., Wrobel, J., Czabanski, R., Jezewski, M., Selected design issues of the medical cyber-physical system for

telemonitoring pregnancy at home. *Microprocessors Microsyst.*, 46, Part A, 35–43, 2016.

14. Laghari, A., Memon, Z.A., Ullah, S., Hussain, I., Cyber Physical System for Stroke Detection. *IEEE Access*, 6, 37444–37453, 2018.

15. Ahn, Y.W. and Cheng, A.M.K., Automatic Resource Scaling for Medical Cyber-Physical Systems Running in Private Cloud Computing Architecture. *5th Workshop on Medical Cyber-Physical Systems*, vol. 36, Schloss Dagstuhl–Leibniz-Zentrum fuer Informatik, pp. 58–65, 2014.

16. Sonntag, D., Zillner, S., Schulz, C., Weber, M., Toyama, T., Towards Medical Cyber-Physical Systems: Multimodal Augmented Reality for Doctors and Knowledge Discovery about Patients, in: *Design, User Experience, and Usability. User Experience in Novel Technological Environments. DUXU 2013. Lecture Notes in Computer Science*, vol. 8014, A. Marcus (Ed.), Springer, Berlin, Heidelberg, 2013.

17. Celdrán, A.H., García Clemente, F.J., Weimer, J., Lee, I., ICE++: Improving Security, QoS, and High Availability of Medical Cyber-Physical Systems through Mobile Edge Computing. *2018 IEEE 20th International Conference on e-Health Networking, Applications and Services (Healthcom)*, Ostrava, pp. 1–8, 2018.

18. Joerger, G., Rambourg, J., Gaspard-Boulinc, H., Conversy, S., Bass, B.L., Dunkin, B.J., Garbey, M., A Cyber-Physical System to Improve the Management of a Large Suite of Operating Rooms. *ACM Trans. Cyber-Phys. Syst.*, 2, 4, Article 34 (September 2018), 24 pages, 2018.

19. Bocicor, M.I., Molnar, A.-J., Taslitchi, C., Preventing Hospital Acquired Infections through a Workflow-Based Cyber-Physical System. *Proceedings of the 11th International Conference on Evaluation of Novel Software Approaches to Software Engineering*, n. pag. Crossref. Web, 2016.

20. Dagale, H. *et al.*, CyPhyS+: A Reliable and Managed Cyber-Physical System for Old-Age Home Healthcare over a 6LoWPAN Using Wearable Motes. *2015 IEEE International Conference on Services Computing*, New York, NY, pp. 309–316, 2015.

21. Sultanovs, E., Skorobogatjko, A., Romanovs, A., Centralized healthcare cyber-physical system's architecture development. *2016 57th International Scientific Conference on Power and Electrical Engineering of Riga Technical University (RTUCON)*, Riga, pp. 1–6, 2016.

22. Mirkouei, A., A Cyber-Physical Analyzer System for Precision Agriculture. *J. Environ. Sci. Curr. Res.*, 3, 016, 2020.

23. Liu, R., Zhang, Y., Ge, Y., Hu, W., Sha, B., Precision Regulation Model of Water and Fertilizer for Alfalfa Based on Agriculture Cyber-Physical System. *IEEE Access*, 8, 38501–38516, 2020.

24. Guo, P., Dusadeerungsikul, P.O., Nof, S.Y., Agricultural cyber physical system collaboration for greenhouse stress management. *Comput. Electron. Agr.*, 150, 439–454, 2018.

25. Selmani, A., Oubehar, H., Outanoute, M., Ed-Dahhak, A., Guerbaoui, M., Lachhab, A., Bouchikhi, B., Agricultural cyber-physical system enabled for remote management of solar-powered precision irrigation. *Biosyst. Eng.*, 177, 18–30, 2019.
26. Dusadeerungsikul, P.O., Nof, S.Y., Bechar, A., Tao, Y., Collaborative Control Protocol for Agricultural Cyber-physical System. *Procedia Manuf.*, 39, 235–242, 2019.
27. Pandey, A., Tiwary, P., Kumar, S., Das, S.K., A hybrid classifier approach to multivariate sensor data for climate smart agriculture cyber-physical systems, in: *Proceedings of the 20th International Conference on Distributed Computing and Networking (ICDCN '19)*, Association for Computing Machinery, New York, NY, USA, pp. 337–341, 2019.

7

Cognitive Computing

T Gunasekhar* and Marella Surya Teja

Department of CSE, K L E F, Guntur, Andhra Pradesh, India

Abstract

The advancement of network-empowered sensors and Artificial Intelligence (AI) gives rise to different human-focused smart techniques that offer excellent quality services, for example, productive collaboration, self-governing driving, and brilliant medical services. Considering cognitive computing as a crucial innovation to build up these smart frameworks, this paper proposes human-focused cognitive computing supported by cloud computing. To begin with, we give a complete evolution description and analysis of the cognitive computing system including its advancement from data discovery, big data, and cognitive cloud. At that point, the architecture of cognitive computing is proposed, which comprises three basic innovations including IoT (networking), big data analytics (which enables technologies like reinforcement learning, deep learning, and image understanding), and cloud computing. At last, it portrays the applications of human-focused cognitive computing, involving chatbot creation, expressive communication structure like sentiment analysis & face/emotion detection, medical cognitive techniques, and risk assessment.

Keywords: Cognitive computing, artificial intelligence, internet of things, cloud computing, reinforcement learning, deep learning, sentiment analysis, natural language processing

7.1 Introduction

Recently, cognitive computing has obtained significant attention in industry and research areas with a sudden development in information

*Corresponding author: tgunasekhar@kluniversity.in

Kolla Bhanu Prakash, G. R. Kanagachidambaresan, V. Srikanth, E. Vamsidhar (eds.) Cognitive Engineering for Next Generation Computing: A Practical Analytical Approach, (189–218) © 2021 Scrivener Publishing LLC

technologies, artificial intelligence, and big data. Cognition is a mental process of creating knowledge and understanding by achieving a conceptual model of the world. Theoretically, cognitive computing has several definitions according to several researchers [1].

It tries to create machines that will have reasoning abilities identical to a human brain. It is the innovation of self-learning techniques that exploit data mining, natural language processing, and pattern recognition to reflect the way the brain of human functions. It can be done using strategies from biology, psychology, information theory, physics, mathematics, statistics, and processing of signals. It is a centralized, universal mechanism motivated by cognitive informatics, analytical intelligence, and psyche abilities. It includes information processing of the biological nervous system (processing of a human brain), decision making, reasoning, and natural language processing in real-time to tackle real-world problems. It can also be defined as a way of summarizing detailed behavior, goals, plans, limitations, and techniques to a high degree.

In industry, such a cognitive system could learn from records without supervision and perform natural language processing. But modern cognitive computing is still far behind to realize like human intelligence such as emotional sentiments and intellect. Without continuous requirement and upkeep of big data, it is difficult to discover knowledge for the growth of machine learning. Most of the prevailing AI-based industrial applications are based on neural networks and deep learning but not extended enough to realism yet. It is considered important for AI to be able to wipe out the constraints of data. A human-intelligence like cognitive computing should consist of both, hardware facilities and a storage space comprised of information. It can interact with machine and human intelligence at a deep level of the algorithm using that space and wipe out the dependency of machine learning on data and explore the human needs enabling deep human cognition. Thus users are provided with a more intelligent cognitive system [2].

In order to attain a better understanding of cognitive computing, it is required to define its relevant areas and understand all the terms. According to different definitions of cognitive computing, it is an overall combination of cognitive sciences, cognitive informatics, cognitive psychology, knowledge, reasoning, nervous system, the human brain, biological processing, decision making, neurobiology, Artificial Intelligence (AI), behavioural science and manipulation of a large amount of information such as big data. AI is correlated with reasoning and its fundamental processes of thinking, beliefs, and emotions in order to create an intelligent system that can behave and understand in a rational way just like humans. The reasoning is a succession of steps helps in obtaining conclusions or knowledge. And knowledge is the interpretation of a problem or a topic attained through study or experience. Expanding such knowledge from a large amount of data to support decision making is the big data where decision making is defined as the process of analyzing and selecting the best alternative from a given set of possible choices based on some standard or conditions to achieve an objective. The nervous system is composed of neurons, reacts to physical impulses, and exchanges electrochemical signals between neurons to organize body reactions. These are all naturally related to cognitive computing where mind and brain are two different things. The mind is comprised of a set of actions enabling humans to think, understand, and feel whereas the brain is an organ that provides humans with an ability to think, understand, and feel. Therefore, cognitive computing should emphasize on simulating the brain mechanism to improve computers with all the brain's ability.

Cognitive computing describes era systems that combine gadget learning, reasoning, natural language processing, speech, vision, human–pc interaction that mimics the functioning of the human brain and facilitates to improve human selection making. Cognitive computing applications link data evaluation and adaptive page presentations to modify content material for a particular form of audience.

The motivation behind cognitive computing is to reproduce human thought strategies in a computerized model. Using self-learning algorithms that use information mining, sample recognition, and natural language processing, the computer can mimic the way the human mind works.

7.2   Evolution of Cognitive System

Cognitive computing speaks to the third innovation of registering. In the primary period, (19th century) Charles Babbage, also known as 'father of the computer' delivered the concept of a programmable computer. Used in the navigational calculation, his pc was designed to tabulate polynomial features. The second technology (1950) experienced digital programming computer systems including ENIAC and ushered a generation of modern-day computing and programmable systems [3]. The evolution of cognitive computing started 65 years ago, [4] with a test performed by Alan Turing known as validation of computing machine intelligent behavior and detailed analysis of the chess play as a search which was done by Shannon. The Lisp inventor, John McCarthy coined the concept of Artificial Intelligence during the second conference of Dartmouth. The development of the first smart programs like the checker's play takes place during the 50s. McCarthy and M. Misky found the MIT lab. Masterman and colleagues designed semantic nets for machine translation at the University of Cambridge. In the early

60s, the Solomonoff put AI's mathematical theory by introducing the universal Bayesian techniques for prediction and inferences. Danny Bobrow, a student at MIT demonstrated that computers could be programmed to recognize natural language well enough to solve hard algebraic problems accurately. Before the first database system ever begun, due to the complexity and inadequacy of developed technologies, machine translation was getting negative reports at that time. In the late 60s, J. Moses illustrated the strength of symbolic reasoning and the first good chess-playing program.

Then in the 70s, Perceptrons were developed by Minsky and Papert, realizing the limitations of fundamental neural network systems. Though, at about the same period, Robinson and Walker furthermore defined a powerful NLP group. The first machine learning algorithms were introduced during the 80s. It brought probability and decision theory into Artificial Intelligence by this moment and neural networks came to be broadly adopted with backpropagation algorithms. A neural network is a gadget of hardware and software mimicked after the vital nervous gadget of humans, to estimate capabilities that rely upon the big amount of unknown inputs [5].

Then in the early 90s, a successful reinforcement learning-enabled creation of robust gammon software. The era of the 90s observed suitable advancements in all regions of AI with the combination of semantic classification and probabilistic parsing.

In 2000, QA systems got importance. Watson is an elegant work performed by IBM for further development and enhancement of Piquant

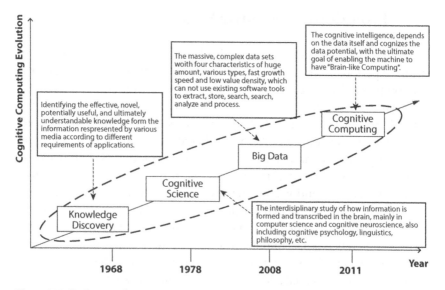

Figure 7.1 Evolution of cognitive computing [6].

(Practical Intelligent Question Answering Technology). The above Figure 7.1 clearly depicts the evolving of cognitive in years. From effectively solving checkers to the advancement in robotics, everything is granting computers the ability to identify images and videos with great accuracy. And now coming to cognitive computing that works on deep gaining knowledge of algorithms and large data analytics to provide the insights. In this way, the brain of a cognitive system is the neural network, the basic thought behind profound becoming acquainted with.

7.3   Cognitive Computing Architecture

Architecture is a hypothesis motivated by the human intellect in which systems operate together with the necessary resources to obtain intelligent behavior in any complicated environment. Cognitive architecture [7] directs on developing both, artificial intelligence and the inherent intelligence. It should be able to incorporate intelligence and capabilities from interactions and represent entities from the short-term as well as the long-term memories about the assumptions, motives, ideas and knowledge of the system. It should be able to define clearly the functional methods based on the operations available in the system, which contain mechanisms of learning and performance. The assumptions related to cognitive architecture could alter in time, just like the human mind. It supports recognizing the infrastructure essential for an intelligent system. Some cognitive architecture is based on mind–computer similarity principles, while others are based on general principles. An ideal cognitive architecture should be able to improve the decision-making potential by learning. It should be competent in developing plans and solving problems for intelligent systems to achieve their expected purposes. Traditional AI is formulated to learn by functioning on the basis of rules while cognitive architecture uses bio-stimulated methods, more specifically for interaction-based learning.

Researchers in IBM are developing a new computer architecture that can process data productively for AI workloads [7, 8]. The researchers insist that traditional computers were invented on Von Neumann architecture, having a central processor that executes arithmetic and logic, storage, a memory unit and input–output devices. However, the recent industry requirement has made the heterogeneous computing architecture essential rather than depending on the homogeneous architecture leading to an intensified research in neuroscience along with applied materials. It requires a new heterogeneous architecture that requires a change in already existing computing architecture for the AI workload. There are two important requirements for AI workloads which have originated a curiosity in brain-stimulated computer architecture:

Memory: The main challenge for such computing is that multi-core processors have attained their performance and efficiency threshold. The AI workloads depend on the processing of a large amount of data and expect faster memory access. The traditional processors are having multi-level cache architecture and are not suited for AI.

Parallel Processing: The architectures for AI workloads have to be designed in such a way that can execute and compute parallelly. The parallel computing technologies are required for such architecture which can successfully operate AI functionalities for such large amount of data.

It has led to increasing in the development of cognitive architecture modeling that simulates the brain, cognitive architecture design in which the system learns in a specific environment and applying them to the products. Such cognitive architecture works on three features. First are the brain's memory and processing that simulates a memory device to execute computational tasks in it. The second is the structure of the brain's synaptic network that can be developed as arrays devices to fasten the training process for deep neural networks. And the last one is the stochastic nature of neurons as well as synapses to generate an influential computational substrate for altering neural networks. These systems are expected to be more efficient than conventional computers. Researchers found that the brain-simulated memory strategy in unsupervised learning is 200× faster in performance than conventional computing systems.

Figure 7.2 shows the system designing of cognitive computing. With the help of fundamental advancements, for example, 5G system, mechanical autonomy, and profound learning alongside IoT/cloud frameworks, undertakings including human-machine collaboration, voice acknowledgment, and PC vision will be executed for a huge scope. The upper applications upheld can be wellbeing oversight, subjective social insurance, savvy city, keen transportation, and logical examinations. Thereinto, each layer in the framework engineering is joined by comparing mechanical difficulties and framework prerequisites. Subsequently, the significance between cognitive computing and each layer is considered and examined in detail in this paper [9].

7.3.1   Cognitive Computing and Internet of Things

The Internet of Things (IoT) and Cognitive Computing are ideas that have been creating since the 1950s with differing terminology. Empowered by propels in innovation, for example, the advancement of lower cost, lower

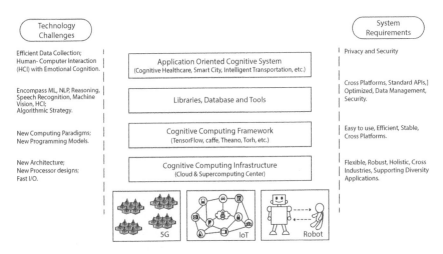

Figure 7.2 The system architecture of cognitive computing.

power, smaller microchips and microcontrollers, cell/remote chips, and the enablement of progressively across the board machine-to-machine correspondences, IoT advances are presently more broadly sent. It is the next stage in improving the precision and potential of complex-sensor-operated systems by learning and implanting more human awareness into the highly communicated devices and settings. Cognitive IoT utilizes the data generated by connected devices and actions performed by them in a combination with cognitive computing technologies and a new standard of computing called cognitive computing. Cognition implies thinking that will lead IoT to the most advanced level, making it more intelligent and more interactive. Thus, the Cognitive IoT is contemplated as a combination of the modern IoT with cognitive and unified mechanisms that are focussing at increasing the all-around performance and obtains intelligence.

The IoT is an important aspect of AI-enabled cognitive computing which enhances the two opposing and critical outputs of data-centered processes such as machine-automated activity and human decision making. Nonetheless, the inclusion of IoT and its data sources in cognitive computing allows automation to improve the process of decision making and gives the best of their potentials. For the automation of the data modelling requirements, machine learning and neural networks are the best sources that can produce targeted algorithms and refine data control and management characteristics of integration and transformation speeding up the initial data consumption in the predictive analytics. The omnipresence of the IoT is predictable due to its potential of producing real-time activity from data. IoT's applications when supported with cognitive computing automation establish an ultimate predictive analytics precision for best decision making.

It is obvious from the above-portrayal that cognitive computing depends on data. The area of contact emphasizes information processing while the world of computers emphasizes knowledge consumption. In real cognitive computing applications, the information is conveyed mainly by data containing various structured and unstructured data [10]. Cognition embodies three key elements—interpreting, reasoning and learning. In terms of computing, interpretation represents the capability of taking structured and unstructured data in a huge amount in order to obtain meaning from it like setting up a prototype of ideas, entities (elements) and relationships among them. The reasoning is to employ that specific prototype to be able to attain conclusions and decipher similar problems without having the already programmed specific solutions. And learning is the ability to automatically comprehend new knowledge from the information and stands as a crucial component in understanding.

The IoT collects diverse real-time valuable information of objects' concerns in the objective world, forms a huge internet network that interconnects large sensing systems in order to make co-fusion between the data world and the physical world. Currently, some advanced distributed information fusion technologies can also be employed to improve the accuracy of the sensed large-scale network information [11]. Firstly, the IoT obtains knowledge about tracked artifacts through perception technologies such as RFID and a wireless sensor, satellite positioning and WiFi, and fingerprint tracking. Secondly, it disseminates relevant information within the network using various efficient means of communication and shares and integrates. Finally, it performs knowledge collection and retrieval utilizing advanced software technology such as cloud storage, deep learning, and data mining to realize intelligent decision-making and control in the information fusion framework [12].

Cognitive computing is essential to the IoT for some of the important reasons. Some of them are rating and scaling of data initiation. Learning makes the system or processes more structured depending on merging sensor data about the system with their actions that can affect the human ability to recognize necessary patterns and understandings. The scaling is done using machine learning in order to improve it. Another reason includes moving computation into the physical world as people from various demographics and different level skills communicate with IoT, there is a need to move beyond existing machine interface that requires human to learn interface concepts for communicating with machines. A human-centred interface is needed where the system can communicate with humans in natural language. And the last reason is integrating multiple data sources and categories that may give associated information for better understanding and decision-making. It is having the ability to understand and control numerous kinds of data such as digital sensor data, textual data, audio, video, and location data and so on to perceive the several correlations across these data-types, for example, linking data from sensors with acoustic data.

The IoT knows how information is deciphered and appropriated. The popularization and mainstream usage of IoT would produce more and more evidence that will offer valuable sources of knowledge for cognitive computing. In addition, cognitive computing, as a modern form of computing style, can have higher and better energy-efficient means of action for data interpretation and processing in IoT.

7.3.2 Cognitive Computing and Big Data Analysis

Within the production of huge records, the relentless growth of numbers, and the constant creation of computer processing resources are inevitably apparent [13]. Stood out from the advancement of traditional structured data, the surge of unstructured data, for example, social networking and mobile internet data continue to expand exponentially. Structured and unstructured data form cognitive big data and can be defined by 5V, i.e. quantity (large volume), pace (rapid shift and high speed), range, meaning (meaning-oriented), and veracity. Meanwhile, these features create a number of difficulties during knowledge collection and delivery. Big data modeling and semantic engineering provide powerful approaches, though. We present the connection between huge information preparing and cognitive computing, and contrasts.

However, the biggest problem of big data is that there is not enough skill to manage and exploit such a large amount of data. The perpetually rising demand for such skill cannot behold up by stock of data scientists or analysts. There are a lot of advanced data platforms available but due to a shortage of experienced professionals who can manage and operate them, they are of no use. The solutions can include training people and computers to manage them so that less experienced ones can handle such complexities of the data. This approach can be successful with the help of improvements in cognitive computing.

Cognitive computing gives rise to an extreme level of flexibility to analytics and natural language processing makes the machine communication a lot easier. Less experienced who are not knowledgeable of data language and processing that are necessary for decent analytical function can also interact with the data platform and related programs in a similar way how human interacts. It is done by providing easy commands and employing natural language in the AI technology-based data platforms that could interpret regular speech, conversation and requests into a query language and then delivering feedbacks in the same way they were attained. Such functionalities make it easier for everyone to manage any platform.

Cognitive computation emulates senses in humans. One correlation between Big Data Processing and cognitive computation is the deep data thought of humans. During human life, knowledge is continually accumulating. On condition that the amount of information from different communications is high, the individual in question may embody the big data thought of humans, which is hierarchical as deep learning. The first degree analyzes the amplification of material existence and state. The second level is about the advancement of hallowed qualities and the third stage is about the nature of life. The quantity of top-level people is the least noteworthy. As of now, the reasoning that is reproduced by machine knowledge basically centers on the first and second levels to concern the expectation for everyday comforts and the passionate condition of people. The relating applications are wellbeing checking, savvy medicinal services, brilliant home, keen city, and enthusiastic consideration [14]. The third level is further profound that worries the significance of life and advances customized proposals for consumer life-long growth to motivate the consumer to enable the client to acknowledge cheerful yet increasingly important life. It is impossible by machines at present and is an extraordinary test in man-made reasoning later on. Under the situation where informational collection consents to highlights huge information, the most receiving the new machine learning technique is the immediate path to breakdown and analyze the information [15].

The main argument for separating the large data modelling from semantic analytics is the data processing approach of "brain-like" computation. The approach that focuses based on the meaning capacity of data should be used to allow the computer to achieve the third level by knowing the connotation of data and the picture knowledge found in such data and realizing the environmental details much as a human being does.

One difference between big data analysis and cognitive computing is data size. Big data processing is not inherently semantic computation, in allusion to any data collection. Big data analysis stresses extracting the interest and gaining information from a huge amount of data. The accuracy and toughness of conjectures cannot be guaranteed as a source of perspective, without a colossal measure of information. Remembering the measurement of an assortment of cognitive computation information does not suggest that the information scale is contingent.

Cognitive science, based on reasoning and intuition like the human brain, aims to address the challenges of fluffiness and confusion in the biological framework. In this manner acknowledges different degrees of procedures, for example, cognizance, memory, reasoning, thinking, and critical thinking. Despite the fact that the information size isn't sufficiently enormous however the cognitive computing can at present be utilized to process the information. With respect to ordinary citizens and space specialists, it is accepted that the information is indistinguishable yet the significance of information got by average folks may vary from that got by area specialists. Since the stature of reasoning is unique, the edge to decipher the information may likewise be extraordinary. The machine can mine increasingly concealed importance from restricted information utilizing cognitive computing [16].

Some of the solutions already exist with some very remarkable examples to demonstrate such as Watson, DeepMind (Google's project) and Zeroth platform by Qualcomm. Watson is a cognitive computing system having an already internally constructed natural language processing (NLP), hypothetical production-analysis and active learning. It is extra advanced than the artificial assistants on our mobile device. In evidence, the system works so adequately, it enables users to ask questions in simple and ordinary speech, which this system then translates into the data query language.

DeepMind is the advanced computer invented to reflect some of the short-term memory characteristics of the brain. Practically, the computer system is constructed with a neural network that interacts with external memory adaptively. It stores memories that it can later procure and utilize to understand new information and perform unexpected chores that it was never programmed to do. It is having a brain like potentials so that analysts can lean on information and commands. The program can compare such information with past data queries and respond to without any need for continual supervision.

The Zeroth [17], a Cognitive Computing Platform, is invented to depend on optical and acoustic cognitive computing so that it can reflect human-based thinking and actions i.e., a device operating the platform could identify objects, examine handwriting, recognize people and comprehend the across-the-board context of a situation and environment. For example, the device such as a mobile phone could adapt automatically while taking snapshots at a cloudless seaside or a trek in the moon brightness. It could also automatically modify its microphone configurations whenever there is a lot of background noise to provide satisfactory sound quality. Its ability to reproduce instinctive experiences gives several chances in the sentiment analytics. Its ability to interpret scenes, events and context show that it has supported with right image technology devices, it could untangle how a person is feeling based on facial moods and expressions and can recognize levels of stress or anger based on their voices.

At last, shifting from cognitive platforms to on-device decision reduces the number of back and forth cloud communications and transmissions. The devices can improve performance and security while saving power. Therefore, the advancements in cognitive computing, and implanting AI, machine learning and deep learning into big data platforms and mechanisms, will not only facilitate less experienced professionals to deal with the complexities of data analytics but also enhance the resulting quality. Large amounts of data, information and a lot of work could be transferred to our machines will allow us to respond rapidly and real-time decisions can be made employing real-time analytics.

7.3.3 Cognitive Computing and Cloud Computing

Cognitive computing is supposed to be highly resource-intensive that requires powerful and effective servers, involving strong computers, deep technological expertise, profound technical agility, and frequently leads to a high level of technological obligation and sometimes contributing to a large degree of professional debt. For instance, creating machine learning models not only consumes substantial computing power but also expands specific responsibilities such as technological obligations with the ever-increasing learning process. Therefore, such computing was restricted to huge business industries and ventures for quite a while, for example, the Fortune 500s. But this has been entirely reversed by the cloud.

The cloud absolutely overturned everything. The Cloud helps developers to produce semantic templates, check structures, and integrate without a physical basis into established systems. The Cloud enables architects to create cognitive models, experimenting solutions, test, debug and incorporate with current systems without requiring physical infrastructure. Hence, due to the resource expenses and asset costs are still involved, businesses can flexibly advocate clouding resources for cognitive development and can downscale as whenever important [18].

Conventionally, enterprises are benefiting from cognitive in the sense of ROI perspective only. They would dedicate quantitative time, effort, and stakes in research and development. They could afford delays or any kind of uncertainties in quality production. Presently, even small or mid-size industries can employ the cognitive cloud to apply AI for their daily information technology ecosystem, instantly producing quality without an infrastructure of broker reliances. Generally, from a basic ROI point of view, Cognitive will only bode well for massive endeavors. They should apply tremendous energy, commitment, and R&D desires, and in respect, age could handle the expense of deferrals/vulnerabilities. Currently, even small-to-moderate companies may use the Cognitive Cloud to add AI as a part of their everyday IT biological program, easily creating an opportunity without the merchant circumstances being created.

Processing in the cloud virtualizes processing, data, and bandwidth. This also reduces the expense of delivery for information infrastructure and encourages industrialization and facilitates intelligent computer technologies. In addition, cloud computing's strong computing and storage capability provides cognitive computing with dynamic, flexible, virtual, shared, and efficient computing resources services [19].

In fact, for huge amounts of information created in the wake of analyzing large information about the distributed computing stage, innovations are being received; for example, machine learning to perform information mining and the discoveries are being updated in different zones. The different data classes compare with different innovations in handling. For example, the literal information and the pictorial data compare individually to characteristic language preparation and machine vision.

IBM's cognitive help for Google's use of language and psychological processing underlines the recognition of brain-like cognition and judgment by conveying a model of cloud administration to provide accurate dynamic assistance. Cloud infrastructure and IoT provide computational processing with a foundation for the software and hardware, while large-scale knowledge analysis offers strategies and thought to recognize and interpret potential technology possibilities and benefits [20].

Conventional cloud-based communications give ground-breaking cloud computing managements. However, only supporting intensive data processing isn't enough, particularly when a limit is restricted and superlow latency is required. Hence, it is basic to propose another Artificial Intelligence empowered heterogeneous systems, including different terminal networks and clouds. Gotten from cognitive science and information analytics, cognitive computing can copy or increase human intellect. At the point when such cognitive knowledge is integrated with communications, conventional services will be redesigned with higher accuracy and lower inactivity.

With the assistance of cognitive cloud computing, we can:

1. Advance resource usage: Enterprises no longer need to spend on the cognitive prepared framework. The Cognitive Cloud can be utilized whenever required and discontinued when inactive.
2. Access more extensive ranges of abilities: Instead of employing a data scientist or AI modeling master, enterprises can partner with Cognitive Cloud sellers at an adaptable month to month rate. This is especially valuable for those confronting slow digital transformation.
3. Speed up investments: The overlong arranging, planning, speculation, and set-up period is substituted by a prepared to send solution. Some cloud merchants significantly offer adaptable default AI models.

7.4 Enabling Technologies in Cognitive Computing

7.4.1 Cognitive Computing and Reinforcement Learning

You can split modern machine learning approaches into supervised learning and unsupervised learning. In those strategies, the machines train those models with information that are frequently in a fixed organization, and machines total errands, for example, regression, classification, and aggregation. The information that machines can reach is nevertheless restricted. It is hard for machines to learn data in nonlinear cases since they can just lead expectations as indicated by the got data. The tag for related knowledge may even be varied under varying circumstances, which means that the user-friendliness of machine-learned data is distinctive among specific clients. Conventional supervised learning and unsupervised learning rely on planning to shut down with input of knowledge. These conventional learning techniques can't meet the needs of economic improvement in machine insight. Reinforcement learning has now become a popular work branch in the area of machine learning.

Finding out about activities and results essentially shapes social cognition and behavior. For instance, to help other people, we have to know how our choices remunerate or abstain from hurting another person. Before we choose what to decide for ourselves, we can participate in observational learning by viewing the positive or negative things that happen to others, and we can gather others' psychological states by following their activities and results after some time. One of the most significant impacts on brain research, neuroscience and financial aspects has originated from associative or reinforcement learning hypothesis that exactly and numerically depicts how decisions are associated with results over some time. Analysts proposed their learning model which portrayed how learning happens by means of a prediction error, the error between what we hope to occur and what really occurs. This error rectification learning cycle can also be portrayed numerically.

Maybe answer to inquiries of reinforcement learning, these expectation mistakes can be social in nature, for example, social-predicted mistakes, for example, the desire that my activity will help somebody versus the result that it did or didn't or my desire that I will be enjoyed by another person and the result that I was or was definitely not. While mind regions traditionally connected with reinforcement learning, for example, the ventromedial prefrontal cortex and ventral striatum have been connected to handle both social and non-social predicted mistakes, there may likewise be social expectation error signals in areas fairly particular for social preparing. A more broad conversation about the distinction between mind areas coding social and non-social expectation error is covered in a few other ongoing audits.

Reinforcement learning is linked to making reasonable moves in order to boost awards in a given circumstance. Various programming and machines use it to locate the most ideal conduct or manner it should take in a given circumstance. We may find the situation, for example, anytime an infant finds out how to talk. When a kid gets acquainted with a phrase, usually an adult will read the word, over and over, allude to something addressed by that word or play out the activity addressed by that word. In case the interpretation of the kid is not right due to off-base judgment, the grown-up will be an immediate correction. When the teenager strikes the target on the ear, it gives the grown-up a reward. Equally, the underlying environment is a major influence during the human learning process. At this stage, reinforcement learning takes the model and can draw from nature and find behavior. The remuneration has various sections, i.e. when certain action becomes beneficial for practical reasons, and some control becomes implemented beyond what might be predicted. Along these lines, the choice at each time isn't really the ideal, yet it must be useful for the machine to acquire rewards.

How about we take AlphaGo, [21] for instance, subsequent to engrossing a huge number of rounds of chess for profound learning, and it plays chess with itself by support learning. During the self-learning stage, each progression isn't really ideal. However, the progression is well on the way to cause the last win according to worldwide arranging. In this procedure, the machine isn't just subject to past understanding yet would likewise attempt new ways to amplify the objective prize. Much the same as drawing learning, the unpremeditated play would be included once the essential aptitudes are aced. Information is produced during the time spent endeavours of the machine; the last goal isn't relapse, grouping, or accumulation yet the greatest prize. For this reason, both fruitful and ineffective endeavours are significant for the machine. It would gain as a matter of fact in past endeavours at each ensuing advance.

Yet if a computer interacts solely with itself, then its intellect becomes unsatisfactory. Thus, if a learning arrangement pays little attention to outer conditions; it is not a good system of cognitions. Therefore, a neural machine can specifically interact with humans. Unless a human was directly appointed to interact with a computer, however, it will take a great deal of time and manpower. Fortunately, the crowd-sourcing approach will render machine–human contact normal.

One standard case is the Foldit game. In this game, an objective protein is given, the players lead to getting together with various amino acids until this bit of protein's whole body is sorted out. The players volunteer to engage in the amino corrosive get together procedure. In addition, the collective intelligence of this crowd of unprofessional players will surpass that of a few professionals if there are enough players. This methodology can be utilized in specific territories of innovation to improve computer insight by encouraging users to interact implicitly with the system by personalized cognitive computing applications. The complex knowledge generated by the users who engage in crowd-sourcing unintentionally often remits the reliance on cognitive learning on information and simultaneously offers an alternate kind of data processing tool.

Significantly, the utility of reinforcement learning (RL) models has been supported by their neural credibility—the revelation that the phasic action of dopamine neurons in the midbrain encodes a prediction error. In addition to the fact that this model has changed the old style neuro-imaging investigation procedures. Model-based FMRI might help connect various degrees of clarification from the cognitive and behavioural to the neural. Studies in the field of social neuroscience have started to apply these models to see how and whether quantities predicted by reinforcement learning are represented in the brain during social circumstances.

7.4.2   Cognitive Computing and Deep Learning

Innovative revolution, PC integration and the progressions on the Internet saw after the industrial revolt has become a sensation in all parts of our everyday lives. Aside from that, digital devices have assisted with forming our social orders. This has been acknowledged because of the fixed presence of digital information and a change that has been seen with the manner in which people think and act.

Besides, the majority of the digital integration procedures have seen the development of many processing disciplines which have achieved adequacy. One outstanding region that has changed the impression of computer behaviour and how machines work is the control of Deep Learning which is a subset of Artificial Intelligence. Deep learning makes it workable for multi-layered neural systems which can be applied in tuning machines so as to achieve some ideal undertakings. In reality, deep learning has been envisioned as a state-of-the-art approach that can convey numerous precise derivations, which have likewise changed the manner in which intelligent choices are made by computers. For instance, an appropriate conventional system or approach through which deep learning cognitive computing ideas and strategies can be incorporated into cyber forensics so as to acknowledge adequacy during criminological examination utilizing AI approaches.

Deep Learning is an Artificial Intelligence work that can mimic the methods of processing the human brain. It basically includes AI methods that are utilized to speak to realities. They additionally feature that deep learning is an ongoing advancement in AI that can be applied in various fields.

7.4.2.1   Rational Method and Perceptual Method

The human cerebral cortex is partitioned into two hemispheres with clearly different capacities. The left brain, as in most individuals, is responsible for vocabulary, concepts, reasoning, etc, while the right mind is answerable for considerations and visual recognition. People with developed left brain usually have strong logic and are more rational (for example, scientists). Although individuals with a trained-right brain usually have high imagination, space, and entity forms (e.g., artists) are excellent at cognition. Subsequently, the human perspective is separated into coherent reasoning and visual reasoning. The explanation for human regular world change is a lot of sensible techniques and visual apparatuses owing to the interesting multifaceted embodiment of reasoning [22].

The reasonable approach is focused on strict principles and interpretation, whereas the perceptual approach is characterized as a certain mapping connection between input and output. It is still unclear how the human brain knows the knowledge coding, transmission, and storing of 100 billion nerve cells. However, human brain thinking can be simulated

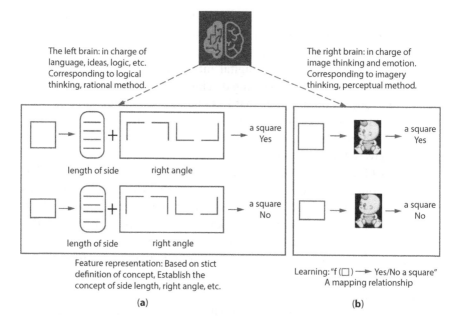

The left brain: in charge of language, ideas, logic, etc. Corresponding to logical thinking, rational method.

The right brain: in charge of image thinking and emotion. Corresponding to imagery thinking, perceptual method.

length of side   right angle

a square
Yes

length of side   right angle

a square
No

a square
Yes

a square
No

Feature representation: Based on stict definition of concept, Establish the concept of side length, right angle, etc.

(a)

Learning: "f (☐) ⟶ Yes/No a square"
A mapping relationship

(b)

Figure 7.3 Perceptual and rational method to recognize a square. (a) Rational method. (b) Perceptual method.

in the cognitive system by means of data analysis. The method for the manual design of features is specifically specified. The learning technique for the component is to get familiar with the mapping connection between information and yield. It's a kind of cognitive strategy, that is, its fasters the human's ability to actually perceive.

Recent examination demonstrates that perceptual learning, experience-induced transformations in complex cognitive operations and neuroscientific research held relationships among cognition, perception, and learning. We diagram three updates to regular suppositions about these relations. Firstly, the Perceptual systems give unpredictable and theoretical depictions of the real world. Second is that perceptual descriptions are frequently amodal and not restricted to methodology-specific-sensory-characteristics and lastly, the perception is particularly choosy [23]. These three properties empower relations among perception and cognition that are both dynamic and they make possible perception learning calculations that adapt information extraction to enhance task execution. Researchers have illustrated a developing perception learning innovation that has just delivered sensational learning profits in an assortment of scholarly and expert learning settings, including arithmetic, science, avionics, and medical fields. The above process was illustrated in the Figure 7.3.

Proceeding with logical advancement and reasonable uses of perception learning, it will be encouraged by a superior comprehension of the relations between perception, cognition, and learning. One may accept that these relations are surely known, yet in reality, they are most certainly not. An essential explanation is that progress in understanding observation in the previous few years requires a reconsidering of a portion of these relations, nullifying a few different ways of reasoning and making ready for new experiences. Consequently, before the most recent couple of years, in the event that somebody proposed a part for perception in learning mathematics that included shaded charts to outline fraction that may permit students to have some solid acknowledgment of rational numbers. These applications are not quite the same as the possibility of overall learning by which students dynamically change the manner in which they remove structure and relations from symbolic equations. Lately, there have been patterns in cognitive science claiming for a nearby connection among perception and cognition.

Cognition is arranged. Psychological movement happens with regards to a true domain, and it naturally includes perceptions and actions. We off-burden cognition work onto nature by exploiting it to control data and information for us, and we collect that data just on a need-to-know premise. The atmosphere is essential for the cognitive framework. The data stream among mind and the world is so thick and consistent that, for researchers considering the idea of intellectual activity, the mind alone is definitely not an important unit of analytics. Cognition is for activity. The capacity of the mind is to direct activity, and intellectual components, for example, observation and memory must be perceived as far as their definitive responsibility position suitable behaviour. Perception is body-based. In any event, when decoupled from the atmosphere, the action of the mind is grounded in devices that developed for connection with nature.

7.4.2.2   Cognitive Computing and Image Understanding

On the off chance that the machine will tackle issues, in reality, the most ideal path is to mimic the thinking more about the human cerebrum. In the psychological framework, the highlights can either be removed from unique information for grouping and forecast model utilizing the technique for manual component configuration to recreate the legitimate thinking capacity about the human cerebrum or can be learned through profound figuring out how to reproduce the capacity of visual considering human mind.

There are two strategies for highlight extraction in face pictures: manual element structure and feature learning. In the manual feature design method, the computer simulates the rational method for recognition and determines which features on the architecture and extraction of the functionality are very problematic owing, for example, to elements expression, making up, beard, glasses, change in illumination, and photographing angle [24].

Be that as it may, when a person conducts face acknowledgment, the individual in question only here and there thinks about explicit highlights in the picture, rather, the person makes judgment absolutely by ethicalness of instinct. The articulation, light, capturing edge, and glasses in the photos would not impact their perception impacts a tall [25].

In other words, effective data features cannot be designed with a manual feature design method and it is quite difficult for a computer to realize the feature expression. Image feature extraction is the base for understanding the image paying little heed to use. For instance, we should take face recognition [26].

Conventional image processing is a field of science and innovation created to encourage human-focused image management and control. Be that as it may, today when enormous amounts of visual information immerse our environmental factors because of the unstable development of image capturing tools, expansion of Internet correspondence means and video sharing administrations over the World Wide Web (WWW), human-focused treatment of big data becomes impossible. In this way, it must be substituted with a machine upheld companion. Obviously, such an artificial partner must be outfitted with some cognitive abilities, normally characteristics of a person. Cognitive image understanding unquestionably will be one of its fundamental responsibilities. Today, the progress from a 'computational data-processing worldview' to a 'cognitive information-processing worldview' influences numerous fields of science, innovation, and designing. This change is an honoured oddity, yet its prosperity is hampered between the idea of information and the thought of data. As the computer applications are getting increasingly complex, the specialists understand that numerous issues in genuine that are straightforward by people are hard to portray with judicious strategy making the sane scientific technique incapable or totally unimaginable computer. At the end of the day, the successful information highlights can't be planned with manual component structure procedure and it is extremely difficult for a computer to comprehend the component articulation.

It very well may be summarized that the mapping connection between the info and the yield (i.e., who is that individual) is set up with this acknowledgment strategy for humans by uprightness of instinct. At the point when picture order is directed with profound learning, the perceptual strategy for people for picture acknowledgment is mimicked [27].

7.5   Applications of Cognitive Computing

7.5.1   Chatbots

Chatbots [28] are applications that can mimic a human conversation with a conceptual perception of contact. The active individual bots are getting pervasive by being inserted in cell phones, wearables, and web of things endpoints, offering self-governing knowledge on more parts of the material world. Maybe the correct name for this kind of smart individual specialist is the cognitive chatbot.

This new inflow of smart individual specialists initiates in the spread of a cloud-based cognitive register environment, for example, IBM's Watson. Through their capacity to utilize AI to drive characteristic language conversations, cognitive chatbots can be recognized from the long queue of "chatterbots" that preceded. What's more, as characteristic language conversational bots like Siri and Amazon's Alexa flourish in the customer world, I consider these operators as part of cognitive IoT chatbots. As engineers move their concentration to Cognitive chatbots, they have to receive crisp reasoning, practices, and systems for building these capacities as reusable management for arrangement in the cloud, portable, IoT, and different situations. At the point when you take other cognitive chatbot advancement natives—past those related with the UI—it's ingenious one that is generalizable enough to serve a wide scope of utilization cases. The examples depend on how much individual bots learn, continue, and follow up on substance and state factors related to explicit clients, channels, and discussions. For instance, a hand animating and entertaining thought expert for investigation escalated Twitter chatbot applications.

Developments in cognitive chatbot advancements, calculations, and applications are coming to advertise at a surprising pace. As space develops throughout the following quite a while and best practices take shape, coordinated improvement systems will very likely rise.

7.5.2 Sentiment Analysis

Sentiment Analysis (otherwise called sentiment mining or emotion AI) refers to the utilization of regular language preparing, text examination, computational phonetics, and biometrics to deliberately recognize, extricate, measure, and study emotional states and abstract data.

Sentiment evaluation is the examination of spotting sentiments expressed in a message. Sentiment evaluation is popularly used to evaluate social network messages which include posts, remarks, ratings, grievances, etc.

The sentimental investigation is generally applied to the voice of the client entities, for example, audits and overview reactions, on the web and online media, and medical care materials for applications that run from promoting to client care to clinical medication. The sentimental investigation, nonetheless, assists organizations with understanding this unstructured content via naturally labeling it.

The sentimental examination is an AI method that recognizes extremity (for example a positive or negative feeling) inside content, regardless of whether an entire archive, passage, sentence, or statement. For instance, utilizing sentimental examination to consequently break down more than four thousand audits about your item could assist you with finding if clients are active about your valuing plans and client care. It's assessed that eighty percent of the world's information is unstructured and enormous volumes of text information such as messages, uphold tickets, visits, online media discussions, reviews, articles, records, and so forth is made each day yet it's difficult to examine, comprehend, and also monotonous and costly.

Understanding individuals' feelings are basic for organizations since clients can communicate their musings and emotions more transparently than any other time in recent memory. Via consequently examining client input, from study reactions to web-based media discussions, brands can listen mindfully to their clients and fasten items and management to address their issues.

Hence, Cognitive AI includes feeling investigation, relevant references to comprehend, distinguish and mine the information, for example, linguistic structure, time, area, space, business prerequisites, a particular client need, undertakings or objectives and mixes thereof emulating human perception far beyond the AI we know. Intellectual AI may draw inductions from various information models, outside sources of the data, including organized and unstructured information and visual, hearable or machine information and metadata.

7.5.3   Face Detection

The specialized stage of picture processing is facial recognition. A cognitive system utilizes facial data such as shape, contours, eye color, etc. to separate it from others.

Apple has obtained Emotient, a face detection startup that utilizes man-made consciousness innovation to survey feelings by using individuals' outward face appearances. It can be utilized by Doctors to decipher the agony of patients who can't communicate. It can also be used by the organization to check the responses of purchasers on the items in its stores.

7.5.4   Risk Assessment

Risk management in financial services includes the expert experiencing market patterns, chronicled information, and so on to foresee the vulnerability associated with a venture. In any case, this is examination isn't just identified with information yet in addition to patterns, gut feel, conduct investigation, and so forth. Organizations and open area associations are utilizing progressively enormous measures of inner and outer information to face a more precaution challenge position. Notwithstanding, with that expansion in information volume, the viability of conventional examination strategies is decreasing. Cognitive capacities including AI, regular language handling, and numerous different kinds of intellectual innovation give an advanced option in contrast to customary examination and are being applied to monstrous informational collections to help discover markers of known and obscure dangers. Cognitive computing can assist organizations with identifying and assessing rising essential dangers that can threaten any or all of what administrators care generally about before those dangers cause conceivably critical harm or lead to greater expenses or speculations.

Simultaneously, Cognitive processing is especially compelling when taking care of and assessing unstructured information or the sort of data that doesn't fit conveniently into organized lines and segments. Cognitive innovations, for example, natural language processing, semantic analysis and image understanding utilize progressed calculations to break down unstructured information to determine experiences and beliefs. Since about ninety percent of information produced today is unstructured, utilization of cognitive processing can put organizations directly on the edge of the threat. This is the place where cognitive analysis and the risks unite. Cognitive processing can assist organizations with distinguishing other rising patterns, understand the danger/reward tradeoffs naturally in esteem innovation, and improve investing options and resource selection.

Pioneers who influence cognitive abilities can increase the upper hand and use risks to control their associations' exhibition.

Also, as cognitive fraud identification frameworks keep on learning, they can identify more perplexing misrepresentation, a preferred position that may have the greatest effect on hazard the administrators. By uncovering developing examples that people would never distinguish, cognitive advancements make new examples to search for an upright cycle that in principle never closes, which is a genuine favorable position when fraudsters are unstoppably advancing their extortion plans.

7.6 Future of Cognitive Computing

The cognitive analysis is normally similar to that of the human idea and perspective in a modernized domain. It is a totality of self-learning frameworks that fuses design acknowledgment, information mining and natural language processing (NLP) to imitate the manner in which the human mind works. The fundamental goal of cognitive computing is to make self-working modernized frameworks that are capable of taking care of even complex issues with no human assistance or interruption [29].

The cognitive cycle can be appreciated in a much basic manner as the component which utilizes the current information for producing new information. The fundamental topic of perception is firmly identified with unique ideas, for example, psyche, mentality, recognition and knowledge. It resembles understanding the commitment of a human cerebrum and taking a shot at the humankind of issues. Such frameworks and set-up consistently gain information from the data. The cognitive processing framework merges information from differing and incidental data sources while thinking about setting and conflicting proof to recommend the best achievable answers.

It is one of the characterizations of advancements that use AI and Natural Languages Processing (NLP) to empower individuals and machines to communicate and increase understanding all-around for amplification of human skill, observation, and perception.

Utilizing computer systems to unwind the diverse class of issues that people are generally worried about, requires a broad measure of organized and unstructured data taken care of by AI calculations. With the progression of innovation, cognitive systems can refine the manner in which it recognizes designs and the manner in which it measures information to get fit for catching new issues and outline the potential arrangements.

To achieve this capability, cognitive analytics must have these five key qualities, as recorded by the Cognitive Computing Consortium [30].

• Versatile
This is the initial phase in making an AI-based cognitive framework. The arrangements should copy the capacity of the human cerebrum to adapt from the environmental factors. The frameworks can't be modified for a segregated task. It should be dynamic in information gathering, getting objectives, and prerequisites.

• Intelligent
Like the mind, the cognitive arrangement must collaborate with all components in the framework—processor, devices, cloud administrations and client. Cognitive frameworks ought to associate in an Omni-directional manner. It ought to understand human information and give significant outcomes utilizing natural language processing and machine learning.

• Iterative and Stateful
The framework should 'recall' past collaborations in a cycle and return data that is appropriate for the particular application by then. It ought to have the option to characterize the issue by posing inquiries or finding an extra source. This component needs a cautious utilization of the information quality and approval procedures so as to guarantee that the framework is constantly furnished with enough data and that the information sources it works on to convey dependable and cutting-edge input.

• Relevant
They should understand, recognize, and remove logical components like language structure, time, area, proper space, guidelines, client's profile, cycle, errand, and objective. They may draw on numerous sources of data, including both organized and unstructured advanced data, just as tangible information sources like visual, gestural, hearable, or sensor-based.

Some of the scopes of cognitive computing are as follows:

1. Engagement
It is the capacity to gain clear insights into the subject and to offer professional assistance. The Cognitive system has tremendous stores of organized and unstructured information. These can grow profound area experiences and give master help. The models work by these frameworks remembers

the relevant connections between different elements for a framework's reality that empower it to shape speculations and contentions. The chatbot innovation is a genuine case of commitment model. A large number of the AI chatbots are pre-prepared with space information for fast selection in various business-explicit applications [31].

2. Decision

There is an independent decision-making through improved thinking. A step in front of responsibility systems, these have dynamic abilities. These systems are displayed using support learning. Decisions made by cognitive systems constantly develop being dependent on new data, results, and activities. Self-sufficient dynamic abilities rely upon the capacity to follow why the specific selection was made and change the certainty score of a system's reaction. For instance, giving options help to improve the abilities and diminishing desk work that allows clinicians to invest more energy with patients.

3. Discovery

Through a method, the program will recall past experiences and return knowledge. Discovery is the most progressive extent of cognitive computing. The vision includes discovering bits of knowledge and understanding a tremendous measure of data and creating aptitudes. These models are based on profound learning and solo AI. While still in the beginning phases, some discovery capacities have just developed, and the offers for future applications are convincing.

7.7   Conclusion

To summarize, Cognitive Computing doesn't carry an extreme curiosity into the AI and Big Data industry. Or maybe it inclined towards advanced answers for meeting human-driven prerequisites: act, think and carry on like a human so as to accomplish the most extreme harmonious energy from human-machine communication.

In this paper, we attempted to clarify this expansive and high-level idea into detailed automated difficulties which give some broad sense proposals where they can be tended to. We accept that soon every computerized system will be estimated on its cognitive capacities. Like user experience was the following huge advance for improving application comfort. Cognitive Computing will be a noteworthy advance towards automated digital humanism. The impact of cognitive technology on organizations will absolutely be anticipated to rise altogether in less than 5 years. Notwithstanding all the obstacles and barriers, we cannot neglect the advantages of cognitive technologies. Starting the transformation cycle and embracing revolutionary technologies for a promising and far more productive future would be in support of both the organizations and society at large [31].

References

1. Octavio, J. and Lopez, Cognitive Computing: A brief survey and open research challenges. *3rd International Conference on Applied Computing and Information Technology*, IEEE, 2015.
2. Karie, N.M., Kebande, V.R. and Venter, H.S., 2019. Diverging deep learning cognitive computing techniques into cyber forensics. *Forensic Science International: Synergy*, 1, 61–67, 2019.
3. Chen, M., Mao, S., Liu, Y., Big data: A survey. *Mobile Netw. Appl.*, 19, 2, 171–209, 2014.
4. Leonel, J., *Cognitive Computing: Basic concepts and timeline*, Retrieved from Medium: https://medium.com/@jorgesleonel/cognitive-computing-reflects-a-new-computing-era-4945aeb0e843.
5. Johnston, V.S., *Why we feel: The science of human emotions*. Perseus Publishing, 1999.
6. Chen, M., Mao, S., Liu, Y., Big data: A survey. *Mobile Netw. Appl.*, 19, 2, 171–209, 2014.
7. Techopedia, *Cognitive architecture*, Retrieved from Techopedia: https://www.techopedia.com/definition/6537/cognitive-architecture, 2017.
8. Bhatia, R., *Brain-Inspired Cognitive Architecture is now solving computational challenges faced by AI*, Retrieved from Analytics India Magazine: analyticsindiamag.com/brain-inspired-cognitive-architecture-is-now-solving-computational-challenges-faced-by-ai/, 2018.
9. Chen, M., Hao, Y., Hu, L., Huang, K., Lau, V., Green and mobility-aware caching in 5G networks. *IEEE Trans. Wireless Commun.*, 16, 12, 8347–8361, 2017.
10. Chen, M. and Y.M., Narrow band Internet of Things. *IEEE Access*, 5, 20557–20577, 2017.
11. Sheth, A., Internet of Things to smart IoT through semantic, cognitive, and perceptual computing. *IEEE Intell. Syst.*, 31, 2, 108–112, 2016.
12. Tian, D., Zhou, J., Sheng, Z., An adaptive fusion strategy for distributed information estimation over cooperative multi-agent networks. *IEEE Trans. Inf. Theory*, 63, 5, 3076–3091, 2017.
13. Fernández, A., Big data with cloud computing: An insight on the computing environment, mapreduce, and programming frameworks. *Wiley Interdiscip. Rev., Data Min. Knowl. Discov.*, 4, 5, 380–409, 2014.

14. Chen, M., Zhou, P., Fortino, G., Emotion communication system. *IEEE Access*, 5, 326–337, 2017.

15. Chaturvedi, I., Cambria, E., Welsch, R.E., Herrera, F., Distinguishing between facts and opinions for sentiment analysis: Survey and challenges. *Inf. Fusion*, 44, 65–77, 2018.

16. Hurwitz, J., Kaufman, M., Bowles, A., *Cognitive Computing and Big Data Analytics*, Wiley, Hoboken, NJ, USA, 2015.

17. Delgado, R., *Cognitive Computing: Solving the Big Data Problem?*, Retrieved from KDnuggets: https://www.kdnuggets.com/2015/06/cognitive-computing-solving-big-data-problem.html, 2015.

18. Zhou, L., On data-driven delay estimation for media cloud. *IEEE Trans. Multimedia*, 18, 5, 905–915, 2016.

19. Armbrust, M., *Above the clouds: A Berkeley view of cloud computing*, vol. 53, no. 4, pp. 50–58, Eecs Dept. Univ, California Berkeley, 2009.

20. Botta, A., Donato, W.D., Persico, V., Pescapé, A.E., On the integration of cloud computing and Internet of Things. *Proc. IEEE Int. Conf. Future Internet Things Cloud*, pp. 23–30, 2014.

21. Silver, D., Mastering the game of go with deep neural networks and tree search. *Nature*, 529, 7587, 484–489, 2016.

22. Chen, M., Herrera, F., Hwang, K., Cognitive Computing: Architecture, Technologies and Intelligent Applications. *IEEE Access*, 6, 19774–19783, 2018.

23. Kellman, P.J. and Massey, C.M., 2013. Perceptual learning, cognition, and expertise. In *Psychology of learning and motivation* (Vol. 58, pp. 117-165). Academic Press.

24. Fasel, B. and Luettin, J., Automatic facial expression analysis: A survey. *Pattern Recognit.*, 36, 259–275, 2003.

25. Chen, M., Hao, Y., Kai, H., Wang, L., Wang, L., Disease prediction by machine learning over big data from healthcare communities. *IEEE Access*, 5, 1, 8869–8879, 2017.

26. Charte, D., Charte, F., García, S., Jesus, M.J., Herrera, F., A practical tutorial on autoencoders for nonlinear feature fusion: Taxonomy models software and guidelines. *Inf. Fusion*, 44, 78–96, 2017.

27. Chen, M., Shi, X., Zhang, Y., Wu, D., Mohsen, G., Deep features learning for medical image analysis with convolutional autoencoder neural network. *IEEE Trans. Big Data*, 2017.

28. Leonel, J., *Cognitive-computing-reflects-a-new-computing-era*, Retrieved from Medium: https://medium.com/@jorgesleonel/cognitive-computing-reflects-a-new-computing-era-4945aeb0e843.

29. Makadia, M., *What-is-cognitive-computing-how-are-enterprises-benefitting-from-cognitive-technology*, Retrieved from Towards Data Science: https://towardsdatascience.com/what-is-cognitive-computing-how-are-enterprises-benefitting-from-cognitive-technology-6441d0c9067b, 2019.

30. *Cognitive Computing Definition*, Retrieved from Cognitive Computing Consortium: https://cognitivecomputingconsortium.com/definition-of-cognitive-computing/, 2018.
31. Witan World, *Cognitive computing*, Retrieved from Witan World: https://witanworld.com/article/2018/10/08/cognitive-computing/, 2018.

8

Tools Used for Research in Cognitive Engineering and Cyber Physical Systems

Ajita Seth

School Of Automation, Banasthali Vidyapith, Jaipur, Rajasthan, India

Abstract

The word cognition was derived from Latin and Greek origin. Cognition is the ability to understand the information that we receive from different sources (perception, experience, beliefs, etc.) in the environment, process it and convert it into learning. This context of the term refers to the human cognition with the help of neurons. Over the years humans have realized computers have a potential to mimic them when they are highly programmed for that processing of structured and unstructured data set, they output it with integrated hardware and tool. Now you can understand the vision behind cognition of data by computers i.e. cognitive computing. The technology was implemented first in the Second World War but since the computers did not have large memory and processing capability back then, people lost hope in the future of cognition. Now when the computers are becoming compact, powerful and fast day by day, cognition models have started to take shape in various fields like medical sciences, industries, physical systems and big data analysis.

Keywords: Cognition, environment, humans, compact, powerful, fast, industries, physical systems, data analysis, analysis

8.1 Cyber Physical Systems

This content covers basic knowledge of a cyber physical system for a rookie. This will help the reader to understand the basics of research in the field and have a grasp on the new functioning technology.

Email: ajitaseth1999@gmail.com

Kolla Bhanu Prakash, G. R. Kanagachidambaresan, V. Srikanth, E. Vamsidhar (eds.) Cognitive Engineering for Next Generation Computing: A Practical Analytical Approach, (219–230) © 2021 Scrivener Publishing LLC

1. Industry 4.0
2. System
3. Autonomous Automotive System
4. Robotic System
5. Mechatronics

8.2   Introduction: The Four Phases of Industrial Revolution

I hope you have understood some basic facts about cognitive computing. The underlined part up till now is "Computers process of acquiring knowledge from a set of collected data is called cognition [1] of computers" and this is the only part you will need to understand this topic called Cyber Physical Systems.

What is an industry? An industry [2] is the activity of producing goods and services from raw material for the generation of the economy and fulfilling needs of a group of people.

Mankind realized years ago that they are prospering day by day, in terms of numbers, needs, culture, etc. This evolution of mankind resulted in mass production of goods and services that cover the frequent requirements of human beings. These industries not only provide a product but also generate employment for people and the economy for the nation.

Now since industries started establishing all over the world, research and development for more efficient and more productive industries was growing with it. All these years have passed and the same thought is still carrying the industries forward. The development of industries has been categorized into 4 phases by the researchers and industry personnel. The first three revolutions being [3]:

(i) Industry 1.0: the invention of the steam engine.
(ii) Industry 2.0: the invention of electricity and adoption of mass production by division of labor.
(iii) Industry 3.0: the combining development of computers with information technology (IT) to automate things has brought a lot of changes to industrial developments.
(iv) Industry 4.0: which includes with the advent of the Internet of things (IoT) and cyber-physical systems (CPS), both industries and governments have started investing huge amounts in related projects to develop the Internet of everything in all sectors.

There are many basic features that are kept in mind while designing an industry 4.0 [4, 8] but the key implementations observed are:

1. The links between mechanical apparatus, devices, sensors, people and communication between them.
2. Highly Integrated Systems
3. Complex and Data Driven
4. Cyber Capability and networked at multiple levels
5. Automation, Control loop and feedback system
6. Error elimination
7. Decentralized control
8. Decision making algorithms so that the system can make its own decisions according to the data collected from the environment.

8.3 System

A system is an independent item communicating in network and working together in an organized pattern completely forms a system [5, 7].
Examples of a system:

1. The water cycle
2. A car
3. A factory
4. Laser printer.

8.4 Autonomous Automobile System

You might have heard sometime from your friends, read it from a book or watched it in a sci-fi movie where people predict and say the future of vehicle is something that has no human involvement other than external commands, that is capable of reading the environment, that can make its own decision of motion, that follows all the safety regulations.

In the era of Industry 4.0 it's possible to design such Automobiles that are Autonomous and work as a whole system.

Breaking down the meaning of the topic the first point I will like to discuss is: what is a vehicle?

A vehicle is a system that is used to carry humans and cargo from one place to another.

Till now a vehicle is human driven, the person driving the vehicle [5] is called a driver. But as the industry is growing towards more automation, the idea of self-driving vehicles is increasing [5, 6].

8.4.1 The Timeline

If you look at the timeline for the idea of auto driven cars the idea is age old [4].

1926: World's first auto driven car 'Linrrican Wonder' which drove in the streets of Manhattan

1939: General Motors sponsored Norman Bel Geddes's presented 'Futurama' at the World's Fair, which depicted embedded-circuit powered electric cars (radio driven).

1953: A miniature autonomous car built by RCA Labs

1960: General Motors presented a car controlled by an electronic guide system.

1987 to 1995: Prometheus Project on autonomous vehicles. Autonomous control to direct a robotic vehicle at speeds of up to 31 km/h United States

1991: Congress passed the ISTEA Transportation Authorization bill.

1995: The Carnegie Mellon University's Navlab project achieved 98.2% autonomous driving on a 5,000 km cross-country journey in a semi-autonomous vehicle.

1966: Alberto Broggi of the University of Parma launched the ARGO Project.

2000: Autonomous public road transport system was in operation and autonomous vehicles, mostly for military usage. Demo I (US Army), Demo II (DARPA), and Demo III (US Army), were funded by the US Government (Hong, 2000).

2010: VIAC or VisLab Intercontinental Autonomous Challenge witnessed 13,000 km trip with four autonomous vehicles and negligible human intervention.

Features of an autonomous automobile system are [5]:

1. These systems are self-driven i.e. they don't require a human driver.
2. The control of the system is remote or by a highly data-driven, environment operated algorithm.
3. There are 3 components of this type of system: the physical system (hardware), the cyber system (the software) and the interfaces between them.

4. Environment is one of the components of the physical system.
5. The system has its own decision making algorithm wholly or partly.
6. It should have voice control so that the user can manually operate the logic accordingly.

Application:
The self-driving technology has impacted various domains of the industry like transportation, military, health, welfare and environment.

1. Autonomous food trucks and vans for food delivery.
2. Autonomous private cars.
3. Autonomous military patrolling trucks
4. Auto-flights.

Advantages:

1. Safety at road transportation will be at higher percentage and the accidents will reduce to a drastic level because the human error while driving will be zero. Human error causes 90% of the accidents in the world.
2. The traffic at roads will decrease and will be more organized.
3. People can have time to invest in other activities during their travel rather than fully focusing on driving.
4. The estimation of time in travelling will be more accurate as there is negligible or partly human involvement and negligible traffic. Even if a human instructs a path of travel to the control the estimated time can be accurately calculated.

8.5 Robotic System

A robot [9, 10] is a machine and robotics is a field of study and research on this machine.

A robot is designed for complicated, difficult and creative tasks that were earlier performed by humans.

Humans are an advanced animal and it has built a highly diverse and advanced environment for itself over years.

Since we are moving forward we have started developing systems that can work in the same way as we do, these systems are called robotic systems but the idea of a robot existed since 400BC.

The term robot was coined in 1920. The first robot was a humanoid, invented by W.H. Richards and presented in an exhibition of model engineers society in London. It was named Eric. It was electrically operated by electromagnets and a single motor. The first electronic autonomous robots with complex behavior were created by William Grey Walter in 1949 and the first digitally operated and programmable robot was invented by George Devol in 1954.

Characteristics of a robot [10, 16]

1. A robot has its own senses
2. A robot has its own intelligence
3. A robot has a physical aspect like humans for e.g. limbs but now with the growing research it isn't necessary to have one which looks like a human physic.
4. A robot is independent of his work and requires no human involvement.
5. A robot is power driven and operated.

The robotic industry [11] is a believer of three laws which are kept in mind while designing, integrating, instructing a robot. These laws are called laws of robotics.

The Three Laws are [9]:

1. A robot may not injure a human being or, through inaction, allow a human being to come to harm.
2. A robot must obey the orders given it by human beings except where such orders would conflict with the First Law.
3. A robot must protect its own existence as long as such protection does not conflict with the First or Second Laws.

Application of a robot [11, 12]:

1. Industry: most of the application of the robot lies in the industries. Car production automated production line. Packaging robot or a series of robots, mass production of electronics like PCBs, etc. These autonomous production by robots is preferred mainly because of the high amount

of cleanliness standards required while production that can't be maintained by humans at this rate.
2. Space probe robot
3. Tele operational robot
4. Domestic Robots for household work.
5. General purpose robots
6. Military robots including patrolling robots.
7. Healthcare and medical robots that can perform surgeries.
8. Research robots.

Advantages of using a robot [10, 11]:

1. Robotic production has higher cleanliness standards because of zero human presence. Once a robotic autonomous line is established and fully packed and vacuumed from inside not even a dirt particle can enter and this can be maintained, as long as we want. This can't be done by humans at this rate.
2. Robots can be used and sent to do tasks at high risk places to save human lives. For e.g. military guards at Siachen Glacier, health workers during COVID-19 epidemic.
3. The quality of product designed and built by a robot is more than a human.
4. The rate at which humans developed a product is less than a robot
5. A robot can teach or design another exact self or other type of robot and replicate without human help once fed with initial data.
6. Intelligent robots do not require large amounts of data to perform all possible tasks in a scenario.
7. Robots are useful when the manpower at an industry or a place required is not enough.

8.6   Mechatronics

Mechatronics is a systematic integration of mechanism, electronics and software and establishes a high communication between them to give an automated result.

The term mechatronics was coined by Mr. Tetsuro Moria, a senior engineer [8].

The purpose of mechatronics [13] was to research and design a more reliable system using a multidisciplinary approach.

These engineers are trained according to industry standards and embody the knowledge to create a fully automatic product.

Mechatronics is the most used and finest disciples of industry 4.0. It is the study where we learn how to fully or partly automate a production line, a home, a camp, etc. in all phases of products from design, testing up to manufacturing constitutes in it.

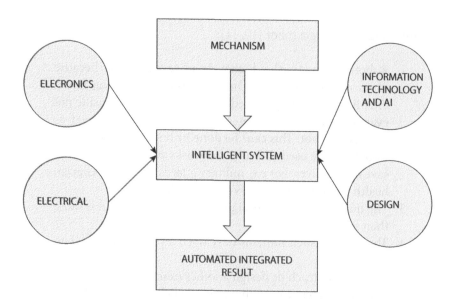

Characteristics of a Mechatronics System [13, 14, 16]:

1. It is a combination of mechanics, electronics and computing.
2. The result of multidisciplinary application in one product is automated or intelligent system capable of performing human like tasks (complex tasks).
3. Mechanism of a system is enhanced using electrical and electronics applications.
4. The precision of the system is high and is highly reliable.
5. Safety of the humans working, the system itself and its environment is taught to the system or programmed accordingly.
6. The task will be performed with improved efficiency.
7. The cost of production will be deceased using the system.

8. Cleanliness guidelines and environmental guidelines are met by the system.
9. The system can adapt and safeguard other humans.
10. It's easy for humans to control the system and handle its wear and tear over years, especially with intelligent systems.
11. The system embodies satisfaction and comfort to mankind.

Elements of mechatronics:

1. Mechanical System
    1. Actuators
        1. Solenoids
        2. Voice coils
        3. Motors
        4. Hydraulics and pneumatics
    2. Sensors
        1. Switches
        2. Strain gauge
        3. Digital encoder
        4. Accelerometer, etc.

2. Electrical system
    1. Input signal conditioning
        1. Time discrete system analysis
        2. Amplifiers
        3. DAC and ADC
    2. Digital controllers
        1. Logic circuits
        2. Microcontrollers
        3. PLC
        4. Control algorithms
        5. Artificial intelligence
        6. Data analysis
        7. Communication, etc.

3. Output signal conditioning
4. Graphical display
5. Error elimination and controllers
6. Modelling analysis and integrated design testing

Application of mechatronics systems [14]:

1. Consumer product
    1. Smart Home security
    2. Automated Washing machines
    3. Automated dishwashers
    4. Climate control curtains and air conditioning
    5. Home helper bot
    6. Smart toaster, etc.

2. Medical
    1. Smart medical assistance
    2. Implant devices

3. Manufacturing
    1. Painting machines and robots
    2. Assembly robots
    3. Packaging machines and robots
    4. Smart distribution in production line or factory
    5. Mixing of chemicals and preparation of drugs in a fully automated production line, etc.

References

1. Lee, E.A. and Seshia, S.A., *An Introductory Textbook on Cyber-Physical Systems*, Proceedings of the 2010 Workshop on Embedded Systems Education, 1, 1–6, 2010. https://doi.org/10.1145/1930277.1930278.
2. *Industry*, Wikipedia, The Free Encyclopedia, https://en.wikipedia.org/wiki/Industry_(economics)
3. Pouspourika, K., *The Four Industrial Revolutions*, June, 2019, https://ied.eu/project-updates/the-4-industrial-revolutions/.
4. Wikipedia contributors, *Fourth Industrial Revolution*, Wikipedia, The Free Encyclopedia, 2020, September 2020, from https://en.wikipedia.org/w/index.php?title=Fourth_Industrial_Revolution&oldid=976126916.
5. Tempo Automation, *Features of Today's Best Autonomous Cars*, < https://www.tempoautomation.com/blog/features-of-todays-best-autonomous-cars/>, April 2019.
6. Martínez-Díaza, M. and Soriguerab, F., Autonomous vehicles: theoretical and practical challenges. *XIII Conference on Transport Engineering, CIT 2018*, https://doi.org/10.1016/j.trpro.2018.10.103, October 2018.

7. GeeksforGeeks, *Self-Driving Car Technology*, https://www.geeksforgeeks.org/self-driving-car-technology/#:~:text=Self-driving%20means%20the%20autonomous%20driving%20of%20a%20vehicle,by%20Google%2C%20Uber%2C%20Tesla%20and%20other%20technology%20companies, Jun, 2019.

8. Wikipedia contributors, *Mechatronics*, Wikipedia, The Free Encyclopedia, 2020, September 2020, from https://en.wikipedia.org/w/index.php?title=Mechatronics&oldid=976384613.

9. Wikipedia contributors, *Laws of robotics*, Wikipedia, The Free Encyclopedia, 2020, September 2020, from https://en.wikipedia.org/w/index.php?title=Laws_of_robotics&oldid=953846832.

10. Wikipedia contributors, *Robot*, Wikipedia, The Free Encyclopedia, 2020, September 2020, from https://en.wikipedia.org/w/index.php?title=Robot&oldid=976688128.

11. Wikipedia contributors, *Robotics*, Wikipedia, The Free Encyclopedia, 2020, September 2020, from https://en.wikipedia.org/w/index.php?title=Robotics&oldid=978394327.

12. Wikipedia contributors, *Robot Operating System*, Wikipedia, The Free Encyclopedia, September 2020, from https://en.wikipedia.org/w/index.php?title=Robot_Operating_System&oldid=974664176.

13. Pelliccio, A., Ottaviano, E., Rea, P., Digital and Mechatronic Technologies Applied to the Survey of Brownfields, https://www.igi-global.com/dictionary/digital-and-mechatronic-technologies-applied-to-the-survey-of-brownfields/48869, 2015.

14. Thorat, S., Advantages and Disadvantages of Mechatronics System, https://learnmech.com/advantages-and-disadvantages-of-mechatronics-system/.

15. Thorat, S., Example Of Mechatronics System, GMT, https://learnmech.com/what-are-some-example-of-mechatronics-system/, Sep 2020.

16. Emery, C., 5 Defining Qualities of Robots, https://www.techopedia.com/2/31572/trends/5-defining-qualities-of-robot, September 2016.

9

Role of Recent Technologies in Cognitive Systems

V. Pradeep Kumar[1]*, L. Pallavi[1] and Kolla Bhanu Prakash[2]

[1]Department of Computer Science and Engineering, B.V. Raju Institute of Technology, Narsapur, Medak, Telangana, India
[2]Department of Computer Science and Engineering, K.L. Deemed to be University, Vijayawada A.P, India

Abstract

Cognitive Computing is a new computing paradigm which has its unique nature of simulating the thought process of human brain. Its evolution depends on the usage of artificial intelligence algorithms, data mining techniques for analytics and automation of the natural language processing need to understand the nature of human beings usage of language. It goes beyond computing where it frames rules and programs for taking decision at different critical instances and analyzing different forms of digital information. Linguistic analysis in natural language processing provides details of its importance in building cognitive systems. The critical part of cognitive system lies in generating rules by using different methodologies of knowledge representation. The processing of huge digital information by cognitive systems was done through support of cloud and distributed computing technologies. Importance of cognitive analytics was highlighted by studying the automatic fraud detection with support of fuzzy systems and design of health care decision support system for detection of cardiac disease. Finally advanced application using cognitive systems were highlighted with facts.

Keywords: Cognitive systems, natural language processing, knowledge representation, cloud computing models, fuzzy systems, machine learning

*Corresponding author: 1pradeepvadla@gmail.com

Kolla Bhanu Prakash, G. R. Kanagachidambaresan, V. Srikanth, E. Vamsidhar (eds.) Cognitive Engineering for Next Generation Computing: A Practical Analytical Approach, (231–264) © 2021 Scrivener Publishing LLC

9.1 Introduction

Cognitive computing is a computing domain which tries to simulate the complex thought process of the human brain. In simple terms, this computing model was trying to mimic the human brain in taking effective decision at critical situations. It is trying to build highly automated systems in IT industry without any involvement of human in decision making for some critical tasks in business processes. The initial generations of computing systems were concentrating in solving high computation tasks like solving polynomial functions and developing programmable systems like ENIAC to compute digital data. Cognitive computing models itself as new era of computing belonging to third type of generation of systems where huge amount of simulations of computing was done through building a complex neural network taking unknown inputs. It mimics the human brain central nervous systems and performs analytics in providing good insights for effective decision making.

9.1.1 Definition and Scope of Cognitive Computing

Cognitive computing doesn't have any specific definition like earlier computing models. Most of the cognitive computing systems carry a specific characteristic of solving a complex problem by analyzing the context where they are applied. Thus the definition of cognitive computing would be like building a computing system for computing a complex problem which has nature of carrying ambiguity and uncertainty while providing a solution and it is highly context computable means it performs analysis depending upon the applicability of solution with specific information for particular situations and finally it acts as a genuine assistant for the users who are involved in solving these critical problems or situations.

The scope of cognitive systems was studied by IBM for business value—"Your Cognitive Future" [1], they stated it comprises of engagement, decision and discovery. In engagement the cognitive systems will use their huge repositories of data which is structured or unstructured, frame rules based on the language the user interacts with the system and it even creates hypothesis to analyze the information which it is communicated to the user. Most of the Chabot's creation is a good example for this type of scope of cognitive systems. The decision making scope of cognitive systems comes with use of reinforcement learning technique where in any new information is added it gets self-reorganize its results and actions and build an automatic decision support system. The discovery scope of cognitive systems is a very advanced task which involves building efficient understanding of large amount of information and gain insights using deep learning mechanisms.

9.1.2   Architecture of Cognitive Computing

Figure 9.1 gives the layered architecture view of cognitive computing. Layer 1 is the physical layer which holds the components with which cognitive systems will gather information with interaction. It comprises generally 5G networks for communications, Internet of Thing devices (Sensors and Actuators) to gather sensors data from the external environment of the products and Mechanical Robots which performs actions based on the instructions of cognitive systems. Layer 2 represents the infrastructure layer where cloud is used to store huge volumes of data generated from those IoT devices and it even consists of workstations for high end systems for processing the data and send information to mechanical robots to take automatic decisions depending on the current context. Layer 3 is a cognitive computing framework where large amount of machine learning and deep learning

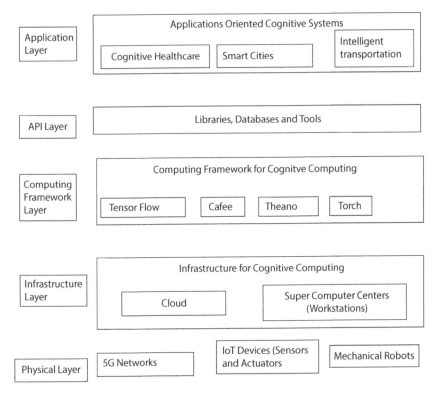

Figure 9.1 Layered Architecture of Cognitive Computing [2].

algorithm implemented tools like tensor flow, torch, etc. are used for processing the data and generate results according to the context where these cognitive systems are built. Layer 4 comprises of huge libraries, databases and tools for support of implementation of cognitive systems. Layer 5 represents the application oriented cognitive systems layer where cognitive systems are used in real time world for managing critical tasks of the users. Like example for doctors are the users who use cognitive health care system interface to understand the patient health conditions and monitor through specific sensors without his physical presence in hospital. Like-wise smart cities and intelligent transportation where cognitive systems are playing critical role in automating various tasks like smart controlling of wastage of water usage, automatic street lights, providing traffic less congestion routes for the users while on drive to their office or home etc.

9.1.3 Features and Limitations of Cognitive Systems

The prominent features of cognitive systems are been framed based on its motivation of automating the tasks without intervention of human brain in solving complex problems. The cognitive computing consortium has recommended following features to be incorporated for any commercial or research oriented built cognitive system.

Adaptability—All the cognitive system more or less meant for mimicking the human brain which takes decision very dynamic by understanding the current context or environment where the task need to be performed. Many tasks which need to be handled by cognitive system are not isolated tasks they are more dynamic in nature of gathering data, fixing goals of systems and collecting requirements of system.

Highly Interactive—The built cognitive system has many elements like processing units, memory, specific devices, cloud storage and user interface. Thus all cognitive systems provide good interactive interfaces where users will provide inputs through text, voice or images and it should analyze these inputs with Natural Language processing or computer vision processing mechanisms to provide desired results for users.

More iterative and state fullness: The cognitive system should run for more iterations for gathering the correct inputs for specific tasks at different instances and save the state of the system at that iteration such that any changes or failures are happened with the system it will recover from the saved and continue its tasks without any stoppage. Thus cognitive system does more input data validation and check for its quality with various stated methodologies and provide reliable information to the users or system to take decision accordingly.

Highly Contextual: The cognitive system should understand the current context of the system inputs such as the type of data, profile of users, processes, critical tasks, format of data, syntax and semantic of data and its specific goals. It deals with both structured and unstructured data or digital information along with some sensory inputs like vision, gestures, audio or video which are provided by specific sensors in the cognitive system.

Limitations of Cognitive Systems

Minimized Risk Analysis—The cognitive systems are typically doesn't have in built risk management mechanisms to analyze risks when unstructured data provided as input.

Diligent Training Process—Cognitive systems are more dependent on the training the systems with huge set of data input and much of its computation is getting wasted in training the system itself and understanding the nature of input.

High Usage of Augmented Intelligence Then Artificial Intelligence—Most of the cognitive systems are fulfilling its scope of engagement and decision factors. Majority of them are not trained to handle the scope of discovery which need high usage of artificial intelligence algorithms to take accurate decision and they are remaining as only intelligent assistant which are only giving suggestions not taking critical decisions.

Security—At the point when advanced gadgets oversee basic data, the subject of security naturally comes into the image. With the ability to deal with a lot of information and dissect the equivalent, psychological processing has a noteworthy test concerning information security and encryption. With an ever increasing number of associated gadgets coming into the image, intellectual registering should consider the issues identified with a security break by building up a full-evidence security plan that likewise has a component to distinguish dubious action to advance information honesty.

Adoption—The greatest obstacle in the way of progress for any new innovation is intentional reception. To make psychological figuring fruitful, it is fundamental to build up a drawn out vision of how the new innovation will improve cycles and organizations. Through joint effort between different partners, for example, innovation designers, undertakings, government and people, the reception cycle can be smoothed out. Simultaneously, it is basic to have an information protection system that will additionally help appropriation of psychological figuring.

Change Management—Change the executives are another pivotal test that intellectual figuring should survive. Individuals are impervious to change as a result of their normal human conduct and as psychological figuring has the ability to learn like people, individuals are frightful that machines would supplant people sometime in the not so distant future. This has proceeded to affect the development possibilities to a significant level. In any case, intellectual innovation is worked to work in a state of harmony with people. People will support the innovation by taking care of data into the frameworks. This makes it an extraordinary case of a human-machine cooperation that individuals should acknowledge.

Lengthy Development Cycles: Probably the best test is the time put resources into the advancement of situation based applications through intellectual figuring. Intellectual registering at present is being created as a summed up arrangement—this implies the arrangement can't be actualized over various industry sections without ground-breaking improvement groups and a lot of time to build up an answer.

Extensive advancement cycles make it harder for littler organizations to create intellectual capacities all alone. With time, as the improvement lifecycles will in general abbreviate, psychological registering will secure a greater stage later on without a doubt.

9.2 Natural Language Processing for Cognitive Systems

Cognitive computing deals with more computation of unstructured data. It needs high capability to analyze on various contexts. Most of the business organizations generate unstructured data which are very complex to parse and difficult to tag with the meaning. Different tools are used to categorize the words, thesaurus, dictionaries, catalogues, and language models. Natural Language processing deals with text-based data for the cognitive system. It helps in establishing relationships by using different techniques.

9.2.1 Role of NLP in Cognitive Systems

NLP uses specific techniques for handling textual data. Generation of meaning from the unstructured text data is a critical task; it needs to mention grammar rules for the word, phrases, sentences, or document for creating the predictable patterns with in the language. NLP apply inference rules by using known rules and patterns in the context of co-occurring of words. Further these rules are applied to all over the documents in the database by establishing relationships.

Context Importance

In general a cognitive system will use tools to extract data from different sources of its availability for understanding the relationships among the other text elements of a document and then use that information for giving answers to the questions posed by the user. NLP supports cognitive systems in providing wide variety of mechanisms to understand the terms in the documents and generate meaning to those terms. It even performs pattern checking for establishing relationship among those terms according to the context. Context plays a prominent role in answering the questions as human's way of reading and putting comments in the text-based documents depends on it for assigning meaning to those terms. Context in general helps the cognitive system in understanding the patterns and relationships among those terms of text based documents and remove the ambiguity in using of those terms in documents.

NLP has the ability to build an effective psychological framework from the text documents. The word or term available in a sentence will constitute to get the knowledge of expressions made by the authors through their comprehensive writing and even specific goal is clearly mentioned for easy archiving in knowledge base. The genuine significance of text based information is evaluated by analyzing the knowledge base. The critical task is to retrieve connections between words and expressions which are identified in a document with relevant to the article goal. Most of cognitive systems try to establish relationship between words to decide meaning with perfect assessment. The huge uncertainty in language is caused because of different words having different implications rely on the article being written with different words in a context of expression, sentence or section. For example if a truck driver want to use such cognitive system which is built with support of NLP he tries to enquire about much options for his safe and fast travel to reach his destination with in an optimized time. At first he queries for seven day weather report on the route of his travel locations and then looks for any road repairs or permissions on that road for amount of tons of goods he is carrying in his truck. The results for the enquiries posted by truck driver in that cognitive system will provide him with different options from its knowledge base and provide more accurate results towards focused solutions. The same queries what the current truck driver posts will not be similar when he starts for return journey. Hence knowledge base needs to be reconstructed for depending on driver posts by studying his psychology of his mood of travel in a hurry tour or like vacation tour and provide variable results from the system.

Connectivity of Words

Fixing the context based on the words usage in text based documents is a complex task as humans general tendency of using different words depending on the perceptiveness of understanding the same context differs among two individuals. Generating absolute rules for such terms is difficult for any systems. Thus NLP uses different language rules in understanding those contexts by generating more questions to users and gather good insights of that usage of terms in the context. It tries to connect among those similar context terms for generating a meaning to those sentences used by users while analyzing the documents.

9.2.2   Linguistic Analysis

Performing the analysis of language to understand the meaning of the terms is automated in NLP by using its statistical techniques and building language models on rules. NLP purely focus during this linguistic analysis to understand the underlying meaning of those terms by using grammatical rules of that language.

Identification of Language and its Tokenization

The first step in analyzing any text present in the documents is to identify the language which is used for writing or speaking with the help of specific terms. The terms are represented with a sequence of characters used by the language and these are called tokens. Tokenization gets its prominence because most language uses many types of separator in their phrases and sentence generations.

Phonetics and Structure of Words

Phonetics or the notations used in many languages for fixing the ascent of the words or terms while pronunciations and study of these mechanisms is called phonology. It plays very prominent role while building speech to text recognition cognitive systems where they track the pronunciation of users while uttering those terms and study the patterns of usage of words for different feelings of an individual like he is in angry, confused or happy etc. Most of the ascent of words and their articulation will emphasize the feeling of the users while using the system.

The other mechanism which is very important in understanding a language is morphology the study of structure of usage of words. Morphology comes out with many language options depending on the usage of words like singular, plural and many other features of language. Each word in a language is partitioned in to a segment known as morphemes which help in understanding the meaning of the terms. Cognitive computing uses these language features to understand the user's questions and find answers from its repository of knowledge base. Depending on the language morphology constructs a dictionary of words and adds many words based on change of language rules. Most prominent mechanism of NLP used by cognitive systems for understanding words of any language is parts of speech tagging. It helps in categorizing words with definite meaning for different disciplines using that language.

Lexical and Syntactic Analysis of Language

The popular mechanisms in linguistic analysis for understanding particular language are lexical, syntactical and semantic analysis. Lexical analysis builds the language dictionary based on words occurring in a particular context. It generally does analysis of stream of characters and generated tokens and assigns a language specified tags for easy understanding of the term. The lexical analyzer uses regular language grammar rules of natural language and determines the acceptance of term or word as a valid word of language. It checks further this term in the corpus or database of language words and then finalize its occurrence in the context. Syntax analyzer uses context free language grammar rules to check the terms contextual occurrence and infer language rules to associate a meaning to the term in that context. Depending on domain knowledge or discipline where these terms are used the syntax analyzer will assign new infer rules for the terms acceptance for that context. Syntactical analysis of NLP supports the cognitive systems in understanding the meaning of term occurring in the context and makes the job of question-answering process easy.

Grammar Construction

Grammar construction in linguistic analysis is an important approach for cognitive systems. The interpretation or parsing of syntactic analysis needs specific grammar rules to generate a meaningful sentence or phrases from those word or terms. Grammar construction need to even have a check of optimizing the way of representing relationship between words and their meaning of occurring in a context. The grammar construction need to use all the features of linguistic analysis like phonology, morphology, syntactic, semantics, pragmatics, discourse and prosodic characteristics for generating efficient rules for defining deep structure for particular language.

Discourse and Pragmatic Analysis

Discourse and pragmatic analysis are very important in cognitive computing in dealing with complex issues of understanding the contexts. Most of the terms usage will change according to their occurrences in specific domains. Discourse will determine the association of terms for a particular context based on their relationships with the domain. Pragmatic analysis does similar task of discourse but it reframe the inference rules for easy parsing by syntactic analyzer to make the context more meaningful.

Managing Ambiguity of Words

NLP uses efficient algorithms for managing the ambiguity of words and resolving their occurrence in a specific context. Statistical techniques are used to compute the probability factor of occurrence of terms for removing the ambiguity in the usage of terms in a particular context. Many uncertainties of terms occurrence are managed by probabilistic algorithms, machine learning algorithms and hidden Markov model techniques to ensure the accuracy of generating meaningful sentence.

9.2.3 Example Applications Using NLP With Cognitive Systems

NLP has become an efficient tool to manage the human interaction with computers or machines. The cognitive computing uses these tools for building applications for betterment of society and understanding the human nature for facing particular situations. Top MNC's like IBM, Microsoft and Google have established special research development centers for building cognitive system dependent applications for their customers. Following are some of the example applications of NLP with cognitive systems.

Improving the Shopping Experience of Customers

Many of the shopping web-site builds their applications integrated with NLP to analyze the searches of consumers and take their comments about the products. The cognitive system will try to work on improve the search experience of customer by providing more options for categorized search .NLP used to analyze the customer experience by creating a chat window where in customer will share his views of product directly and web-site will come with more options as it interacts with the customer and provide ultimate satisfaction to the customer with the words and options which are provided to them.

Utilizing the Wide Features of Connectivity of Internet of Things Devices
Internet of things has made available of sensors equipped with many
mechanical and electronic devices and made them able to take decisions
at critical situations and change its state conditions. Automatic Traffic
re-routing mechanism inside the car will use NLP to interact with traffic
sensors and get the latest updates about the traffic from different part of
city. This cognitive system even can generate chat with traffic police men or
key managers of traffic and get instant updates about bad weather, rallies,
and concerts happening in city and provide alternate route options for car
drivers. Efficient analysis need to be done by cognitive system as it needs
to integrate the chat with traffic managers to interpret there textual data
and weather prediction application perform correlation and finally recommend the next action of re-routing your car with safe and happy drive.

Consumer Analysis
Consumer analysis is a big critical task for any manufacturer. Most of the
consumers of any type of goods they move to social networking web site
to share the views about the products what they purchased. They not only
share their feedback some consumers even post its working scenarios or
failure situations so that others get acknowledged before buying that product. Cognitive system combines the sentiment analysis of consumers with
NLP to understand the key terms used by the consumers in explaining his
view of usage of product. Many companies can employ employee to understand the consumers feedback about their products by not only through
social networking web site but also through their customer representative
who will a have direct dialogue with consumers and finally correlate all the
facts and analyze the manufacturing of their new product and predict it
sales in future to achieve good satisfaction for consumers.

9.3 Taxonomies and Ontologies of Knowledge Representation for Cognitive Systems

Cognitive computing gives more importance to gaining of knowledge from
the data. It quite often does reconstruct and update the data according to
the application requirements. It considers data as more important aspect in
studying the context or environment where it is collected and represent in
different forms for analysis. It always improves the decision making mechanism by taking the inputs from the knowledge base where the updated
data is used for further processing. It builds the systems with important

facts and figures as similar to human being concern. It should follow some standard way of representing the data as objects for establishing relationships using taxonomies and ontologies.

9.3.1 Taxonomies and Ontologies and Their Importance in Knowledge Representation

Taxonomies are a hierarchical way of representing data of information belonging particular domain of study. Each path from top to down of hierarchy represents separate set of classification with similar properties. Most of the hierarchical structure represents the parent-child relationship among the category of elements and all child category elements will inherit the properties from the parent elements. Ontologies does different job apart from representation like taxonomies. Ontologies try to associate rules for each of the category of elements such that it denotes the conditions for transition from one category of information to another with certain criteria. Most of the ontologies represent the semantic information which is used for decision making and problem solving. As cognitive computing deals with information which gets very frequent updates depending on the context hence it need taxonomies to categorize the data in specified hierarchy and generate useful information by using some rules for decision making and problem solving in that environment. Figure 9.2 gives the example of taxonomy of text media where different categories are shown. The category of books hierarchy is elaborated where similar attributes of data can be gathered like author, publisher, and publication dates and maintained as separate data in knowledge base. Ontologies for this taxonomy are like fixing rules for selecting certain category of books with specific study that can be done by users like example here if user wants to select a category of a book of programming languages it will move in hierarchy from text media to books and from books category we move to the computer books where user can clearly achieve his solution of finding the programming language books.

The other form of knowledge representation is shown in Figure 9.3 for a Tic-Tae-Toe game in which rules were defined in one table and the movements of the users are shown in another part of figure in the form of a tree where the possibilities of players are captured. The game rules are like each player fills the marks and the player who gets his all marks in a row (up, down or cross) will win the game. The movements can be captures with alphabets representing column and row as B1, B2, B3 and A1, A2, A3.To implement this game the developer can use this rules and matrix representations and process all possible moves to win the game.

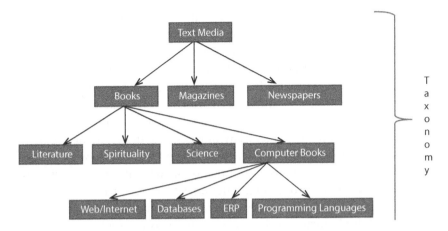

Figure 9.2 Taxonomy of Text Media.

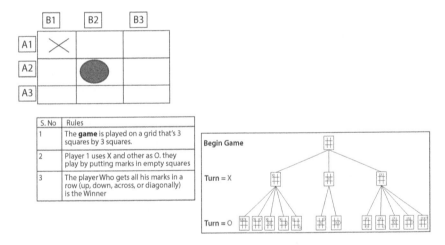

Figure 9.3 Knowledge Representation of data for Tic-Tac-Toe game along with rules.

9.3.2 How to Represent Knowledge in Cognitive Systems?

The knowledge base is constructed in cognitive systems by following scheme of representation in terms of taxonomies and ontologies. Planning the representation of data in the cognitive systems is a critical step for achieving the goal of the solution to a problem occurring in a context. Domain knowledge plays a prominent role while establishing relationship between elements of information stored in knowledge base. Most preferable form of storing the information happens in terms of objects which are having specific attributes as its properties. After creating objects it becomes easy for the cognitive system in building relationships among the objects. Any updates on creating new properties or establishing relationships based on the behavior of systems will change as it gains knowledge with new information added to knowledge base. The cognitive computing uses different representation of data structure to hold these elements like simple lists, database records, multi-dimensional structures data in form of hierarchy of trees. The designers of cognitive computing data models for a particular context will decide what type of data modeling tools to be used for operational data. It can be in terms of procedural form, list processing, functional or object-oriented to specify the structure to be implemented depending on the requirements of the context. Multiple forms of data need to be incorporated in knowledge base because system relies on its operational tasks in domain where the context of accessing data changes depending on the user's intention of usage data by a system in different perspective.

Building Knowledge From Multiple Views of a System
In the Washing Machine diagnostics example covered for three issues as shown in Figures 9.4(a), (b) and (c) represent three separate knowledge models for each issue and treat them as subsystem. All expert manuals are been arranged by the study of subsystems. The manuals are constructed based on analysis made by the knowledge of mechanic and how they approach to address a specific issue by doing diagnosis for a particular problem occurring in a system. As many of system issues dependent on each other so whenever issue raises thinking in on only subsystem point of view may not find good solution to resolve the issue. Multiple subsystems need to be studied simultaneously in order to identify the issue. For an analogy let us consider the healthcare system which considers two subsystems for diagnosing blood pressure and diabetes. But these subsystems are inter-dependent for some specific patient's case. Oncology is one complex domain where similar complications involving several subsystems are needs to be studied by referring to different journals, articles, discussions with other colleague's expert in the domain to understand the case. One view of representation of problem will need more relevant knowledge to build the system for effective diagnosis.

Most of the Cognitive systems are built on developing knowledge by segmenting it into different subsystem study and whenever any analysis needed it will consider the complete system as one view and take decision. As new inventions are carried out for solving specific issue they may take up the study of integration of other subsystems to build the knowledge base in cognitive system. In general in healthcare treatment for cancer patients will differ based on the organ infected with it. Many studies are performed to analyze the cancer infection at the organ boundaries and brief study of patient's genome is considered to study the attributes which to be compared. Similitude investigation for social insurance diagnostics is a significant utilization of machine-learning algorithms. This has prompted the disclosure of promising examples between patients, genomes, malignant

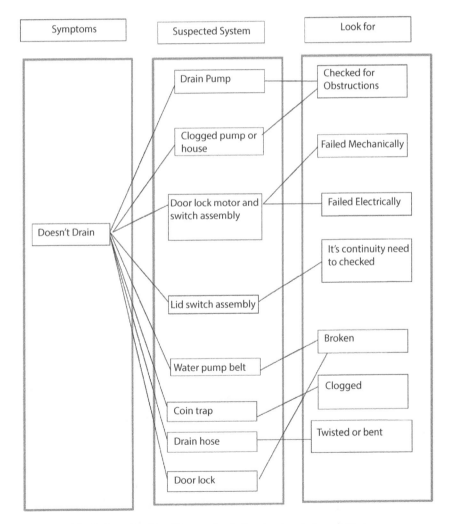

Figure 9.4(a) Washing Machine Diagnostics & Repair when is doesn't Drain.

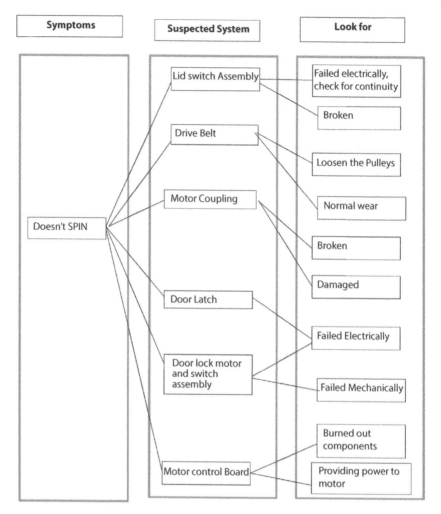

Figure 9.4(b) Washing Machine Diagnostics & Repair when is doesn't Spin.

growths, medicines, and results. Thus, new connections have been found and new medicines have been applied. This sort of revelation calls attention to the incentive in conceding apportioning as long as conceivable to forestall missing connections.

Figures 9.4(a), (b) and (c) discuss about the automated diagnosis of knowledge base building for washing machine repair for specific issues like when it doesn't spin, doesn't drain and water pumping is slow the respective subsystems sequences are analyzed and the final cause of the component which need to be repair is identified.

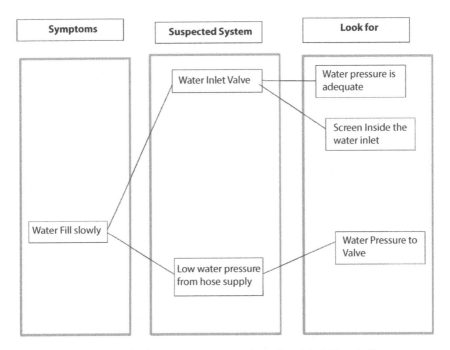

Figure 9.4(c) Washing Machine Diagnostics & Repair when Water Flow is Slow.

9.3.3 Methodologies Used for Knowledge Representation in Cognitive Systems

The knowledge representation in cognitive systems can be as simple as a chart or complicated with a full complex terms used in a domain field of interest with different representations and definitions. This section provides different methodologies of representing knowledge in cognitive systems.

Taxonomies

Taxonomy is a representation of knowledge based data in a hierarchical form of objects of a particular domain. It provides the details of relationship among the objects with specified attributes for categorization. The categorization of data objects is done with specified rules which would provide the information with nature of consistent, complete and unambiguous. The cognitive systems use the taxonomies as reference objects arranged in a tree structure which represents parent–child hierarchy of object oriented programming and stored information in either tables or lists. The rules which are framed in taxonomies are to be consistent throughout the life time of data stored for a particular context.

Ontologies

Ontology is mechanism adding more elaborative information than taxonomy. It provides details like vocabulary, definitions and rules belonging to a specific domain. It need more detail domain knowledge to fix the rules and get the agreement from all designers who are building the knowledge base for that domain.

Simple Trees

It is a logical data structure that denotes the parent and child relationships. It is a model in which relationships are more formalized and rigid. The details are stored in a table with (key, value) pair where key would be parent and element is the value and it is more efficient way to access. It is popularly used by data analytic tools.

Semantic Web

Most of the web documents are unstructured and they are maintained in resource description framework (RDF) and addressed with specific URLs. The semantic information will add specific meaning details to those web documents. The cognitive systems which are mostly depend on web interface interaction of users will uses this form of semantic web documents without extensive pre-processing to hide unstructured details.

9.4 Support of Cloud Computing for Cognitive Systems

The cognitive computing depends on huge computational services for meeting the needs of distributed applications. The large computational resources which are specific to hardware, software and networking services of cloud computing can be made available to cognitive computing for balancing the workload. Large scale cognitive can be operational by using cloud computing technology.

9.4.1 Importance of Shared Resources of Distributed Computing in Developing Cognitive Systems

Current cognitive computing models need a wide variety of platforms for consolidating the massive amount of information from various sources for processing in a sophisticated manner. The cognitive system must implement advanced analytics on huge and complex data for processing.

The cloud computing is the only choice for cognitive system for managing that huge data and complex processing abilities with less cost-effective and high efficiency. The cloud is a method for providing distributed shared resources for cognitive system. It not only manages the shared resources but also makes large storage capabilities, networking, and distributed software, variable deployment models for different business processes.

Cloud providers develop a standard interfaces for managing large cognitive workloads with high efficiency. The cloud consumers like firms who are using these cognitive systems build applications to get benefit from the cloud model with pay as you use services. Any instant scalability of resources is also possible in this cloud model distributed environment.

9.4.2 Fundamental Concepts of Cloud Used in Building Cognitive Systems

Cognitive computing have become more operational with the nature of distributed model of cloud computing. Most of the web data is stored in cloud and used by cognitive system to analyze them to generate patterns depending on the environment where it is operational. Cloud environment provides good orchestration environment where cognitive system uses its high processing abilities to solve complex problems of business on demand. Cloud computing is a service-provisioning model which provides services at any degree to which cognitive system can access and manage its data for efficient processing. Workload balancing of cloud computing is one of the important task which provides many cognitive systems to be operational without any delay of executing them for operational environments. The operational cost of cognitive systems has become more reliable based on its usage with help of cloud computing principle pay as you usage concept.

Cloud Computing Deployment Models

Table 9.1 gives more information on various attributes of cloud deployment models. As cognitive computing needs more flexibility in terms of knowledge base management it prefers to depend more on hybrid cloud model where in dynamically cloud provides will collaborate or integrate with others to provide efficient computing or storage services for fulfilling the system needs. Cognitive systems need a wide variety of workloads with less cost effective and it depends on multiple sources of data with elaborative API services for handling the situations occurring in the real time environment and providing solutions with the flexibility of hybrid cloud

Table 9.1 Features of Cloud Deployment Models for building Cognitive Systems.

Types of cloud / Key Factors	Public cloud	Private cloud	Manage service providers	Hybrid cloud
Managed Mode	Multi-Tenant and Shared Environment	Isolated own Company Data Center	Managed by third party based on industry specific needs	Multiple vendors like private ,managed and public providers in combination
Workload	Difficult to Optimize the services for different applications	Effective optimized services as they are managed for single organizations workloads	Workloads are automated based on the organization needs	Automated Scalability of workloads are managed depending on customers request
Payment Model	Pay based on Usage of all Services	Fixed payment model at once when it is created for organization	Automated payment services based on the demand	Hybrid payment model constructed for all sort of customers demand requests
Services and Security	Provides automated service and security management with agreed SLA (Service Level Agreements	Optimized services in terms of both security and services offered to customers	More effective mechanisms are provided for automated services and security	Still Research is happening in building effective service and security management

deployment model. It builds the system from heterogeneous sources of big data and provides reasonable results with low cost in an effective manner. The Managed Service Provider model is one of the effective cloud models with more set of machine learning algorithms supporting for building cognitive systems. It ensures to provide more satisfied customer requests for continuing their services without any delay. Cognitive system building requirements of single organization depending on their private cloud or global management of their resources through public cloud are analyzed to server multiple customers with good infrastructure facilities.

Cloud Computing Service Models

The business intelligence services are the most prominent service which were used by business organization to perform analytics on large amount of data and is provided by one of the service models of cloud computing for giving more efficient results then earlier. Increased data storage and managing good view of dashboard for more analytics is really made possible using software as a service. High end storage systems are available using Infrastructure as a service and more efficient APIs, computational algorithms and advanced analytics are provided through platform as a service. Table 9.2 gives concept mapping representation of cloud service models with their details about characteristics, advantages and disadvantages.

Workload Management

Resource management and provisioning is an effective feature in cloud computing where workload management is performed by using high end load balancing algorithms for managing the resources usage effectively in cloud. The cognitive computing needs flexible workload management to perform wide variety analytics on huge data. Data is consistently updated depending on the requirements of the environment and large amount of resources are utilized to achieve this task effectively through workload management of cloud computing.

Cloud API Management for Text Analytics

Table 9.3 highlights the text analytics covered by the top cloud service providers for building the cognitive systems. The cloud providers built APIs for managing text processing more effective manner.

Cloud Security

Cognitive computing is widely used by business organizations to manage their services more efficiently. As much amount of information or

Table 9.2 Concept Mapping Representation of Cloud Service Models.

	Paradigm design	Features	Benefits	Limitations
IaaS Model	It provision physical infrastructure requirements of cloud consumers like Compute, Storage and Network	• Virtualized environments. • Computer hardware and network facilities. • Effective Service Level Agreements. • Utility Computing Payment Model.	• Pre-configured environment. • Latest Technology for infrastructure equipment's. • Secured computing platform. • Ability to manage huge service demand.	• Dependent on vendor capabilities. • Huge costs. • Security measures in terms of utilization of its services.
PaaS Model	It provides licensing administration of utilizing developing platforms	• Building applications support. • Licensing administrations.	• Services for concurrency, scalability, failover. • Ability to share code. • Integration with web based services and databases. • Pay Per Usage billing models	Security issues need to be incorporated while sharing code among heterogeneous platforms.
SaaS Model	It provides application delivery model of one to many and network based management of commercially available software's	• Network –based management of commercially available S/W. • Application Delivery. • Centralized Enhancement and patch updating	• CRM Management • Shared with application vendors. • Reduced administration and management burdens • Increase availability of applications	Security impact of users who are using those application services.

Table 9.3 Features of Text Analytics Covered by the Top Cloud Service Providers.

Features	Amazon Comprehend	Google Cloud Natural Languages	Microsoft Azure Text Processing Analytics	IBM Watson NLP for Text Processing
Entity Extraction	✓	✓	✓	✓
Sentiment Analysis	✓	✓	✓	✓
Syntax Analysis (Spell Check etc.)	✗	✓	✓	✗
Topic Modeling	✓	✓	✗	✗
POS Tagging	✓	✓	✓	✓

data of knowledge base is made available online in cloud storage open to many users. The content of knowledge base need to be secured and only authenticated users need to be provisioned to use those applications of business and access the data. Cloud computing has come up with the effective identity management system and high end encryption techniques to safe guard the knowledge base from hackers or unauthorized users who want to access for corrupting it or removing to defame the business activities.

Data Integration in Cloud
Data integration in cloud provides wide variety opportunities for building cognitive system to manage data analytics at an increased phase and provide results to as many people in the organization to access it while taking decision at critical situations. Different data sources need to be integrated as data is managed in different forms at different locations of the organization. All these data need to be processed at critical situations and make available to all the stake holders of the organization without any delay.

9.5 Cognitive Analytics for Automatic Fraud Detection Using Machine Learning and Fuzzy Systems

Fraud detection has more relevance in application of data science particularly to analyze the framework model for understanding the frauds made by the hackers for their financial gain. In contrast of stir demonstrating, proposal framework, credit scoring and comparable frameworks, misrepresentation discovery displaying is considerably more perplexing for programmed arrangement advancement. Absence of target factors, shrouded rare patterns, indications rather than sureness adds to difficulties around there when we are discussing programmed extortion location arrangements. Arrangement on experimental information demonstrates effectiveness of proposed strategy even with restricted utilization of strategies. This methodology mimics human cycle of taught surmise. Intellectual strategies like proposed system have assignment to be comfortable with human insightful instrument with capacity to take care of explicit issues. Use of some basic strategies in various ways, remain solitary or as indispensable piece of fluffy master framework, add to thought of development intellectual information science answer for extortion recognition

9.5.1   Role of Machine Learning Concepts in Building Cognitive Analytics

Benford's law is one of the popular probability factor considerations in computing analytics of fraud detection. An efficient framework is built for accomplishing the psychological evaluation of fraudsters in doing their frauds. The people who are specialists in identifying the fraud in finance sector are falling short of proofs from the information what they have. Big challenge is that to build a framework for fraud detection using cognitive system. Benford's law as a whole can't work as an effective component of cognitive system in building framework for fraud detection and the components like fuzzy system computation, study of social network can be integrated to give efficient results.

The job of fundamental measurement techniques in fraud detection location is significant in various parts of utilization [7] considering accomplishing instinct; one of the factual measures which can be extremely helpful is normalized values. Tale about misrepresentation, are frequently anecdote about boundaries. That implies if for instance hoodlum take charge card he will attempt in brief timeframe to make whatever number as could be allowed exchange with high cutoff use. That is outrageous conduct, and it tends to be perceived by computation of boundaries and normalized values on customer level. Customer level implies that every proprietor of Visa has exceptional social attributes and computation of boundaries on populace level won't offer us a response. Convincing the suspicious cases involved in fraud detection by implementing Benford's law is not an adequate sign with respect to fraud detection. The convergence of information from irregular sources and factual measures are becoming complex to build knowledge base for fraud detection.

The factual data which uses organizational information along with Benford's law and other considerations of fuzzy systems are used for creating psychological misrepresentation with location framework. All components which are part of analyzing the fraud detection are compared with natural of way of detection by people prefers to consider more benchmarks on critical factors for building an effective knowledge base with varied objectives.

9.5.2   Building Automated Patterns for Cognitive Analytics Using Fuzzy Systems

Primary reason for the master fraud models was acknowledgment of dubious exercises on singular customer level. Conventional methodology, which inclines toward prescient models as a base for misrepresentation discovery models, couldn't be inadequate. Principle purpose behind that lays actually that prescient model contains hardly any most prescient traits as essential part of prescient models. Reasons why they cause prescient model to suggest truth that those qualities shows most elevated effect on point variable. The custom strategy which was estimated by utilizing the factual information for evaluation has its extreme effects on variable measurable for factors highlighting the facts. Some measures are very clear in providing suspicious data for early sign of notification. The fraud patterns which are unidentified for longest time frame makes critical information are not significantly examined.

On the off chance that some pattern or occasion occurs on person level, and it is false movement, it is difficult to remember it with customary measurable prescient models. For fundamental pattern acknowledgment, and false example acknowledgment which has mass trademark those procedure is acceptable enough [8, 9] yet, for early complete extortion location arrangement it isn't adequate. It doesn't mean that prescient models ought not to be utilized for extortion displaying; it just implies that prescient models ought not to be just component or base for extortion location frameworks.

Fuzzy master frameworks offer capacity to extortion recognition models to perceive potential doubts exercises dependent on human master information which is coordinated inside programmed arrangement. Venture forward is to improve fluffy master frameworks in approach to join components like Benford's law with factual estimations for finding silly designs which shows on dubious exercises. In that manner some possible low visit and surprising examples which demonstrate on misrepresentation can be perceived. This approach gives open door for discovering non express misrepresentation designs without planning express guidelines for every likely fake case.

9.6   Design of Cognitive System for Healthcare Monitoring in Detecting Diseases

Health Care Monitoring carries huge information [10] of patients, doctors, diseases and hospital infrastructure details. The information generated in healthcare system is more dependent on each other for perfect diagnosis of patients with the disease what they are suffering. The information of healthcare system extends [11, 12] beyond the clinical data with many factors of management policy, health policy and funding agency [10, 13]. It also includes information beyond hospital maintenance like home care and primary care for different category patient treatment [12].

Building cognitive system of health care system by considering all factors need more analysis to understand the technology behind its management. The health care cognitive system demands for more strategies to be constructed to make the job of practitioners easy. Despite the vital role of cognitive system automating the health work system will remove current techno-centric approaches to distribute information among different knowledge bases to support any failure tasks to get observed and analyze the causes of failure during the design of system itself.

9.6.1 Role of Cognitive System in Building Clinical Decision System

The role of cognitive system is analyzed by going through following case studies in clinical decision system.

Case Study 1: Patient Evacuation in Multi-Specialty Hospital
The patient evacuation in multi-specialty hospital is a critical task for healthcare staff they need to physical schedule by checking the availability of free lift slots, make of beds and emergency transport. The first kind of its automated system was built at U.S military to relieve healthcare staff in scheduling patients for evacuation as primary care facility [14]. This system becomes feasible during peak time during emergency shift of critical situation patients for emergency treatment to a specified facility where his treatment can be carried smoothly. The automated system need to adjust for the next schedules of the patients after completion of the emergency case evacuation through specific aircraft for fulfilling the urgent requirements.

The challenge with this automated scheduling system is to respond the dynamic adjustment of patients shifting during emergency. The process of manual scheduling will check for available resources options and resolve conflicts to adjust the schedule for meeting new demands. The less knowledgeable cognitive system will be trained to learn the awareness about the situations to check for available resources to avoid conflicts and take decisions. The current automated scheduling system not only learn the situations but considers different constraints and build a system of effective choosing options by not blocking the staff to take decision during critical situations for different adjusted schedules when they are demanded.

Resource scheduling is a critical challenge in multi-specialty hospitals. For example, it is often tough to manage situations to meet the demands of new beds in intensive care [16]. These are some of the ideal situations where computerized support will present their solution by taking concerns of all the process while building effective cognitive system for handling critical issues with good satisfaction.

Case Study 2: Patients Self-Management of Type II Diabetes
The patient's self-management of type II diabetes system challenges were studied by Klien and Lippa [19]. They explored the demands of patients by interviewing them to understand their concerns for disorder in managing the diabetes. The study helped them to build a macro-cognitive system to structure to check for sugar level management by designing activities and decisions to support patients. The results of the system design were contributed with more relevant documents, websites, surveyed interviews of diabetes patients. The contribution of training data set was collected from American Diabetes Association chat room where patients shared their issues related to diabetes. They have come up with a detail picture of minute cognitive system that impact the effectives of patients self-management for type-II diabetes.

The analysis of the information gathered by Klien and Lippa indicates explicit knowledge of patients from different sources for self-management of diabetes. The patients found it difficult to deal with routine checkup for illness. The knowledge base encountered with different challenges of generating data with explicit knowledge for handling constraints imposed by non-routine events. The dynamic changes of diet and other factors affect changes in sugar level affecting the patients' health.

Klien and Lippa [19] gave a conclusion about the education for diabetes self-management by specifying rules and procedures to respond dynamic challenges faced by patients. The sugar level management is analogous to the regulation of a complex dynamic system. The rule set created by them doesn't prove to be adequate they get changed depending on the patients requirements for changing his routine to decrease the illness with the instructions of knowledge associated with the support of dynamic control of the cognitive system. Finally, they build a cognitive system which was using their knowledge base to respond to the dynamic control by effective feedback system and trends to check for maintaining the sugar levels in the blood [20].

Summarizing the Cognitive Challenge
The problems described in the above case studies are resulted initial failures without adaption of cognitively relevant systems approach as a solution. The computerized solution will guarantee the cognitive demands of healthcare work and provide functionality which was ignored earlier.

The solutions where these design projects are implemented with high technological factors with more apparent concerns for facing the challenges posed by the work. The developers of the automated scheduling systems were unaware about the concerns of conflicts and found after implementation about minimal cognitive work. These were disappointments of disregard, ones that could have been dodged with the correct kind of examination and plan aptitude. The need to configuration modernized frameworks so they don't disturb psychological work and don't include burdensome intellectual errands might be testing, however the structure endeavors behind the frameworks of our contextual analyses show no proof that this test was even perceived.

Facing the Challenge
The plan work attempted by Powsner and Tufte was, notwithstanding, aimed at a generally basic and surely known work issue and didn't utilize any top to bottom investigation of intellectual issues. Psychological building is planned for creating inventive intellectual help answers for work that has unpretentious and shrouded complexities. That requires both extensive examination and inventive plan.

In the accompanying investigation, we center around ventures that pre-owned Decision-Centered Design since it is an experienced structure that is generally utilized outside of medical care and is similarly straightforward. Choice Centered Designer goes astray from an option psychological building procedure of extensive investigation [18] by zeroing in on influence focuses, those difficult work exercises that offer open doors for considerable execution improvement whenever tended to with inventive intellectual structure arrangements.

9.7   Advanced High Standard Applications Using Cognitive Computing

Examples of Applications Using Cognitive Computing

Royal Bank of Scotland Using Cora Intelligent Agent
Royal Bank of Scotland built a cognitive system of an intelligent chat bot by IBM Watson for taking care of 5,000 queries per day for assisting their customers in mutual investments. Utilizing intellectual learning capacities, the right hand enabled RBS to break down client complaint information and make a vault of normally posed inquiries. Not exclusively did the aide

investigate inquiries, in any case, it was additionally fit for giving 1,000 distinct reactions and comprehend 200 client goals. The computerized aide figured out how clients pose general inquiries, how to deal with the question and move to a human operator on the off chance that it is excessively confused.

Healthcare Concierge by Welltok
Welltok built up a proficient medicinal services attendant—CafeWell that refreshes clients' applicable wellbeing data by handling an immense measure of clinical information. It encompasses the wellbeing information populated in its knowledge base to help medical coverage supplier to assist their clients with significant data to improve the quality of well-being of their customers. It builds its information system by gathering the information of their customer's health status from different sources and provides offers which are fixed or custom wellbeing proposals and act as a remainder for their good health. The Welltok's CEO, Jeff Margolis stated by examining the CafeWell services quoted that it would act as deliberate considerable framework for their patients and then streamline their health status information. The 85% population of their country were utilizing there cognitive system on day to day basis of decision making on their health status.

Personal Travel Planner by WayBlazer
WayBlazer's Travel Planner is a good example of intellectual innovation where it tries to explore the customers for their interested tour or any expected trips by querying them in their native language. The application poses many questions to gather information regarding his previous travel experience and current thoughts of travel. This cognitive system provides wide variety options for custom flight booking and hotel stay for their travelers without browsing different sites for booking. Travel Planner has been effectively utilized and more profit was gained by WayBlazer to attract customers with wide variety of options during their chat.

Edge Up's Smart Tool to Manage Fantasy Football Teams via Mobile App
Fantasy football is a demanded sport activity which was popular among 33 million people all over the world. Edge Up has come up with a mobile app to build an intelligent system for its users to understand their interests in formation of dream groups by gathering the player's information of their popularity across different media like paper, news channels and social media by inquiring with details in common language.

Tesla Motors Self-Driving Vehicles

Tesla has come with innovation in manufacturing vehicles with various advanced sensors, artificial intelligence; Computer vision to make it fully programmed vehicles. All sensors communicate to each other and computer vision uses supersonic sensors and radars to make vehicle to identify living articles track/street markings and sign boards. It ensures the good mechanisms to communicate other vehicles on street, items and turnings. The various pictures caught by the camera are handled by the neural system to view the article on the way. The knowledge based of this cognitive system has good control of vehicle engine, expanding and diminishing speed, turning and so forth.

The vehicle provides connection to individual cell phones to create a personalization for setting the path to take a tour without any driver. Now these types of vehicles are full of IoT gadgets/Things. This gadgets incorporate intelligence to the car as an individual systems and learn from the knowledge base by shared learning [24].Tesla thus shown that AI empowered with IoT will lead the future where car are of interest is grown among people [25].

Encompassing Helped Living

Encompassing Helped Living is an application started by European innovation and development. This application targets the individuals who want good condition home for living. It has improved the nature of living tenants, particular to the older ones [26], utilizing the good innovations and far off considering many factors for building personal satisfaction autonomy, social inclusion and decreased expenses for careful wellbeing of tenants. It particularly targets the physical disabled persons to improve the day to day lives with new innovated rooms. Encompassing helped living to remunerate a portion of inabilities by the use of savvy gadgets with IoT technology. Surrounding knowledge permits things to utilize all the usefulness to improve the conditions of living with automated devices without being dependent [27]. This technology of knowledge base of cognitive system is valuable for older people who use it for wellbeing without any dependence on the others for their work at home easily.

Building Emotional Communication Systems

The current world is interconnection of web, mobile phones and other electronic items. Building the psychology of individuals who are using above components to connect to digital world follow the study of patterns for developing future system [21]. The material life of today is progressively plentiful and individual have move to their focal point from physical world to imaginable world i.e. to the world of internet. For example the first version of smart home was mainly concentration of control of machine to machine interaction which is electronically and automatically managed. The second version of smart home has moved to human to machine interaction with keen advances of electronic components used for home automation. The second version of smart home enhances the technical savvy of home framework to a feeling of users who are getting assistance for observation and guideline on feelings of clients in connection with growth of plants, watering it, checking for waste of plants for its manures. Feeling of individuals becomes a quick reference for building emotional intelligence catering their automated needs. Thus feeling cognizance has a significant utilization of intellectual processing. Thus it stands for good example for human to machine cooperation.

The human to machine interaction has incorporated the visual separation of knowledge base to analyze the perspective of individual in its problem space. An effective framework of visual separation is different from human to machine association for enthusiastic correspondence framework with different mode of operation then voice to voice approach then with cushion robot [23]. The individual framework has a bunches of utilizations, for example a kid of 6 years young has lost her mother and she misses her mother so much that her dad gives her a voice-based cognitive system which simulates her mother voice in taking care of her wellbeing so that she never mentally thinks about her mother's death. Like when she is going for school she wishes her mother voice-based system and it cautions about weather update and ask her to carry the umbrella because of heavy rain forecast. It also helps her in solving math homework like her mother helps her. The touch of her mother's feeling comes with the voice-based system and meets all her requirements. The virtual reality augmentation can be also being done to simulate a voice and video and cause visual separation to make her feel the presence of her mother virtually.

9.8   Conclusion

Cognitive Computing with brief overview was covered in this chapter. Features and limitations of this computing are highlighted with in detail about its architectural components of cognitive computing. The support of Natural Language Processing with its efficient language characteristics and representation of knowledge base data in different database objects were acknowledged. The support of cloud computing with its wide variety characteristics like built-in storage capacity with effective analytical algorithms through APIs provide cognitive system an affordable environment to analyze the problem or situations and support for good decision making. Finally some brief case studies were highlighted in terms of fraud detection and health support decision system and high standard example applications.

References

1. https://marutitech.com/cognitive-computing-features-scope-limitations/.
2. Chen, M., Herrera, F., Hwang, K., Cognitive computing: Architecture, technologies and intelligent applications. *IEEE Access*, 6, 19774–19783, 2018.
3. Ahmad, M.O. and Khan, R.Z., The Cloud Computing: A Systematic Review. *Int. J. Innovative Res. Comput. Commun. Eng.*, 3, 5, 4066–4075, 2015.
4. Chhabra, S. and Dixit, V.S., Cloud Computing: State of The Art And Security Issues. *ACM SIGSOFT Softw. Eng. Notes*, 40, 2, 1–11, 2015.
5. Kaur, K., A Review of Cloud Computing Service Models. *Int. J. Comput. Appl.*, 140, 7, 15–18, 2016.
6. Khurana, S. and Verma, A.G., Comparison of cloud computing service models: SaaS, PaaS, IaaS. *Int. J. Electron. Commun. Technol. IJECT*, 4, 121–127, 2013.
7. Fawcett, T. and Provost, F., Adaptive Fraud Detection. *Data Min. Knowl. Discov.*, **13**, 3, 291–316, 1997.
8. Duffield, G. and Grabosky, P., The psychology of fraud, in: *Trends and Issues in Crime and Criminal Justice*, vol. 199, Australian Institute of Criminology, Australia, 2001.
9. Jennings, C.R. and Poston, R.J., *Global Business Fraud and the Law: Preventing and Remedying Fraud and Corruption*, May 2016 Edition, Practising Law Institute (PLI), Amazon Digital Services LLC, Springer, Cham, 2016.
10. Rahadhan, P., Poon, S.K., Land, L., Understanding unintended consequences for EMR. *Stud. Health Technol. Inform.*, 178, 192–8, 2012, https://doi.org/10.3233/978-1-61499-078-9-192.
11. Vanderhook, S. and Abraham, J., Unintended Consequences of EHR Systems: A Narrative Review. *Proceedings of the 2017 International Symposium on Human Factors and Ergonomics in Health Care*, 2017.
12. Vincent, C. and Amalberti, R., *Safer healthcare: Strategies for the real world*, Springer Open, London, 2016, (eBook). https://doi.org/10.1007/978-3-319-25559-0.
13. Greenhalgh, T., Potts, H., Wong, G., Bark, P., Swinglehurst, D., Tensions andparadoxes in electronic patient record research: A systematic literature review using the meta-narrative method. *Milbank Q.*, 87, 729–88, 2009.

14. Cook, R.I., Woods, D.D., Walters, M. *et al.*, The cognitive systems engineering of automated medical evacuation scheduling, in: *Proceedings of Human Interaction With Complex Systems*, IEEE Computer Society Press, Los Alamitos, pp. 202–7, 1996.

15. Walters, M.E., *The Cognitive Complexity of Event-Driven Replanning: Managing Cascading Secondary Disruptions in Aeromedical Evacuation Planning*, Ph.D. Dissertation, OH, The Ohio State University, Columbus, 1997.

16. Cook, R.I., Being Bumpable, in: *Joint cognitive systems: Patterns in cognitive systems engineering, chapter 3*, D.D. Woods and E. Hollnagel (Eds.), CRC Press, Boca Rotan, 2006.

17. Cook, R.I. and Woods, D.D., Adapting to new Technology in the Operating Room. *Hum. Factors*, 38, 4, 593–613, 1996.

18. Lintern, G., *Joker One: A Tutorial in Cognitive Work Analysis, Melbourne, Australia*, Cognitive Systems Design, Australia Melbourne. http://www.cognitivesystemsdesign.net/Downloads/Cognitive Work Analysis Joker OneTutorial.pdf, Accessed 1 Aug 2013, 2013.

19. Klein, H.A. and Lippa, K.D., Type 2 diabetes self-management: Controlling a dynamic system. *Cogn. Eng. Decis. Mak.*, 2, 1, 48–62, 2008.

20. Klein, H.A. and Lippa, K.D., Assuming control after system failure: Type II diabetes self-management. *Cogn. Technol. Work*, 14, 243–51, 2012.

21. Zhou, L., QoE-driven delay announcement for cloud mobile media. *IEEE Trans. Circuits Syst. Video Technol.*, 27, 1, 84–94, Jan. 2017.

22. Chen, M., Yang, J., Zhu, X., Wang, X., Liu, M., Song, J., Smart home 2.0: Innovative smart home system powered by botanical IoT and emotion detection. *Mobile Netw. Appl.*, 22, 6, 1159–1169, 2017.

23. Chen, M., Zhou, P., Fortino, G., Emotion communication system. *IEEE Access*, 5, 326–337, 2017.

24. Bhardwaj, A., AI could be the catalyst to unleash the power of IoT, http://www.oodlestechnologies.com/blogs/AI-Could-Be-The-Catalyst-To-Unleash-The-Power-of-IoT.Accessed 9 Nov 2016, 20 Oct 2016.

25. Faggella, D., Artificial intelligence plus the internet of things (IoT)—3 Examples worth learning from, http://techemergence.com/artificial-intelligence-plus-the-internetof-   things-iot-3-examples-worth-learning-from/. Accessed 9 Nov 2016, 8 Feb 2016.

26. Chan, M., Estève, D., Escriba, C., Campo, E., A review of smart homes— Present state and future challenges. *Comput. Methods Programs Biomed.*, 91, 1, 55–81, 66, 2008.

27. Nussbaum, G., Smart environments: Introduction to the special thematic session, in: *ICCHP*, 2008.

10

Quantum Meta-Heuristics and Applications

Kolla Bhanu Prakash

A.I. & Data Science Research Group, Koneru Lakshmaiah Education Foundation, Vaddeswaram, Vijayawada, A.P, India

Abstract

Meta-heuristics has various optimization models which resolve various critical problems in an optimal way. The idea of using the principle of quantum computing to solve the problems of classical computers is better because of their meta-heuristic methods that achieve optimal solutions in less time.

This chapter aims to give details regarding current research trends of quantum-inspired meta-heuristics and its applications for feature extraction, signal coding, speech synthesis, speech recognition, on chip intra-system quantum entangled states generator, noise resilience, photonic quantum computing, communications, polar encoding and decoding, cascade semantic fusion for image captioning.

Drug design, cyber security, deep machine learning, code breaking and financial portfolio estimation are some other key applications to look for where quantum meta-heuristics will play a vital role.

Keywords: Quantum computing, meta-heuristics, quantum meta-heuristics inspired algorithms, challenges and applications

10.1 Introduction

In the 1980s, Feynman [1] and Manin [2], expressed the idea of quantum computing, based on Quantum mechanics. A Quantum Computer (QC)

Email: drkbp@kluniversity.in

Kolla Bhanu Prakash, G. R. Kanagachidambaresan, V. Srikanth, E. Vamsidhar (eds.) Cognitive Engineering for Next Generation Computing: A Practical Analytical Approach, (265–298) © 2021 Scrivener Publishing LLC

is different from a conventional computer. Quantum computers are capable of delivering more than the classical machines. A QC may be physically implemented as analog or digital, the former may be further divided into adiabatic quantum computation, quantum annealing, quantum simulation and the latter uses quantum logic gates for computation.

The classical computer uses either 0 (false/off) or 1 (true/on) for data representation, while QC uses the smallest bits of information, known as the quantum bit (Q-Bit), which is the 0- and 1-state superposition and is implemented with the quantum gates (QG) [73]. At the same time the Q-bits exist in the states 0 and 1. When we use n number of Q-bits then the number of states is 2^n at the same time in the quantum machine.

The differences between classical computing and quantum computing mechanics highlight the performance mechanisms in solving the industrial critical problems. The classical mechanisms are much deterministic with end result of solution can be predicted from starting of the problem solution and they give casual solutions where one objective output used for other objective solution. The quantum computing mechanics uses its basics characteristics like superposition, Entanglement and measurement paradox for getting optimal solutions for critical problems. The superposition enables to generate multiple states simultaneously and correlate them to get separate solutions with entanglement and the output of quantum computing mechanics becomes a paradox for giving the measured outcomes for better solutions to critical problems.

The limitations of classical computing is the usage of transistors which are getting doubled for solving any parallelization tasks and the size of transistors are going to be decreased to the size of electron i.e. 1–3 nm by the year 2022 for providing any commercial solution to industry productions. The quantum mechanics overcome these limitations of classical by using 20 Q-bits to store million variable information for performing parallel tasks and these q-bit values are correlated which enables them to get the information by reading only one q-bit and by using superposition and entanglement characteristics it compute all calculations at once to get the solutions at faster rate.

The quantum computing is enabled with high processing power and accurate error correction by using large number of q-bits. The de-coherence property of quantum state supports it performing high computation at faster rate for large scale systems. The accuracy of error identification and error correction gives confident output while computing solutions for large scale systems.

Shor [3] has published an algorithm that can effectively resolve some of the problems mentioned in information security domain related to cryptography and these are considered to be difficult for classical computers [3]. Grover [4] presented a fast search in unstructured database with quantum algorithm. This success shows that QC credibly change the way of computing.

The principles of quantum mechanics has contributed to evolvement of quantum computing which opened doors for much research unsolved optimized problems are been resolved with this computing. The classical computer processes the data in an exclusive binary state of 0 and 1, while the quantum computer processes data with the smallest bit of information known as the quantum bit (Q-bit) that represents the 0 and 1 state superposition [6]. The quantum computers are implemented with the gates of quantum logic known as Q-gates. The Q-bits are used as the order of the quantity gates to be applied and respectively exist in 0 and 1 states. The number of states in a quantum computer for n number of Q-bits is 2^n simultaneously [6]. Using its multiple state existences, quantum computers can thus achieve increased computing power to solve important computational problems.

The quantum computers has their significance in resolving complex problems like mission critical applications in scientific research, dealing with breaking of encryption keys, performing search in huge amount of data etc. Meta-heuristic is a mathematical optimization technique which provides an efficient solution to optimization problem by following a procedure to search, generate or select on partial search of algorithm. The various methods of quantum meta-heuristics like evolutionary, swarm intelligence, physical based and bio-inspired are listed with algorithms and discussed with their applications in different trending domains.

10.2 What is Quantum Computing?

As presented earlier, Q-bit is the smallest unit of information in a QC. The Q-bit is 0 or 1 or superposition of 0 or 1. The representation of the Q-bit state is given by Equation (10.1) [5]:

$$|\psi\rangle = \alpha|0\rangle + \beta|1\rangle \qquad (10.1)\ [5]$$

Where α and β are complex numbers which indicate probability amplitudes of respective states. With Probability, results state 0 and with

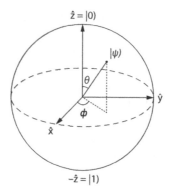

Figure 10.1 Bloch Sphere which represents the Q-bit.

probability results the state 1, thus the =1. Equation (10.1) is rewritten as Equation (10.2) [5].

$$|\psi\rangle = e^{i\gamma}\left(\cos\frac{\theta}{2}|0\rangle + e^{i\varphi}\sin\frac{\theta}{2}|1\rangle\right) \qquad (10.2)\,[5]$$

Where θ, ϕ, γ are real numbers. The numbers θ and ϕ represent a point in three dimensional sphere as shown in Figure 10.1, called Bloch Sphere [5], which presents the visualization of single bit state.

The QG used for quantum computation are AND, OR, NOT Hadamard, Pauli, Y-gate, Z-gate, S-gate, T-gate, controlled-NOT, swap, controlled-Z, Toffoli, Fredkinetc are applied to change the state of a Q-bit [5].

10.3   Quantum Computing Challenges

Table 10.1 lists the important domain areas where quantum computing is influencing with applications and developments. Quantum simulation uses quantum systems for simulating the molecular structure and their composition while preparing drugs and other materials. The challenge for quantum simulation is for large molecules massive numbers of q-bits are required and the results also lead to errors in quantum calculations. Cryptanalysis need prime factorization in order to break keys used during encryption to access intelligent data which were encrypted using RSA. Q-bit scalability is needed for quantum computing to improve the confidence level of encrypted data. Terabyte-size RSA keys are required to encrypt large amounts of data on a quantum computer. The challenge for

Table 10.1 Quantum computing influenced domain areas with applications and development.

Domain area	Limitations of classical computing	Quantum computing applications	Quantum computing developments
Catalyst Reactions and Material Discovery	Classical computing limit is at a molecule with 50 electrons, with errors	Molecules are formed following quantum mechanics' laws. Quantum computers inherently show quantum characteristics and are expected to model larger molecules in the future.	Simulation to date limited to small molecules (beryllium hydride, lithium hydride, and hydrogen)
Drug development	Trial and error—Pharmaceutical companies will take up to 10+ years and billions of dollars to introduce a new drug in to market.	Understanding the interactions of drugs with proteins will be much more accurate, faster and cost effective by harnessing the power of QC	Biogen, Accenture and 1Qbit have showcased in a joint effort to speed up drug discovery for critical and harmful diseases
Cyber Security	Significant share of encrypting currently based on RSA and Elliptic-curve cryptography	Shor's algorithm can solve the factorization problem, but requires powerful computing, such as QC.	Technology resistant to Quantum hacking is being developed already by top universities and startups. The flipside is the increased security that could be offered and needed with quantum-based cryptography.

(Continued)

Table 10.1 Quantum computing influenced domain areas with applications and development. (*Continued*)

Domain area	Limitations of classical computing	Quantum computing applications	Quantum computing developments
Supply Chain and Logistics	Classical computing at its limit trying to solve large scale optimization problems	Quantum gates are able to produce all possible solutions at once using entanglement and superposition	Research to date limited to study and development of algorithms for semi-definite problems, but not implementations or test cases to date
Financial Modeling	Advanced portfolio optimization (returns, risk) done using time-intensive and inefficient Montecarlo simulations	Quantum gates are able to produce all possible solutions at once using entanglement and superposition.	Current size of problems that can be solved is small. Optimizing a portfolio of 3 assets already requires 84+ q-bits
Artificial Intelligence and Machine Learning	Classical computing at its limit trying to solve large scale AI/ML problems	QC enabled algorithms, such as Grover, can accelerate data based search problems	Enormous potential for applications such as Voice, Image and writing recognition

quantum computing to process big data, machine learning and deep learning problems is to improve error correction Q-bits for fast recovery of data for better optimal solutions.

10.4 Meta-Heuristics and Quantum Meta-Heuristics Solution Approaches

Meta-heuristics basic solution approach is shown in Figure 10.2 where initial candidate solution is taken for computation of fitness function for solving specific objective. If any of the solution meets the criteria then its output the solution if not new candidate solution is added to check improved solution

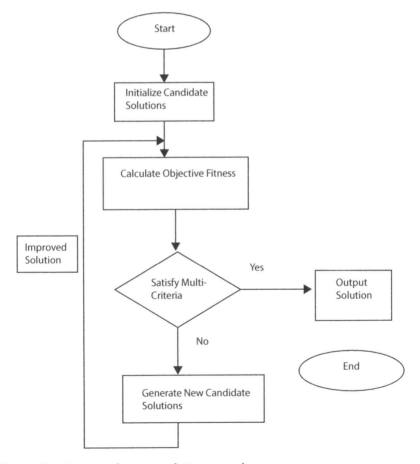

Figure 10.2 Basic meta-heuristics solution approach.

and then once again computed for fitness function to meet the objective of the problem solution. This process of adding candidate solution will repeat until the computed candidate solution meets the criteria.

Quantum meta-heuristics solution approach is shown in Figure 10.3, where initial candidate solution is taken for computation for fitness function

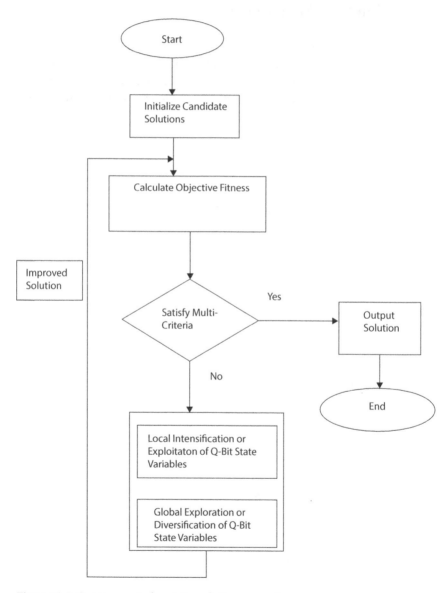

Figure 10.3 Quantum meta-heuristics solution approach.

for meeting specific objective and this result is tested for satisfying multi-criteria if it satisfies the output the solution. If not new candidate solution need to be evaluated by exploitation or local intensification and then apply diversification or global exploration for getting improved candidate solution. Thus new candidate solution is once again evaluated for meeting multi-criteria.

10.5   Quantum Meta-Heuristics Algorithms With Application Areas

The most widely used computational model of evolutionary method is genetic algorithm. It generates more number of solutions called population. The first meta-heuristic of quantum is applied for genetic algorithm where conventional GA is combined with quantum computing for better convergence. The quantum genetic algorithm provides features of rapid convergence of global search ability [60]. It provides optimal cluster centroids for adjusting weights in fuzzy neural networks [61]. The QGA provides improved web object sequence during image analysis in web sites [62]. The NQGA is applied in radar emitter signal recognition for selecting the best feature from subset of features [63].

Particle swarm optimization [73] is a population dependent swarm intelligence calculation in which the word "swarm" denotes population of an entity called as particle and also represented as the candidate solution. The quantum computing is added to particle swarm optimization to improve the accuracy in search ability. The QPSO has improved association rule mining for large databases [64], for retrieving associated records for satisfying complex queries. QPSO enhanced not only the local optimization but increased rapid convergence during DNA encoding [65].

Differential evolution [73] is a population-based optimization algorithm that works iteratively to increase the quality of the candidate solution. It is used for real-valued multidimensional functions, with noisy and non-continuous optimization problems. Quantum computing with differential evolution adds probability factor Q-bit at mutation, cross over and selection operators during solving optimization problems. The QDE (Quantum Differential Evolution) offers better results in terms of convergence speed, search capabilities and competency. QDE enhances the solving of optimization problems in binary valued space through Q-bit string in all its representations for operations [31]. It increased exploitation ability and achieved high convergence performance in optimizing the problem solution for binary valued-space. DE along with variable neighborhood search space is used to enhance local search in permutation flow shop scheduling problem [32] and reduced make span, total flow time of jobs with improved lateness of jobs.

Artificial bee colony (ABC) is a meta-heuristic evolutionary algorithm that first discovers a population with base solution, and iteratively enhances for discarding low standard solutions using fitness functions [73]. Quantum computing discusses the ABC Smart Search Strategy [73] and the process of computational capabilities. The quantum bit, superposition of states, and quantum interference are used to improve ABC's diversity and computational capacity and provide optimal solutions by balancing discovery and exploitation [66]. QABC (Quantum Artificial bee colony) is used to solve complex continuous optimization problems effectively [67].

Gravitational search algorithm is a meta-heuristic which is based on law of gravity and mass associations. The global movements of objects are considered while exploitation and exploration in search space. The quantum computing improves the GSA with adding more robustness to its search space with more coherence. The binary encoded problem is solved using QGSA robust optimization tool [37]. This QGSA is tested for 0/1 knapsack problem, Max-ones, Royal-Road functions and analyze its robustness in optimizing search space to get the effective solution. The mobile computation grid lags the less bandwidth, low battery and computational power which affects while job scheduling on the devices. The QGSA is used for effectively explore the search space for optimal job scheduling in mobile computational grid [68].

Ant colony optimization is one of the common meta-heuristic that solves computational issues based on ants behavior [73] in searching for their food between colonies. The quantum computing enhances the optimal solution attained by ACO at faster rate with improved quality of solution. The QACO is applied for multi-level thresholding on color image. The experimental results are described in terms of fitness function, threshold values and computational time and compared with other optimized algorithms [69]. The Peak signal to noise ratio is analyzed at different threshold levels for real time color image using QACO technique. The convergence rate of obtaining optimal solution for (TSP) travel sales person problem was enhanced using QACO technique [41].

The immune clonal algorithm is meta-heuristic which represents the biological immune system in which both local and global search capabilities are effectively used get the optimized solutions. The quantum computing acts as antibodies on ICA algorithm problem search space to effect less number of population. The QICA causes good improved results with high quality of solution with less cost. The QICA is used for population sub grouping to enhance search efficiency for antibody and achieved high success ratio with reduced computational complexity [70]. QICA with embedded evolutionary game approach used for antibody to solve combinational optimization problem and tested on good population size with less number of iterations [71]. Large scale capacitated arc routing problem is effectively managed with QICA using approximating local optimum and strong stability is achieved for getting optimal solution [72].

Tabu Search is a meta-heuristic method that uses memory units with some set of rules which denote solutions for already visited nodes [73]. Unless the solution is revisited in the span of time and rule is broken, the solution will be labeled as tabu [73] and not considered for optimum solution. Quantum computing uses quantum principles to fix the rules and look for solving optimization problems. The QTS is an efficient algorithm which gets the function minimization problem solved without carried away by local optima solution. The QTS algorithm solves the 0/1 knapsack problem with two step approach in first step it adds probability for worst solutions and update the population and in second step it rotate the solutions not reaching the worst solutions to improve the performance in getting optimal solution [48].

Cuckoo search algorithm is a global method of optimization [73] used to solve the problems of combinatorial optimization. Quantum CSA improves the approach to optimal solutions that solve problems in real life. The QCSA offered a good solution for less iterations and population size in the 0/1 knapsack problem [45]. QCSA worked on non-homogeneous parameters to obtain an optimal solution to increase search efficiency with the exploitation capabilities to lead the optimal solution premature convergence [47].

Harmony search algorithm is a population based meta-heuristic algorithm whose aims is to find harmony among the quality of parameters on which optimization of solution is possible. The influence of fitness function is to increase the harmony for solving an optimization problem. Quantum computing adds intensification and diversification of evolution process to get more effective solutions. QHS provides improved performance in measuring optimized parameters with different population sizes with efficient searching technique. This was tested for 0–1 knapsack problem to achieve good quality solutions [49].

Frog leaping algorithm is a population dependent meta-heuristic algorithm [73] in which the local search for optimized parameters is carried out by reorganizing them for global exploration. This method is mainly used for solving combinatorial optimization problems. Quantum computing improves this approach to produce solutions of higher quality. QFLA is used to solve NP's hard problem of finding minimal attribute reduction by applying quantum properties to the diversity of the frog population and convergence for optimum global resulting in efficient, high-performance solution [50]. QFLA does have ability of good search with high accuracy in detecting sonar images by combining non spatial information with shuffle FLA [51].

Artificial fish swarm algorithm [73] uses the movement of the fish as the base study for understanding instinctive features to attain high convergence speed and accuracy. QAFSA uses the quantum representation and quantum gates to gather features to improve the good quality of search ability. QAFSA is studied for improving convergence speed by performing good searching ability by combining features of quantum with fish swarm algorithm [52]. Glow warm swarm optimization is a meta-heuristic algorithm for multi-modal functions with swarm intelligence. The algorithm makes use of adaptive neighborhood by the estimation of its movement. Quantum computing adds better accuracy and speed for convergence. QGSO is used for solving discrete optimization problem with better convergent accuracy and speed [55].

Social evolution algorithm [73] is a human characteristic meta-heuristic algorithm in which selective interactions based on individual prejudice are given priority to human interactions and re-evaluate indecisive interactions in the second opinion. Quantum computing improves SEA's efficiency with an overall efficient and reliable approach to solve the optimization question. QSEA is tested for 0/1 knapsack problem which resulted high efficient in resolving the optimization with indecisive human interaction methods [53]. Firefly algorithm is a meta-heuristic swarm intelligence which refers to firefly moves and behaviors. When the distance decreases, the attractiveness of the fireflies near each other is proportional to the brightness. Quantum FA computing provides solutions that are of better quality. QFA is checked for the problem of multilevel knapsack that was considered a complete NP problem [56]

Figure 10.4 is meant for categorizing the quantum meta-heuristics methods under four types for having similarity in getting solution to critical problems. The first category is quantum evolutionary algorithms which provide solution by evolution technique among the optimal variables for meeting multi-criteria. The second category is quantum swarm Intelligence which provides solution by specific searching strategies.

The third category is quantum physical based which uses physics concepts of gravitational and harmony search. The fourth category is a quantum bio-inspired algorithm which uses the bio-diversity of birds or animals

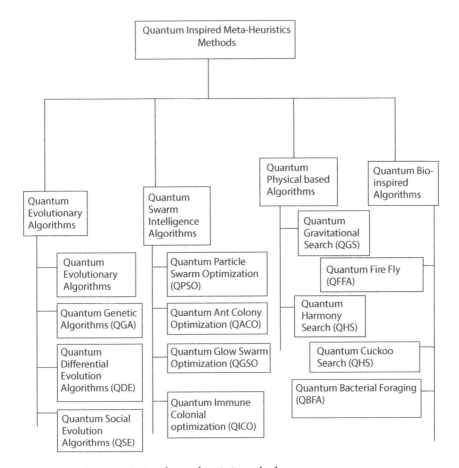

Figure 10.4 Quantum inspired meta-heuristic methods.

for getting the optimal solution. Table 10.2 lists the quantum meta-heuristics methods with author and application area details.

10.5.1 Quantum Meta-Heuristics Applications for Power Systems

For Power Quality Monitors (PQMs) at the power grid during power supply, a quantum meta-heuristic algorithm called quantum inspired lightning search algorithm [74] is used. Placing these PQMs faces crucial observability constraint to increase performance by framing an objective feature with the scope field of topological control. The power quality has important vital impact in industries in order to avoid voltage sag which

Table 10.2 Quantum meta-heuristics methods and application area.

Category	Authors	Application area
QEA	Han *et al.* (2002)	Knapsack problem [6]
QEA	Li (2012)	SAR Image Segmentation [7]
QEA	Talbi (2007)	Multi-objective Image Segmentation [8]
QEA	Ramdane (2010)	Data Clustering [9]
QEA	Chen (2018)	Data Clustering [10]
QEA	Yu (2016)	Fuzzy Interface controller [11, 73]
QEA	Xing (2016)	Dynamic multicast network-coding routing [12, 73]
QEA	Silveira (2017)	Ordering problems [13]
QGA	Han (2000)	Knapsack problem [14]
QGA	Li (2007)	Multi-objective Flow Shop Scheduling [15]
QGA	Xiao (2010)	Data Clustering [16]
QGA	Zhao (2009)	Training of Fuzzy Neural Networks [17]
QGA	Mohammad (2012)	Non-linear Programming [18]
QGA	Dilip (2015)	Website Optimization [19]
QGA	Konar (2017)	Real-time Task Scheduling [20]
QPSO	Wang (2007)	Travelling Salesman Problem [21]
QPSO	Xiao (2009)	DNA Encoding [22]
QPSO	Sun (2012)	Multiple Alignment Sequences [23, 73]
QPSO	Ykhlef (2011)	Laws related to mining associations in broad repositories [24, 73]
QPSO	Sun (2007)	Non-linear Programming problems [25]
QPSO	Dey (2014)	Gray level Image thresholding [26]
QPSO	Li (2017)	Map Reduce Model of Big data [27]
QPSO	Li (2017)	Complex Network Clustering [28]
QPSO	AlBaity (2012)	Multiple Objective Context Analysis [29]

(Continued)

Table 10.2 Quantum meta-heuristics methods and application area. (*Continued*)

Category	Authors	Application area
QPSO	Banerjee (2016)	Reliability Optimization Problem in Power Distribution Systems [30]
QDE	Yang (2008)	Binary Optimization [31]
QDE	Zheng (2010)	Flow Shop Scheduling Problem [32]
QDE	Hota (2010)	Knapsack Problem [33]
QDE	Talbi (2015)	Feature Subset Selection problem [7]
QABCO	Bouaziz (2013)	Numerical Optimization [34]
QABCO	Duan (2010)	Numerical Optimization [35]
QGSA	Soleimanpour-Moghadam (2014)	Numerical Function Optimization [36]
QGSA	Nezamabadi-pour (2015)	Binary Encoded Optimization [37]
QGSA	Barani (2017)	Feature Subset Selection [38]
QGSA	Singh (2017)	Mobile Computational Grid [39]
QACO	Dey (2015)	Multi-level Color Image Thresholding [40]
QACO	You (2010)	Travelling Salesman Problem [41]
QICO	Jiao (2008)	Global Optimization [42]
QICO	Wu (2009)	Evolutionary Game Theory [43]
QICO	Shang (2017)	Problems with large-scale effective arc routing [44, 73]
QCS	Layeb (2011)	Knapsack problem [45, 73]
QCS	Layeb (2012)	Bin Box Issue [46, 73]
QCS	Cheung (2017)	True Optimization of Parameters [47, 73]
QTS	Yang (2013)	Function Optimization [48, 73]
QHS	Layeb (2013)	Knapsack problem [49, 73]
QFLA	Ding (2013)	Attribute Question Elimination [50, 73]

(*Continued*)

Table 10.2 Quantum meta-heuristics methods and application area. (*Continued*)

Category	Authors	Application area
QFLA	Wang (2017)	Sonar Image Detection Underwater [51, 73]
QAFSA	Zhu (2010)	Global search [52, 73]
QFFA	Zouache (2016)	Discrete Performance issues [53, 73]
QBFA	Huang (2016)	Modeling Neuro-fuzzy [54, 73]
QGSO	Gao (2017)	Discrete Performance issues [55, 73]
QSE	Pavithr (2016)	Knapsack problem [56, 73]
QSA	Crispin (2013)	Vehicle schedule [58]
Hybrid	Dey (2014)	Thresholding at multilevel [57]

decreases performance of machinery equipment's during production time. This voltage sag is effectively managed by placing PQM's at every junction of power system. PQM's placement uses Quantum meta-heuristic technique by providing optimal solution using lightning search algorithm with simple, flexible and derivation free approach. Optimal placement of PQMs is achieved using three main components i.e. decision vectors, objective functions and optimization constraints in QLSA.

The power loss at the distributed network in the power delivery center is very important because of the complicated way components like transformers are organized. The optimum location of condensers in the power distribution center will reduce these power losses. An adaptive quantity-inspired evolutionary algorithm [76] is used to evaluate the optimal capacity size and position to eliminate power losses and optimize total net savings in the device.

Shipboard zonal power system [81] has critical impact of reconfiguring themselves on navy ships for managing power effectively. The topology and load priority are two factors considered to analyze while reconfiguring shipboard zonal power system in optimal way. The optimization of power systems on ship board is achieved using quantum particle swarm optimization with belief desire intention agent by considering reconfiguration as main objective. The quantum meta-heuristic QPSO enhances the restoration of power system reconfiguration on ship board with better optimal way than normal PSO technique.

Power distribution system has a critical challenge to distribute or supply electricity to their consumers by maintaining optimal price with high reliability. Quantum meta-heuristics provides a hybrid nature of solution approach for this problem by combining features of Quantum Genetic Algorithm and Quantum Particle Swarm Optimization [30]. The optimal way of power distribution for consumers is achieved with nominal price and high reliability by giving them as inputs through fuzzy model triangular member function and then applied QGA and QPSO for better results.

10.5.2   Quantum Meta-Heuristics Applications for Image Analysis

Visual tracking is the field of computer vision with prominent research area where optimization of main criteria is used to resolve the objects location in an image with different metrics like Structural similarity index [75] for estimating its position. A Meta-heuristic algorithm effectively solves this problem by optimization technique called differential evolution with using Gaussian distribution to make search faster and more accurate.

Image Processing is a domain where more formats of images need to be processed with different perspective of extracting information. This evolutionary approach of extracting information from images is effectively dealt with quantum meta-heuristic principles. The search strategy of maximization of image alignment based on entropic measurement and shared information [79] is performed by optimization of the quantum particle swarm. Experiments on high quality alignment for both mono and multi-modality images were performed for better compatibility with findings using QPSO.

In Image processing domain image segmentation for 1D, 2D and 3D color images need effective way by reducing low signal-to-noise ratio and poor contrast. Image thresholding for color image segmentation needs optimal way of decreasing the effect of noise and weak edges in 3D color images. Quantum meta-heuristic algorithm called cuttlefish algorithm [84] is used for optimal image segmentation for avoiding poor contrast in three dimensional spaces by applying multilevel image thresholding.

Multi-level Color image scheduling is a technique which need to find optimal threshold values at different levels for quick processing of image. Quantum meta-heuristics has got many efficient techniques to experiment with this problem by stating fitness functions with different computational time. QACO turns out to be the best optimization technique to resolve this multi-level color image scheduling.

Image processing is a critical task to be dealt to detect under water objects in sonar images. Quantum inspired shuffled frog leaping algorithm is effectively used to set filtered parameters which normalizes the non-local spatial information to avoid noising effect in sonar images. A quantum inspired shuffled frog leaping algorithm based on new search mechanism to quickly detect sonar images [51]. QSFLA evaluates the fitness function combining inter and intra classes of frog positions accurately for improving search ability and detection accuracy.

Image processing on gray-level images requires optimum threshold values to be calculated by applying correlation coefficient and measurement functions at various gray image levels. Quantum meta-heuristics has come up with various methods to overcome this gray level picture threshold by integrating quantum genetic and particle swarm optimization algorithms with solution approaches [26]. The results of this hybrid approach is compared with QEA in corresponding to fitness and standard deviation of fitness and found to be highly time efficient in getting gray level image threshold values.

In Image Processing, image segmentation is a process of partitioning the image into disjoint regions. The image segmentation can be considered as combinatorial optimization problem as it need form partitioning cluster while processing image. Quantum meta-heuristics has come with new solution approach called quantum evolutionary clustering algorithm based on watershed [7]. At first the image is partitioned using watershed algorithm and on these small pieces of image QEA is applied to form optimal clusters and finally obtain segmentation result.

Figure 10.5 gives basic quantum meta-heuristic genetic evolution approach for Image segmentation where preliminary image data is taken and initialized population of non-dominated set for generation then quantum interference, mutation and rotation of Q-bit is computed and evaluated for non-dominated set and check for conditions and every criteria for image segmentation is met then results are given as output.

10.5.3 Quantum Meta-Heuristics Applications for Big Data or Data Mining

Data Clustering is a popular research area in image processing, data mining, etc.

Clustering is a process of grouping similar things based on certain attributes. Quantum meta-heuristics provides with an efficient algorithm called Quantum inspired evolutionary algorithm for data clustering (QECA) [77] considers different local factors and exploit local search space for a global solution with in less span of time. A novel measurement index called manifold distribution is used for effective computation of cluster centers.

Big data and Internet of Things are the two prominent emerging domains which are progressing towards usage of meta-heuristic techniques to get improved results in solving complex industrial problems. The quanta

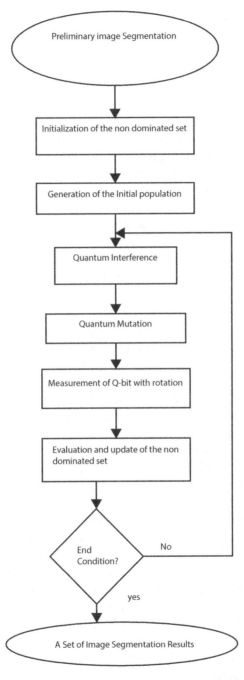

Figure 10.5 Basic quantum meta-heuristics genetic evolution approach for image segmentation.

meta-heuristic algorithm of cuckoo search is integrated with map reduce programming for different instances of crew scheduling problem. The wide exploration of these quantum meta-heuristics techniques in big data domain is used to evaluate quality of results, to improve convergence time of intermediate solutions under different conditions and processing capacity.

Big Data is a domain which deals with huge data for analysis. This domain is full of technological challenges in order to use it with full potential. The beginning stage of data in big data analysis is generation and acquisition. The other phases of big data where criticality lies is with storage and management phase in providing infrastructure, transportation and building conceptual models for complex data. Quantum meta-heuristics would come up with optimal algorithms in solving these challenges in more flexible way and it even provides the nature of adaptability any types of data with different contexts.

Data mining attribute reduction is considered as rough set theory based on feature selection. The minimum attribute reduction is stated as NP-hard problem which effective approximated. Quantum inspired shuffled frog leaping based minimal attribute reduction (QSFLAR) [50] represents the frogs by multi-state quantum bits and applies quantum rotation gate and quantum mutation operators to exploit the diversity and convergence of the frog population to obtain optimum values with good accuracy in attribute reduction.

Data clustering plays vital role in data mining where sensitive data need to be selected for creating initial cluster centroids. Quantum inspired genetic algorithm for k-means clustering uses Q-bit representation to explore and exploit by discrete 0–1 hyperspace using quantum gate with typical genetic algorithm operations [9]. Quantum evolutionary search strategy is to optimize a quality measure by good partitioning of the datasets [10]. Both set of synthetic and real data are identified with valid clusters with effective comparison of quantum evolutionary algorithms.

In Data mining the association rule mining aims at specifying rules for extracting correlation between frequent items. The association of rules from extracting large data sets is considered as NP-complete problem as it need to exploit large number of transactions on items simultaneously. Quantum meta-heuristics has come with hybrid approach called quantum swarm evolutionary approach [24] which extracts best rules in a reasonable time of execution for large data sets.

Big data need a huge parallel computation for getting good performance results while analyzing those data. Map Reduce has been popularly used in big data for improving the performance but parallel computation is really big challenge for it also. Quantum meta-heuristics has come with hybrid approach of combining Map Reduce with quantum particle swarm optimization (MRQPSO) [27] to achieve parallel computation for the improved performance of results with less execution time.

Feature selection is an important task in data mining to get good prediction accuracy of classifiers with less problem size. Quantum meta-heuristics has come with new approach combining binary quantum-inspired gravitational search algorithm with K-means [38] for performing selection of optimal subset of features to improve the prediction results for any large data sets. Bin Packing problem is a popular combinatorial problem in data mining where set of items need to be packed with minimum number of bins. Quantum meta-heuristic proposes quantum cuckoo search algorithm for dealing this one dimensional Bin packing problem [46]. QCSA improves the performance of Bin packing problem by filling the spaces for standard measure operation.

10.5.4 Quantum Meta-Heuristics Applications for Vehicular Trafficking

Quantum Annealing is a meta-heuristic algorithm which is used for solving a capacitated vehicular routing problem (CVRP) [58] to route a heavily loaded vehicles to distribute goods among customers located in different cities. This problem has similarity with TSP (Traveling Sales Person) problem but it is different in terms of providing solution in giving an optimal path to capacitated vehicle. The quantum annealing meta-heuristic algorithm uses spin encoding scheme of quantum and empirical approach of tuning parameters to solve the CVRP. Vehicular routing problem has been dealt with three models of problem solving approach construction heuristics, improvement heuristics and meta-heuristics. Construction heuristics starts building the path for single vehicle serving single customer and distributing the goods .In improvement heuristics the vehicular cost of single vehicular services are merged with similar locality customers and compute the vehicular cost. Meta-heuristic is treated as top-level strategy which optimizes the vehicular cost by scheduling based on some local parameters such as distance, traffic, etc. in that locality of customer. The CVRP is treated as undirected graph with customer as vertices and path of vehicle as edges and local parameters are defined as operators are Boolean or spin variables of quantum and Monte Carlo algorithm is used for computing the configurations in CVRP problem. Finally Quantum Annealing is applied for vehicular scheduling to generate optimum cost.

Visual surveillance has its significance in wireless sensor networks (WSNs) and cyber-physical systems (CPSs) for monitoring traffic and security in civilian areas. Placement of the sensors is a fundamental issue in WSN/CPS and many other factors like quality of service, lifetime and efficiency are considered while deploying them. The optimal deployment of sensors is achieved using Quantum Inspired Tabu Search algorithm with Entanglement (QTSwE) [80] which is pure quantum heuristic algorithm which determine the minimum number of sensors required in different locations of civilian areas. The QTSwE treat this property of placement of sensors as phenomenon dependency based on certain critical factors and iteratively provide the solution.

Dynamic traffic flow management is a critical problem any populated locality. A dynamic transportation network model is used for managing traffic dynamics and it is used by decision makers like transportation planners to decide optimal capacity expansion policies of existing transport network infrastructure with limited resources but while road users will utilize these expansion capacities for their profit. Quantum meta-heuristics come up with efficient solution by applying sub-network for real world road traffic flow problem.

10.5.5　Quantum Meta-Heuristics Applications for Cloud Computing

Workflow scheduling in grid applications [78] need an effective approach for good performance without any delay in satisfying grid computing consumers. Quantum meta-heuristic provides an optimal critical path solution for scheduling the resources to carry out smooth workflow during its allocation. Quantum Particle Swarm Optimization was identified to provide best effective optimal solution in allocating resources dynamically without any performance degradation while providing services to their consumer's QPSO has extended this adaptive work scheduling to hybrid cloud environments to manage dynamic user requirements while allocating resources.

High performance computing is a realization of type of efficient distributed systems where demand of scheduling the critical tasks is given primary concern. Allocation of these high performance computational tasks for particular resources in optimal way is solved very effectively by quantum meta-heuristic technique with many limiting constraints. Quantum Genetic Algorithm for schedule generation (QGARAR) [82] is the quantum meta-heuristic technique which compares the peers under various critical factors or conditions to minimize the makespan value of dependent tasks submission for resource allocation in heterogeneous distributed systems.

10.5.6   Quantum Meta-Heuristics Applications for Bioenergy or Biomedical Systems

Biomedical research domain involves high dimensional data for processing feature selection by improving the accuracy of classification with reduce in measurement of parameters, storage of data and computational demands of information. Quantum meta-heuristics introduced in biomedicine due to its optimized evaluation of search ability among the existing techniques to process the high dimensional data effectively.

Production of bioenergy is increasing day by day in current economies of developed countries to meet their energy needs. The supply chain for bio-energy material has become a challenging issue for manufacturers to gather bio-mass in bulk and generate energy. This problem bio-energy supply chain is considered as large-scale optimization model where effective approaches need to be strategized to find near optimal solutions for less computational resources. Quantum meta-heuristics approaches provide two set of popular approaches called population and trajectory to solve the supply chain of bio-energy. The QACO,QPSO,QBCA,QGA are the quantum meta-heuristics algorithms which uses population approaches for solving supply chain network design problem. The task and truck scheduling is solved using trajectory based approaches by QTS and QSA quantum meta-heuristics algorithms.

10.5.7   Quantum Meta-Heuristics Applications for Cryptography or Cyber Security

Cyber security is a domain where huge amount of data need to be secured from hackers. Anti-symmetric fingerprinting technique is generally used by banking sector industry in order to find traitors who do fraud transactions instead of original customer. Quantum heuristics algorithms are used to improve the efficiency of figure scan and multicast this for checking this information while performing transactions by original customer.

Cryptosystems deals with effective task managing cryptanalysis of algorithms they are considered as NP-Hard problem. These cryptanalysis algorithms are subjected to various attacks because of insufficient resources to manage their computation. Quantum meta-heuristics support these cryptanalysis algorithms with wide optimized resources used while computing the keys for encrypting the data. QPSO algorithm was found to efficient to achieve fast convergence with required limited resources. The QPSO algorithm is extended it support to build strong intrusion detection system to stop the intruders to hack the systems inside the organization.

10.5.8 Quantum Meta-Heuristics Applications for Miscellaneous Domain

Financial portfolio management is the process of selection of optimal allocation of a budget to different criteria of activities under taken in the organization for certain assets like commodities, securities and bonds which will in turn gives organization high returns over time. The solution of financial portfolio problem was to maximize the expected revenue while minimizing the risks. This solution can be obtained optimally by quantum mea-heuristics algorithm called quantum genetic algorithm by defining an objective function for allocation of budget to assets which gives high expected returns in future.

Aviation industry has emerging challenges in performing airside operations for managing like airspace, air traffic flow management, operation of aircraft and surface traffic operation. Quantum meta-heuristics has come with multiple optimized algorithms to provide solutions to the problems of aviation industry. It promises with high efficiency in resolving the issues at faster rate for decision making in airside operations. Figure 10.6 gives the clear idea of type of airside specific operations with mentioned quantum meta-heuristics method algorithms. The three category airspace operations are effectively dealt with various quantum meta-heuristics methods to solve them in optimized way efficiently.

DC motor fault diagnosis is the latest application where quantum meta-heuristics are applied to give robust, sensitive and adequate computational cost solution with in less time. The fault diagnosis is treated as optimization problem and quantum differential evolution method is used for efficient fault diagnosis in DC motors.

E-commerce has revolutionized way of shopping as website became more popular where multiple organizations are competing for their products to attract online customers without losing existing ones and increase their purchases. These online shopping website need to be updated with new features to give more productive information with good visibility of product features to online customers. This website adaptation needs to be optimized by considering multiple criteria like maximizing transaction and visualization of product [84]. Quantum meta-heuristic has come with Quantum inspired ant colony optimization to solve this shopping website multi-criteria optimization problem.

Quantum Annealing is a quantum meta-heuristic that provides multivariable optimization problem with fast convergence and better results for hardware architecture in FPGA circuit synthesis. Multi-dimensional knapsack problem is applied for effective circuit synthesis for placing the

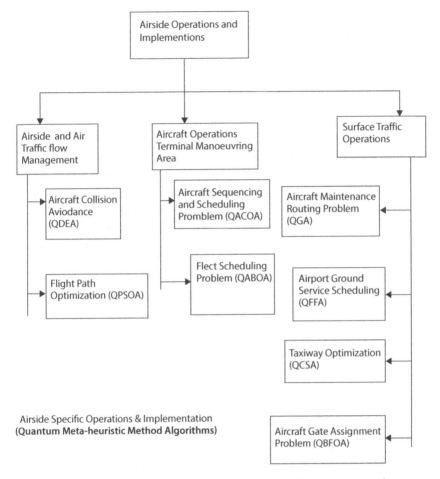

Figure 10.6 Airside specific operations & implementations with quantum meta-heuristic method algorithms.

components in optimal way of taking load and checking power supply for each component on FPGA board.

Website design for online shopping has gained much significance as many users with less knowledge using websites are using these websites for purchases of goods and this opened heavy competition among these online shopping websites to design their websites for attracting their customers with simple navigation procedures. This website design needs to satisfy multiple criteria like lower waiting time, attractive presentation, etc. which are easily achieved using multi criteria optimization of quantum-inspired genetic algorithm [19]. The quantum genetic algorithm applies the quantum mechanics and use q-bit representation for efficient means of optimization.

The fuzzy control needs to solve several stabilization condition problems like linear matrix inequality and sum of squares of polynomial by considering optimal performance requirements. A novel design procedure for polynomial fuzzy controllers is done in an efficient way using quantum inspired evolutionary algorithms [11]. The best stability conditions are analyzed for better performance to achieve good control gains in less period of time. Neuro-fuzzy modeling needs a modified rule generation approach with self-constructing property which is achieved using quantum inspired bacterial foraging algorithm [54]. This quantum meta-heuristic algorithm updates the consequence parameters and tested for modeling fuel gas denitrification efficiently for a thermal plant.

DNA encoding is latest emerging domain where criticality lies with DNA computation. The traditional optimization methods are failed to solve the DNA encoding because of its multiple constraints while evaluation. Quantum meta-heuristics has come with a novel solution approach by combining features of chaotic search, particle swarm optimization and evolutionary to generate a new quantum technique called as Quantum Chaotic Swarm Optimization Evolutionary Algorithm (QCSEA) [22]. QCSEA solved this DNA sequence optimization problem by generation of global optimal solution in later evolution period by keeping rapid convergence performance.

Mobile Computing domain has a critical challenge of managing low power consumption and high power storage in a small sized battery for decreasing their cost in future. The feature of low price made more no of customers to buy these mobile devices but they face a critical problem in terms of processing their applications. Mobile computational grid is created to effectively utilize the processing power of these devices by fixing constraints like bandwidth, battery, job scheduling and computational power. Quantum meta-heuristics has come with evolutionary approach for these problems with Quantum inspired Gravitational approach to schedule the jobs by exploring and exploiting above multiple criteria for effectively using computational power of mobile devices.

Chemical informatics is the latest domain in chemical data computing where prediction of composition of compounds needs high accuracy for reducing toxic effect on the utilization of those chemicals for preparing cosmetics or drugs and food safety. High knowledge discovery of chemical compound data needs to be processed for accurate predictions. Quantum meta-heuristic has come with a new solution approach called Quantum-inspired genetic programming (QIGP) [83] to improve prediction accuracy.

Quantum computers compute the data in terms of states q-bits. The IBM quantum D-wave is used for running quantum tabu search in order to obtain a combinatorial optimization of quantum states. The quantum entanglement states are used for building optimal graph coupling among different states of q-bit and design a teleport circuit. These quantum computers are efficiently used to resolve much of machine learning tasks. The boltzman restricted computations are solved using quantum circuit born machines t by modeling them with probabilistic nature. The portfolio optimization problem was resolved using quantum circuit born machines to work simultaneously on large amount time series data sets to optimize the price in stock market index.

Quantum meta-heuristics local search algorithms are efficiently used for network community detection problem. Two sets of network community data are connected using 16-Qbit IBM quantum computer and D-Wave 2000Q to compare the performance of optimal solutions. The quantum meta-heuristics results quality solutions with more number of iterations for convergence among two quantum computers. The current research trends of quantum are applied for robotics to integrate them with cloud services for fast processing. The impact of quantum meta-heuristics on artificial intelligence and machine learning enabled robots to carry out the sensing perception and kinematics of system diagnosis are effectively optimized.

Basics of quantum computing with their challenges will give quite good overview of latest domain areas where quantum meta-heuristics can be applied for optimizing the analysis of data sets. The current challenges before quantum meta-heuristics are they need to be merged together for hybrid solution approaches which are resulting more appropriate results then applied as individual for optimal solution. All trending domains are utilizing these features of quantum meta-heuristics to optimize their solution approaches in efficient manner. Complex mathematical problems are optimized using quantum meta-heuristics optimization techniques.

References

1. Feynman, R., Simulating Physics with Computers (PDF). *Int. J. Theor. Phys.*, 21, 6/7, 467–488, 1982.
2. Manin, Y.I., Vychislimoeinevychislimoe [Computable and Noncomputable] (in Russian). *Sov. Radio*, 5, 13–15, 1980.
3. Shor, P.W., Quantum computing. *Doc. Math.*, 1, 1000, 467–486, 1998.
4. Grover, L.K., A fast quantum mechanical algorithm for database search, in: *Proceedings of the Twenty-Eighth Annual ACM Symposium on Theory of Computing*, pp. 212–219, 1996.

5. Nielsen, M.A. and Chuang, I.L., *Quantum Computation and Quantum Information*, 2nd ed., Cambridge University Press, Cambridge, 2010.

6. Han, K.H. and Kim, J.H., Quantum-inspired evolutionary algorithm for a class of combinatorial optimization. *IEEE Trans. Evol. Comput.*, 6, 6, 580–593, 2002.

7. Li, Y., Shi, H., Jiao, L., Liu, R., Quantum evolutionary clustering algorithm based on watershed applied to sar image segmentation. *Neurocomputing*, 87, 90–98, 2012.

8. Talbi, H., Batouche, M., Draa, A., A quantum-inspired evolutionary algorithm for multiobjective image segmentation. *Int. J. Math. Phys. Eng. Sci.*, 1, 2, 109–114, 2007.

9. Ramdane, C., Meshoul, S., Batouche, M., Kholladi, M.K., A quantum evolutionary algorithm for data clustering. *Int. J. Data Min. Model. Manag.*, 2, 4, 369–387, 2010.

10. Chen, Y.-R., Tsai, C.-W., Chiang, M.-C., Yang, C.-S., An Improved Quantum-Inspired Evolutionary Algorithm for Data Clustering. *IEEE International Conference on Systems, Man, and Cybernetics*, pp. 3411–3416, 2018.

11. Yu, G.R., Huang, Y.C., Cheng, C.Y., Sum-of-squares-based fuzzy controller design using quantum-inspired evolutionary algorithm. *Int. J. Syst. Sci.*, 47, 9, 2225–2236, 2016.

12. Xing, H., Xu, L., Qu, R., Qu, Z., A quantum inspired evolutionary algorithm for dynamic multicast routing with network coding. *Sixteenth International Symposium on Communications and Information Technologies (ISCIT), 2016*, pp. 186–190, 2016.

13. da Silveira, L.R., Tanscheit, R., Vellasco, M.M.B.R., Quantum inspired evolutionary algorithm for ordering problems. *Expert Syst. Appl.*, 67, 71–83, 2017.

14. Han, K.H. and Kim, J.H., Genetic quantum algorithm and its application to combinatorial optimization problem. In *Proceedings of the 2000 Congress on Evolutionary Computation*. CEC00 (Cat. No. 00TH8512), 2, 2000.

15. Li, B.B. and Wang, L., A hybrid quantum-inspired genetic algorithm for multiobjective flow shop scheduling. *IEEE Trans. Syst. Man Cybern. Part B*, 37, 3, 576–591, 2007.

16. Xiao, J., Yan, Y.P., Zhang, J., Tang, Y., A quantum-inspired genetic algorithm for k-means clustering. *Comput. Appl. Biosci.*, 37, 7, 4966–4973, 2010.

17. Zhao, S., Xu, G., Taoi, T., Liang, L., Real-coded chaotic quantum inspired genetic algorithm for training of fuzzy neural networks. *Comput. Math. Appl.*, 57, 11, 2009–2015, 2009.

18. Mohammed, A.M., Elhefnawy, N.A., El-Sherbiny, M.M., Hadhoud, M.M., Quantum crossover based quantum genetic algorithm for solving nonlinear programming, in: *Proceedings of the Eighth International Conference on Informatics and Systems*, pp. 145–153, 2012.

19. Dilip, K., Multi-criteria website optimization using multi-objective quantum inspired genetic algorithm, in: *Proceedings of the First International Conference on Next Generation Computing Technologies*, pp. 965–970, 2016.

20. Konar, D., Bhattacharyya, S., Sharma, K., Sharma, S., Pradhan, S.R., An improved hybrid quantum-inspired genetic algorithm (HQIGA) for scheduling of real-time task in multiprocessor system. *Appl. Soft Comput.*, 53, 296307, 2017.

21. Wang, Y., Feng, X.Y., Huang, Y.X., Pu, D.B., Zhou, W.G., Liang, Y.C., Zhou, C.G., A novel quantum swarm evolutionary algorithm and its applications. *Neurocomputing*, 70, 4, 633–640, 2007.

22. Xiao, J., Xu, J., Chen, Z., Zhang, K., Pan, L., A hybrid quantum chaotic swarm evolutionary algorithm for DNA encoding. *Comput. Math. Appl.*, 57, 11, 1949–1958, 2009.

23. Sun, J., Wu, X., Fang, W., Ding, Y., Long, H., Xu, W., Multiple sequence alignment using the hidden Markov model trained by an improved quantum-behaved particle swarm optimization. *Inf. Sci.*, 182, 1, 93–114, 2012.

24. Ykhlef, M., A quantum swarm evolutionary algorithm for mining association rules in large databases. *J. King Saud Univ.-Comp. Info. Sci.*, 23, 1, 1–6, 2011.

25. Sun, J., Liu, J., Xu, W., Using quantum-behaved particle swarm optimization algorithm to solve non-linear programming problems. *Int. J. Comput. Math.*, 84, 2, 261–272, 2007.

26. Dey, S., Bhattacharyya, S., Maulik, U., Quantum inspired genetic algorithm and particle swarm optimization using chaotic map model based interference for gray level image thresholding. *Swarm Evol. Comput.*, 15, 38–57, 2014.

27. Li, Y., Chen, Z., Wang, Y., Jiao, L., Xue, Y., A novel distributed quantum behaved particle swarm optimization. *J. Optim.*, 2017, 9, 2017.

28. Li, L., Jiao, L., Zhao, J., Shang, R., Gong, M., Quantum-behaved discrete multi-objective particle swarm optimization for complex network clustering. *J. Syst. Eng. Electron.*, 63, 1–14, 2017.

29. AlBaity, H., Meshoul, S., Kaban, A., On Extending Quantum Behaved Particle Swarm Optimization to Multi Objective Context. *IEEE World Congress on Computational Intelligence*, Brisbane, Australia, June 10–15, 2012.

30. Banerjee, A., Gavrilas, M., Chattopadhyay, S., A Fuzzy Hybrid Approach for Reliability Optimization Problem in Power Distribution Systems. *International Conference and Exposition on Electrical and Power Engineering (EPE 2016)*, Iasi, Romania, 20–22 October, pp. 809–814.

31. Su, H. and Yang, Y., Quantum-inspired differential evolution for binary optimization, in: *Proceedings of the Fourth International Conference on Natural Computation, 2008*, pp. 341–346, 2008.

32. Zheng, T. and Yamashiro, M., Solving flow shop scheduling problems by quantum differential evolutionary algorithm. *Int. J. Adv. Manuf. Tech.*, 49, 5–8, 643–662, 2010.

33. Hota, A.R. and Pat, A., An adaptive quantum-inspired differential evolution algorithm for 0-1 knapsack problem, in: *Proceedings of the Second World Congress on Nature and Biologically Inspired Computing*, 2010, pp. 703–708, 2010.

34. Bouaziz, A., Draa, A., Chikhi, S., A quantum-inspired artificial bee colony algorithm for numerical optimisation, in: *Proceedings of the Eleventh International Symposium on Programming and Systems*, pp. 81–88, 2013.

35. Duan, H., Xu, C., Xing, Z., A hybrid artificial bee colony optimization and quantum evolutionary algorithm for continuous optimization problems. *Int. J. Neural Syst.*, 20, 1, 39–50, 2010.

36. Soleimanpour-Moghadam, M., Nezamabadi-Pou, H., Farsangi, M.M., A quantum inspired gravitational search algorithm for numerical function optimization. *Inf. Sci.*, 267, 83–100, 2014.

37. Nezamabadi-Pour, H., A quantum-inspired gravitational search algorithm for binary encoded optimization problems. *Eng. Appl. Artif. Intell.*, 40, 62–75, 2015.

38. Barani, F., Mirhosseini, M., Nezamabadi-Pour, H., Application of binary quantum-inspired gravitational search algorithm in feature subset selection. *Appl. Intell.*, 47, 1–15, 2017.

39. Singh, K.V. and Raza, Z., A quantum-inspired binary gravitational search algorithm-based job-scheduling model for mobile computational grid. *Concurr. Comput.: Pract. E.*, 29, 12, 2017.

40. Dey, S., Bhattacharyya, S., Maulik, U., New quantum inspired metaheuristic techniques for multi-level colour image thresholding. *Appl. Soft Comput.*, 10, 46, 3–4, 677–702, 2016.

41. You, X., Liu, S., Wang, Y., Quantum dynamic mechanism-based parallel ant colony optimization algorithm. *Int. J. Comput. Intell. Syst.*, 3, 101–113, 2010.

42. Jiao, L., Li, Y., Gong, M., Zhang, X., Quantum-inspired immune clonal algorithm for global optimization. *IEEE Trans. Syst. Man Cybern. Part B*, 38, 5, 1234–1253, 2008.

43. Wu, Q., Jiao, L., Li, Y., Deng, X., A novel quantum-inspired immune clonal algorithm with the evolutionary game approach. *Prog. Nat. Sci.*, 19, 10, 1341–1347, 2009.

44. Shang, R., Du, B., Dai, K., Jiao, L., Esfahani, A.M.G., Stolkin, R., Quantum-inspired immune clonal algorithm for solving large-scale capacitated arc routing problems. *Memet. Comput.*, 1–22, 2017.

45. Layeb, A., A novel quantum inspired cuckoo search for knapsack problems. *Int. J. Bio-Inspir. Com.*, 3, 5, 297–305, 2011.

46. Layeb, A. and Boussalia, S.R., A novel quantum inspired cuckoo search algorithm for bin packing problem. *Int. J. Inf. Technol. Comput. Sci.*, 4, 5, 58–67, 278, 2012.

47. Cheung, N.J., Ding, X.M., Shen, H.B., A nonhomogeneous cuckoo search algorithm based on quantum mechanism for real parameter optimization. *IEEE Trans. Cybern.*, 47, 2, 391–402, 2017.

48. Yang, Y.J., Kuo, S.Y., Lin, F.J., Liu, I.I., Chou, Y.H., Improved quantum inspired tabu search algorithm for solving function optimization problem, in: *Proceedings of the IEEE International Conference on Systems, Man, and Cybernetics*, pp. 823–828, 2013.

49. Layeb, A., A hybrid quantum inspired harmony search algorithm for 0-1 optimization problems. *J. Comput. Appl. Math.*, 253, 14–25, 2013.

50. Ding, W., Wang, J., Guan, Z., Shi, Q., Enhanced minimum attribute reduction based on quantum-inspired shuffled frog leaping algorithm. *J. Syst. Eng. Electron.*, 24, 3, 426–434, 2013.

51. Wang, X., Liu, S., Liu, Z., Underwater sonar image detection: A combination of non-local spatial information and quantum-inspired shuffled frog leaping algorithm. *PLoS One*, 12, 5, e0177666, 2017.

52. Zhu, K. and Jiang, M., Quantum artificial fish swarm algorithm, in: *Proceedings of the Eighth World Congress on Intelligent Control and Automation*, pp. 1–5, 2010.

53. Zouache, D., Nouioua, F., Moussaoui, A., Quantum-inspired firefly algorithm with particle swarm optimization for discrete optimization problems. *Soft Comput.*, 20, 7, 2781–2799, 2016.

54. Huang, S. and Chen, M., Constructing optimized interval type-2 tsk neurofuzzy systems with noise reduction property by quantum inspired BFA. *Neurocomputing*, 173, 3, 1839–1850, 2016.

55. Gao, H., Du, Y., Diao, M., Quantum-inspired glowworm swarm optimisation and its application. *Int. J. Comput. Sci. Math.*, 8, 1, 91–100, 2017.

56. Pavithr, R.S. and Gursaran, Quantum inspired social evolution (QSE) algorithm for 0-1 knapsack problem. *Swarm Evol. Comput.*, 29, 33–46, 2016.

57. Dey, S., Bhattacharyya, S., Maulik, U., Quantum Behaved Multi-objective PSO and ACO Optimization for Multi-level Thresholding. *Sixth International Conference on Computational Intelligence and Communication Networks*, pp. 242–246, 2014.

58. Crispin, A. and Syrichas, A., Quantum annealing algorithm for vehicle scheduling. *IEEE International Conference on Systems, Man, and Cybernetics*, pp. 3523–3528, 2013.

59. Yang, X.S., *Nature-inspired metaheuristic algorithms*, Luniver Press, 2008.

60. Han, K.H. and Kim, J.H., Genetic quantum algorithm and its application to combinatorial optimization problem. In *Proceedings of the 2000 Congress on Evolutionary Computation*. CEC00 (Cat. No. 00TH8512), 2, 2000.

61. Zhao, S., Xu, G., Taoi, T., Liang, L., Real-coded chaotic quantum inspired genetic algorithm for training of fuzzy neural networks. *Comput. Math. Appl.*, 57, 11, 2009–2015, 2009.

62. Dilip, K., Multi-criteria website optimization using multi-objective quantum inspired genetic algorithm, in: *Proceedings of the First International Conference on Next Generation Computing Technologies*, pp. 965–970, 2016.

63. Zhang, G.-x., Li, N., Jin, W.-d., Hu, L.-z., Novel quantum genetic algorithm and its applications. *Front. Electr. Electron. Eng. China*, 1, 1, 31–36, 2006.

64. Ykhlef, M., A quantum swarm evolutionary algorithm for mining association rules in large databases. *J. King Saud Univ.-Comp. Info. Sci.*, 23, 1, 1–6, 2011.

65. Xiao, J., Xu, J., Chen, Z., Zhang, K., Pan, L., A hybrid quantum chaotic swarm evolutionary algorithm for DNA encoding. *Comput. Math. Appl.*, 57, 11, 1949–1958, 2009.

66. Bouaziz, A., Draa, A., Chikhi, S., A quantum-inspired artificial bee colony algorithm for numerical optimisation, in: *Proceedings of the Eleventh International Symposium on Programming and Systems*, pp. 81–88, 2013.

67. Duan, H., Xu, C., Xing, Z., A hybrid artificial bee colony optimization and quantum evolutionary algorithm for continuous optimization problems. *Int. J. Neural Syst.*, 20, 1, 39–50, 2010.

68. Singh, K.V. and Raza, Z., A quantum-inspired binary gravitational search algorithm-based job-scheduling model for mobile computational grid. *Concurr. Comput.: Pract. E.*, 29, 12, 2017.

69. Dey, S., Bhattacharyya, S., Maulik, U., New quantum inspired metaheuristic techniques for multi-level colour image thresholding. *Appl. Soft Comput.*, 46, 3–4, 677–702, 2016.

70. Jiao, L., Li, Y., Gong, M., Zhang, X., Quantum-inspired immune clonal algorithm for global optimization. *IEEE Trans. Syst. Man Cybern. Part B*, 38, 5, 1234–1253, 2008.

71. Wu, Q., Jiao, L., Li, Y., Deng, X., A novel quantum-inspired immune clonal algorithm with the evolutionary game approach. *Prog. Nat. Sci.*, 19, 10, 1341–1347, 2009.

72. Shang, R., Du, B., Dai, K., Jiao, L., Esfahani, A.M.G., Stolkin, R., Quantum-inspired immune clonal algorithm for solving large-scale capacitated arc routing problems. *Memet. Comput.*, 10, 1–22, 2017.

73. Karmakar, S., Dey, A., Saha, I., Use of quantum-inspired metaheuristics during last two decades, in: *2017 7th International Conference on Communication Systems and Network Technologies (CSNT)*, 2017 Nov 11, IEEE, pp. 272–278.

74. Wong, L.A., Ling, T.J., Ramlee, N.A., Optimal Power Quality Monitors Placement using Improved Lightning Search Algorithm, in: *2018 IEEE 7th International Conference on Power and Energy (PECon)*, 2018 Dec 3, pp. 227–230.

75. Xu, F., Hu, H., Wang, C., Gao, H., A visual tracking framework based on differential evolution algorithm, in: *2017 Seventh International Conference on Information Science and Technology (ICIST)*, 2017 Apr 16, pp. 147–153.

76. Manikanta, G., Mani, A., Singh, H.P., Chaturvedi, D.K., Sitting and sizing of capacitors in distribution system using adaptive quantum inspired evolutionary algorithm, in: *2016 7th India International Conference on Power Electronics (IICPE)*, 2016 Nov 17, pp. 1–6.

77. Li, Y., Shi, H., Gong, M., Shang, R., Quantum-inspired evolutionary clustering algorithm based on manifold distance, in: *Proceedings of the first ACM/SIGEVO Summit on Genetic and Evolutionary Computation*, 2009 Jun 12, ACM, pp. 871–874.

78. Rahman, M., Hassan, R., Ranjan, R., Buyya, R., Adaptive workflow scheduling for dynamic grid and cloud computing environment. *Concurr. Comput.: Pract. E.*, 25, 13, 1816–42, 2013 Sep 10.

79. Meshoul, S. and Batouche, M., A novel quantum behaved particle swarm optimization algorithm with chaotic search for image alignment, in: *IEEE Congress on Evolutionary Computation*, 2010 Jul 18, IEEE, pp. 1–6.

80. Kuo, S.Y., Chou, Y.H., Chen, C.Y., Quantum-inspired algorithm for cyber-physical visual surveillance deployment systems. *Comput. Networks*, 117, 5–18, 2017 Apr 22.

81. Zhang, W., Shi, W., Zhuo, J., BDI-agent-based quantum-behaved PSO for shipboard power system reconfiguration. *Int. J. Comput. Appl. Technol.*, 55, 1, 4–11, 2017.

82. Gandhi, T. and Alam, T., Quantum genetic algorithm with rotation angle refinement for dependent task scheduling on distributed systems, in: *2017 Tenth International Conference on Contemporary Computing (IC3)*, 2017 Aug 10, IEEE, pp. 1–5.

83. Darwish, S.M., Quantum Inspired Genetic Programming Model to Predict Toxicity Degree for Chemical Compounds. *Int. J. Artif. Intell. Res.*, 3, 1, 33–46, 2018 Jun 7.

84. Bhandari, A.K., Kumar, I.V., Srinivas, K., Cuttlefish algorithm based multilevel 3D Otsu function for color image segmentation. *IEEE Trans. Instrum. Meas.*, 84, 69, 1871–1880, 2019 Jun 12.

85. Dilip, K., Multi-criteria website optimization using multi-objective quantum inspired genetic algorithm, in: *2015 1st International Conference on Next Generation Computing Technologies (NGCT)*, 2015 Sep 4, IEEE, pp. 965–970.

86. Forno, E., Acquaviva, A., Kobayashi, Y., Macii, E., Urgese, G.A., Parallel Hardware Architecture For Quantum Annealing Algorithm Acceleration, in: *2018 IFIP/IEEE International Conference on Very Large Scale Integration (VLSI-SoC)*, 2018 Oct 8, IEEE, pp. 31–36.

87. Soares, J., Lobo, C., Silva, M., Morais, H., Vale, Z., Relaxation of non-convex problem as an initial solution of meta-heuristics for energy resource management, in: *2015 IEEE Power & Energy Society General Meeting*, 2015 Jul 26, IEEE, pp. 1–5.

11

Ensuring Security and Privacy in IoT for Healthcare Applications

Anjali Yeole* and D.R. Kalbande

Vesit, Mumbai, India

Abstract

Healthcare is a service whose forthcoming appears to be motivated by innovation and data sharing. We can effectively use Internet of Things (IoT)-based healthcare systems for patient monitoring and emergency response services by maintaining security and preserving the privacy of patient's medical records. IoT devices in healthcare can gather patient's body parameters and share information with doctors, nurses and patient's relatives. Most of the time traditional method of manual recording of body parameters and reporting them to the doctors is used. This is obtained by nurses periodically for all patients. Their precious time is for taking care of patients not for recording body parameters all the time. IoT-enabled healthcare industry is the solution for the same. This article focuses on architectures and models for IoT-based Healthcare applications along with security, privacy issues and challenges by considering industry standards. Using IoT devices for health monitoring at a personal level is very easy and comfortable but using IoT at hospital level is challenging hence integration of E-health and IoT will also be discussed in this article.

Keywords: IoT, healthcare, security

11.1 Introduction

With the expansion of the IoT healthcare service is growing. The cause of this chapter is to validate how the IoT is transmuting the healthcare sector as well as the role of Information Technology in healthcare. It is necessary to transform the lives of people with better healthcare services with IoT applications. IoT in

---

Corresponding author: anjali.yeole@ves.ac.in

Kolla Bhanu Prakash, G. R. Kanagachidambaresan, V. Srikanth, E. Vamsidhar (eds.) Cognitive Engineering for Next Generation Computing: A Practical Analytical Approach, (299–314) © 2021 Scrivener Publishing LLC

healthcare mentions to measuring devices used for patients' vital monitoring devices such as pulse rate, body temperature, Oxygen saturation (SPo2), blood pressure, heart rate & activity monitoring and body check-up, such as a thermometer, weight scale, linked to the internet and transform information from the physical world in to the digital world and get saved in the cloud storage for future reference. Following IoT components are used in healthcare.

- To gather patient data like vital body parameters: Sensors.
- To process, investigate and wirelessly transfer the data: Microcontrollers.
- To empower rich graphical user interfaces: Microprocessors.
- To analyze sensor data and sent to the cloud for permanent storage: Healthcare-specific gateways.

Use of IoT in healthcare is clearly separated into two parts: IoT for patient care and IoT for hospital management. IoT is convenient in the healthcare services, but the work of IoT in the healthcare sector is a little bit neglected because of security, privacy, heterogeneity and interoperability issues. First section of this chapter discusses about need of IoT in healthcare. Second section throws light on IoT enabled medical devises. Third section is study of different IoT enable architectures for Smart Hospitals. Fourth section throws light on Challenges and Issues for using IoT. Section five describes proposed architecture to overcome challenges and issues discussed in Section four.

Major contribution of this chapter is to improve security and privacy of data getting exchanged in healthcare using IoT is covered in the last section of this paper. Proposed architecture for medical data exchange gives deep insight of preserving security and privacy with the help of encryption and authentication algorithm in IoT.

Section 11.2 focuses on need of IoT devices in healthcare along with IoT devices available in healthcare. Section 11.3 concentrates on IoT enable architecture for smart healthcare. In Section 11.4 all major challenges faced by IoT enable devices specifically in healthcare are discussed. Section 11.5 mentions new proposed architecture to overcome problems as discussed in Section 11.4. A complete solution for secure use of IoT in healthcare is the main contribution of this paper.

11.2   Need of IoT in Healthcare

Continuous monitoring of the patient is a critical task in care of critically ill patients. ICUs, CCUs, operation room and anesthesia ward need the continuous observation of the patient [1]. The conventional, manual method requires a considerable amount of time. Current investigation shows that the monitoring and recording of the five vital signs manually are most of the times partial which has the potential to worsening health condition of a patient [2]. Whereas continuous electronic monitoring is beneficial and it alarms when patient's health is deteriorating [3]. Although bedside monitors are monitoring vital parameters all the time, these parameters are never directly sent to doctors or nurses or caretaker of the patient on their handheld devices (like mobile). No analysis is performed on this data to alert the patient's health status. Data reading, and it's reporting to the doctor is still a manual process in most of the hospitals. Nurses, assistant doctors are observing those parameters and reporting them to doctors. In the era of IoT, mobile sending vital real-time parameters of the critically ill patient to the doctor will help to give better treatment to the patient [4]. IoT enables health care system to lessen the chance of human errors, delay in communication and helps the doctor to give more inputs at the time of decision making with correct interpretation [5]. We decided to study this and to come up with a solution so that patient and doctors can be connected in minimum cost for better care of a patient.

11.2.1 Available Internet of Things Devices for Healthcare

In IoT applications, essential things like internet and sensors/actuators work in the bottom-most layer of the technology stack of IoT. IoT reads physical data like temperature, humidity to human body parameters like blood pressure, temperature, heart rate, motion oxygen saturation, etc. using sensors and converts it into digital data. Actuators are used to react in the appropriate position like insulin pump injecting insulin. Table 11.1 has listed all conditions where IoT can be used with sensors and their operations.

A new Grand View Research Inc. report says that by 2022, IoT in the healthcare market is projected to accomplish nearly $409.9 billion; another report by Technavio's market expect the global IoT market in the healthcare segment to raise at a marvelous CAGR of about 37% by 2020. Gartner [7] in their report on "Mass Adoption of the Internet of Things will Create New Opportunities and Challenges for Enterprises," discuss security and identity issues represent major IoT roadblock. Nearly 50% of people are reluctant to take IoT because of security and privacy concern. Next 40% are due to lack of a compelling business case.

Then nearly 32% inhibitors to IoT adoption because there is need of obtaining staff and skills to create the IoT strategy and systems. Whereas

Table 11.1 IoT in healthcare scr [6].

Parameter to measure	Sensors details
Diabetes	Insulin injection to inject specific quantity of insulin at specified time.
Wound analysis for advanced diabetes patients	Humidity sensor to check wounds are required so that its bandage can be removed. For diabetic patients it helps in keeping track of their wound recovery.
Heart rate monitoring	Elderly people or people having heart diseases need continues monitoring of heart rate this sensor play major role.
BP monitoring	BP is an important vital parameter to major for all patients where BP monitoring sensor continuously send data to doctor's mobile.
Body temperature monitoring	Continuously keep track of patient's body temperature. This works very well with patients discharged from hospital and toddlers.
Medication management	This can manage how much medicine has been dispatched.
Wheelchair Management	IoT enable wheelchair can take patient from on room to other.
Oxygen saturation monitoring	Oxygen saturation is important vital parameter to measure in serious patients and elderly person. This sensor measures that parameter seriously.
Skin Infection	Sensor for skin infection Keep track of spread of skin infection.
Cough detection	This is an audio system in smartphone which detects changes in voice to detect cough in throat.
Robotic Surgery	Surgical robot system and augmented reality sensor, robot arms help in surgery.

22% are refusing IoT because they are afraid of risk associated with business change and new business model. In this sample, 20% are refusing IoT because they think that they need to deal with new and untried technology and service providers. They feel that initially if services providers are having less number of customers, they will provide excellent service but later on when a number of customers will go on increasing what the is guarantee that all will get seamless service. In this group, 17% of generation is not ready to accept IoT because of workforce resistance to new technologies, practices or procedures.

In western countries, most of the hospitals are IoT-enabled whereas in India very few hospitals have implemented the IoT concept. One of them is Bangalore-based Manipal Hospital which provides a wearable device to pregnant mothers which once connected with a mobile phone app gives fetal heart rate and other key parameters to the doctor every after-fix interval this can be accessed remotely on a tablet or phone [8].

Chennai-based Apollo Hospital is also IoT-enabled [8]. Doctors can access radiology, CT scan reports and ECG reports using IoT-MD [9]. Generally, common sensors can be used to measure following parameters in medical field Body Temperature, Electroencephalography (EEG)/Electronic Cardio Graph (ECG), SpO2, blood pressure, breathing CO, alcohol, positions, local body angle, weight and some momentum sensor on exercise [9].

11.3   Literature Survey on an IoT-Aware Architecture for Smart Healthcare Systems

Daily life, Road traffic monitoring, Security, Transport and Logistics, and Healthcare, are top five applications where IoT is taking a major step. This chapter majorly focuses on IoT in healthcare service. The IoT could be a game-changer for the healthcare industry. Using IoT in healthcare industry has many advantages like, put the focus back on better patient care increasing efficiency, and lowering costs. IoT in healthcare is diverse computing, wirelessly communicating apps and devices that connect patients and health caretakers to identify, observe, track and store vital information and medical information. Different authors have studied and presented IoT-based healthcare systems, some of which are discussed in this chapter.

11.3.1   Cyber-Physical System (CPS) for e-Healthcare

In this framework as shown in Figure 11.1 there are four layers: "IoT device layer", "IoT gateway layer", "IoT service platform layer", and "mobile app". The sensor network is WBAN sending information to the cloud for further processing using the relay network [10].

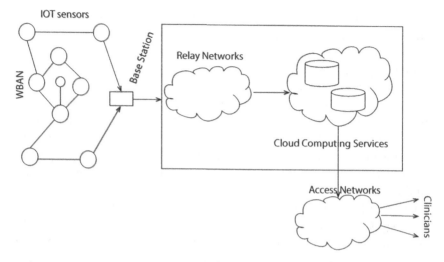

Figure 11.1 An IoT framework for healthcare monitoring systems [10].

11.3.2   IoT-Enabled Healthcare With REST-Based Services

Author has proposed five stages involved in this platform. All sensors should have REST connector API for healthcare. The important module is a "medical sensor" gadget to calculate and send the important data, and the other module is a "virtual medical sensor" which is a "software sensor" having a rational conclusion calculation and mash-up information from different physical medical sensors and server. All segments are talking to one another with API. The virtual sensor is nothing but a software sensor after gathering data from IoT. And actual sensors are like BP sensor, temperature sensor, etc. [11].

11.3.3   Smart Hospital System

In this paper the author has used RFID for identification: the RFID—improved wireless sensor network, named "Hybrid Sensing Network (HSN)" hereafter. The IoT Smart Gateway and the user interface for data visualization and management are the heart of this system. The HSN consists of an integrated "RFID—WSN 6LoWPAN topology [12]". Catarinucci, De Donno *et al.* [12], in their paper titled "An IoT-Aware Architecture for Smart Healthcare Systems," presented and discussed a novel "IoT-aware Smart Hospital System (SHS)". It can promise advanced services for the automatic monitoring and tracing of patients, staffs, and biomedical devices within hospitals and nursing organizations, by exploring the advantages obtainable by the mix use of dissimilar, yet corresponding, technologies and standards, such as Radio-frequency identification, wireless network, smart mobile, IPv6 over Low-Power Wireless Personal Area Networks, and Constrained Application Protocol.

11.3.4   Freescale Home Health Hub Reference Platform

"Freescale Home Health Hub reference platform" is an example of enabling technology for remote monitoring, which is built on "Freescale i.MX applications processing technology and tightly integrates key capabilities—such as power management and wireless connectivity in the telehealth gateway that enables collection and sharing of physiological information [13]".

11.3.5   A Smart System Connecting e-Health Sensors and Cloud

This paper presents the look associated implementation of an e-health good networked system. The system is aimed to stop delays within the arrival of patients' medical info to the health care suppliers, significantly in an accident and emergency things, to prevent manual information getting into, and to extend beds capability in hospitals, particularly throughout public events wherever an oversized variety of individuals are meeting in one place. The design for this method is predicated on medical devices that live patient's physical parameters by exploitation wireless sensor networks (WSNs). These sensors transfer information from patients' bodies over the wireless network to the cloud surroundings. Therefore, patients can have a prime quality service as a result of the excellent e-health good system supports medical workers by providing duration information gathering, eliminating manual information assortment, sectionalize the observation of significant numbers of patients [14].

11.3.6   Customizing 6LoWPAN Networks Towards IoT-Based Ubiquitous Healthcare Systems

Gia et al. [15] in their paper titled "Customizing 6LoWPAN Networks towards Internet of-Things Based Ubiquitous Healthcare Systems", presented for customizing 6LoWPAN for improvement of effectiveness, overall costs, and quality in healthcare. The author has implemented IoT-based architecture and an inclusive system starting from collecting bio-signals using analog front-end devices integrated into 6LoWPAN medical sensor nodes to finally present health and contextual data stored in the cloud server to end-users.

IoT is the state of art technology which has been used almost in all fields. There are many research articles that have been published about IoT in healthcare in this chapter and we studied few of them primarily one to represent different domains like WSN, e-healthcare, RFID based IoT in healthcare, REST-based services for IoT in healthcare, etc.

11.4 IoT in Healthcare: Challenges and Issues

One of the most exciting goals of today's world is enlightening the productivity of healthcare infrastructures systems. The need for delivering quality care to patients while reducing healthcare costs is the main issue. Latest treads in the design of IoT technologies are stepping stone towards the expansion of smart systems to support and improve the healthcare system.

Our world has become more intelligent and interconnected because IoT devices are connected to the Internet which collect data for investigation. Normally we carry on an average one or two mobile devices with us nowadays. Hence, by taking advantage of the increasing presence of mobile devices, the cost of equipment can be reduced meaningfully in many services like healthcare.

In traditional TCP/IP networks, the primary purpose of security is to protect the confidentiality, integrity, and availability (CIA) of data which is getting transferred. Because of advancements in IoT environment, Wireless Sensor Network security needs more than traditional security protection. That results in new and the unique requirements of trust, security, and privacy (TSP). Purchasing IoT-enabled devices is not affordable to many hospitals, as we need specific mechanism or device which will convert existing digital devices into IoT-enabled healthcare device. Security, Privacy and Interoperability are the significant issues faced by IoT in healthcare.

11.4.1 Challenges of the Internet of Things for Healthcare

Khanna *et al.* [16] in their white paper titled "Life Sciences, The Internet of Things for Medical Devices-Prospects, Challenges and the Way Forward, Tata Consultancy Services" discussed, "complex ecosystems could be insufficient to discuss only standard requirements regarding hardware issues and software support of individual elements. In the affected multidisciplinary development area, with intricate vertical and horizontal markets, it is essential a close collaboration between the corresponding stakeholders:

application domain experts, end-users, hardware designers, market specialists, software developers, road mapping strategists and even the association of visionaries to implement successful healthcare ecosystems". The significant challenges in the integration and management of IoT-MD include: "Interoperability and Managing device variety, Data integration, data volume and performance, Scale, Flexibility and development of applications, Data privacy, Need for medical expertise". As shown in Figure 11.2, IoT security is at the topmost position in the list. As many researchers are working on IoT security because people bother to use IoT because of security and next to it is privacy.

Fernandez *et al.* [17] in their paper titled "Opportunities and challenges of the Internet of Things for healthcare: Systems engineering perspective," analyzes the involved system engineering decisions, to build cost-effective Health-IoT platforms that enhance the corresponding medical services, clinical care, and remote monitoring, to respond to new social challenges.

IoT-enabled devices are costly as compared to standard medical devices. Let's take one example BP786 10 Advanced Accuracy per Arm Blood

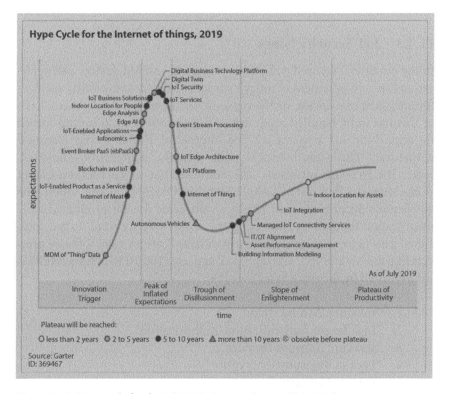

Figure 11.2 Hype cycle for the IoT, 2019. Source: Gartner (July 2019).

Pressure Monitor Bluetooth Connectivity costs Rs. 11,936.00 whereas normal "Omron Digital Blood Pressure Monitor HEM-7130-L" with Large Cuff Size 100% original, 1 Year warranty With Vat Bill costs Rs. 1,990.00. This clearly shows that IoT-enabled devices are costly as compared to the normal one. But for sure once this IoT setup for hospitals is ready, it will lower the cost of care. The health of patients can be monitored on a real-time basis, avoiding unnecessary movement from one place to other.

11.4.2   IoT Interoperability Issues

Tarouco *et al.* [18] in their paper titled "Internet of Things in Healthcare: Interoperability and Security Issues," discussed different issues in interoperability like if the device is Bluetooth-enabled or ZigBee-based there are very few solutions available to connect to internet better to go with WiFi connectivity. With WiFi SNMP or web services can be used for internet connectivity and proposed a middleware to provide an enhanced "AAA (Authentication, Authorization, and Accounting)" service that it is especially important.

11.4.3   IoT Security Issues

In the era of IoT, secured and attack-proof IoT-enabled devices and applications are a requirement of today's world. IoT devices have many surfaces for an attack like device, or the network, or the clients or data, etc. Each of this has to be handled separately. All elements need to be considered for security in IoT projects are The Internet of Things Device (sensors/actuators), The Cloud-storage, The Mobile Application—business logic, The Network Interfaces, The Software, Use of Encryption, Use of Authentication, Physical Security, USB ports. OWSP [19], The "Open Web Application Security Project" [23] is a worldwide not-for-profit charitable organization focused on improving the security of software. It had published a list of top 10 vulnerabilities in different categories of software projects like the Mobile app, Web app, IoT app, etc. Top 10 IoT Vulnerabilities for IoT listed by them are as follows [19].

1. "Insecure Web Interface"
2. "Insufficient Authentication/Authorization"
3. "Insecure Network Services"
4. "Lack of Transport Encryption"
5. "Privacy Concerns"
6. "Insecure Cloud Interface"

7. "Insecure Mobile Interface"
8. "Insufficient Security Configurability"
9. "Insecure Software/Firmware"
10. "Poor Physical Security".

11.4.3.1 Security of IoT Sensors

Few days' back there were news that the insulin pump was hacked. Hacker could do that because logs of insulin pump were not encrypted. This doesn't mean that there are no security measures for IoT. Few Security algorithms those they are in use for IoT are Attribute-Based Encryption (ABE) [20], Tiny Encryption Algorithm (TEA) [21], PRESENT Cipher [22], Scalable Encryption Algorithm (SEA) [24], IPSec, TLS, etc. But the actual need is Lightweight algorithms with improved privacy.

11.4.3.2 Security of Data Generated by Sensors

Yi, Bouguettaya, *et al.* [24], in their paper titled "Privacy Protection for Wireless Medical Sensor Data", have used the lightweight encryption scheme and MAC generation scheme based on SHA-3 for secured communication between medical sensors and data servers along with a proposal for a distributed server approach to split up patient data for privacy preservation.

Bose *et al.* [25], in their paper titled "Why Not Keep Your Personal Data Secure Yet Private in IoT?: Our Lightweight Approach", presented works which make user privacy aware by noticing sensitive content of smart-meter readings as well as deliver privacy conservation using a lightweight, safe channel with mutual authentication by encrypting sensitive content based on resulting confidentiality score.

11.4.3.3 LoWPAN Networks Healthcare Systems and its Attacks

Mohiuddin *et al.* [26], in their paper titled "6LoWPAN based Service Discovery and RESTful Web Accessibility for the Internet of Things", discussed Attacks on RPL: "Selective forwarding attack, sinkhole attack, Sybil attack, hello flooding attack, wormhole attack, clone ID attack, black hole attack, denial of service attack". Attacks on 6LoWPAN: "Fragmentation attack, authentication attack, confidentiality attack, security threat from the internet side". Pongle, Pavan, and Chavan [27] in their paper titled "A survey: Attacks on RPL and 6LoWPAN in IoT", have discussed different attacks on 6LoWPAN. They are listed below:

- Selective Forwarding Attack: This is one type of DOS in the RPL network.
- Sinkhole Attack: Hacker attracts traffic with the help of advertisement node.
- Hello Flooding Attack: When any node joins network, they need to broadcast HELLO message to all neighboring nodes. An attacker can become part of the network and go on broadcasting this message.
- Wormhole Attack: This attack disturbs network formation and the flow of traffic.
- Clone ID Attack: Attacker nodes copies identity of other authentic nodes and make use of it for further communication as if it is an authentic node.

Proposed protocol with confidentiality and authentication technique can fight against almost all attacks. For more details kindly refer our paper [28].

11.5 Proposed System: 6LoWPAN and COAP Protocol-Based IoT System for Medical Data Transfer by Preserving Privacy of Patient

After studying different architectures and their issues we have proposed following system which is cost effective as well as secure.

Figure 11.3 shows system architecture for IoT-enabled secure system for reading patients body parameters like Heart rate, Temperature and Spo2. This system has three important parts border routers for connecting two different networks, RFID tag here it is termed as RFID server indicated by red color in the diagram above and sensors. The circuit diagram is for signal user. For one hospital we will require one circuit for one patient. All of them connecting with border router to send information to cloud. Blue color boxes show security routine running for authentication and encryption.

Protocol used for the communication is "6LoWPAN for personal area network: All the sensors and local devices are connected through this protocol". Constrained Application Protocol (CoAP) is used to expose data to the outside world. "6LoWPAN" is an abbreviation of "IPv6 over Low-Power Wireless Personal Area Network". Routing of 6LoWPAN works with near neighbor discovery allows any node coming in the range of edge router to transfer data. Any new node can register to the edge router and start broadcasting of data. Because of which many attacks are possible on this network. Authentication module will avoid this problem.

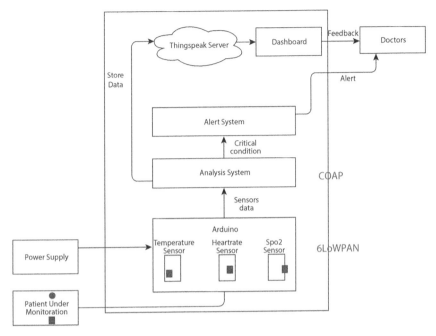

Figure 11.3 Architecture of IoT-based secure system for medical data transfer.

- *Authentication module* will check only sensor installed on patient body is sending data to respective RFID server by means of challenge response protocol. MAC ID of all sensors are saved on RFID server. If challenge and MAC ID matches that is an authentic sensor to send data to RFID server. As authentic sensor only can transfer data which avoids multiple attacks like DDOS, Selective Forwarding Attack, Sinkhole Attack, Clone ID.
- *Encryption model* will encrypt data send by sensors and will be transferred in the network thus will preserve privacy. Symmetric key encryption is used. Encrypted data transferred to the ThingSpeak cloud at an interval of a few seconds.

Data generation is enormous, so we considered sample size as data generated in 5 min by a patient in a day it was collected three times for 10 days, for 10 patients. Figure 11.3 shows a photo of one patient reading these body parameters. Readings given by IoT devices and readings by conventional devices are compared to check the accuracy of data. Whatever medical data is getting transferred in this network is encrypted using encryption algorithm. RFID server attached to the patient's body carries out authentication

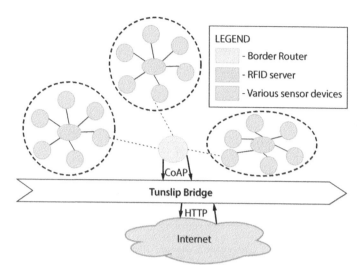

Figure 11.4 IoT network architecture for above hospitals [28].

of each sensor before accepting data from that sensor. Figure 11.4 shows complete network architecture of above system. Details of this architecture are given in our chapter [28].

11.6   Conclusion

In this chapter, we focused on the usage of IoT devices in healthcare as well as security and privacy awareness of IoT devices for healthcare. The increasing usage of IoT-enabled devices in healthcare requires focus on few points, namely: a) Need to design IoT-enabled Low cost device for healthcare, b) Need for a Lightweight Security protocol to take care of Trust, Security and Privacy for medical data, c) Need a data compression and data filtering layer in protocol to improve battery life and network bandwidth and d) Need to design intelligent Intrusion Detection System for IoT. Proposed system takes care of all aspects. In future proposed architecture should be expanded for secure medical image transfer at high speed without added overhead.

References

1. Barro, S., Presedo, J., Félix, P. *et al.*, Intelligent telemonitoring of critical care patients. *Dis. Manag. Health Out.*, 10, 291, 2002, https://doi.org/10.2165/00115677-200210050-00003.

2. Cardona-Morrell, M. et al., Vital signs monitoring and nurse–patient interaction: A qualitative observational study of hospital practice. Int. J. Nurs. Stud., 56, 9–16, 2016.
3. Medical buyer's guide MedTech care http://www.medicalbuyer.co.in/index.php/buyers-guide/buyers-guide-medtech/4542-bg-patient-monitoring-equipment.
4. Jara, A.J., Zamora, M.A., Skarmeta, A.F.G., An architecture based on Internet of Things to support mobility and security in medical environments. IEEE CCNC, 2010.
5. An Intelligent Real Time IoT-Based System, https://www.researchgate.net/publication/319161021_An_Intelligent_Real_Time_IoT_Based_System_IRTBS_for_Monitoring_ICU_ Patient [accessed Apr 29 2018].
6. Riazul Islam, S.M. (Member, Ieee), Kwak, D., Kabir, Md. H., Hossain, M., Kwak, K.-S. (Member, IEEE), The Internet of Things for Health Care: A comprehensive Survey, International Conference on Information and Communication Technology for Intelligent Systems, march 18, Received April 4, 2015, accepted May 8, 2015, date of publication June 1, 2015, date of current version June 4, 2015. Digital Object Identifier 10.1109/ACCESS.2015.2437951.
7. https://www.gartner.com/doc/2994817?ref=SiteSearch&sthkw=inhibitors&fnl=search& srcId= 1-3478922254.
8. Pongle, P. and Chavan, G., A survey: Attacks on RPL and 6LoWPAN in IoT. Pervasive Computing (ICPC), 2015 International Conference on, IEEE, 2015.
9. Khanna, A. and Misra, P., White Paper Life Sciences, The Internet of Things for Medical Devices -Prospects, Challenges and the Way Forward, Tata Consultancy Services, July 1, 2014.
10. Sawand, A., Djahel, S., Zhang, Z., Abdesselam, F.N., Toward Energy-Efficient and Trustworthy eHealth Monitoring System. IEEE/CIC ICCC2014, 1 Paris Descartes University, Paris, France, 2 University College Dublin, Dublin, Ireland, 3 TELECOM Lille, France.
11. Singh, D. and Gour, R., An IoT Framework for Healthcare Monitoring Systems. IJCSIS, 14, 5, 6, 2016.
12. Catarinucci, L., Danilo De Donno, L., Mainetti, L., Palano, L., Patrono, M., Stefanizzi, Tarricone, L., An IoT-Aware Architecture for Smart Healthcare Systems. IEEE Internet of Things Journal, 2, 515–526, 2015.
13. Niewolny, D., How the Internet of Things Is Revolutionizing Healthcare. Healthcare Segment Manager, Freescale Semiconductor, White Paper.
14. Jassas, M., Qasem, A., Mahmoud, Q., A smart system connecting e-health sensors and the cloud, in: Canadian Conference on Electrical and Computer Engineering, 712–716, 2015, 10.1109/CCECE.2015.7129362.
15. Gia, T.N., Thanigaivelan, N.K., Rahmani, A.-M., Westerlund, T., Liljeberg, P., Tenhunen, H., Customizing 6LoWPAN Networks towards Internet of-Things Based Ubiquitous Healthcare Systems, IEEE, ©2014, 978-1-4799-5442-1/14/$31.00.

16. Shton, K., That 'Internet of Things' Thing, In the real world, things matter more than ideas. *RFID J.*, 22 June 2009, Available from: http://www.rfi djournal.com/articles/view?4986.

17. Fernandez, F. and Pallis, G.C., Opportunities and challenges of the Internet of Things for healthcare Systems engineering perspective. *International Conference on Wireless Mobile Communication and Healthcare—Transforming healthcare through innovations in mobile and wireless technologies (MOBIHEALTH)*, ICST, © 2014.

18. Tarouco, L.M.R., Bertholdo, Granville, L.Z., Arbiza, L.M.R., Carbone, F., Marotta, M., de Santanna, J.J.C., *Internet of Things in Healthcare: Interoperatibility and Security Issues, (ICC)*, IEEE, 2012.

19. https://www.owasp.org/index.php/OWASP_Internet_of_Things_Project#tab=Main.

20. *Understanding the Internet of Things (IoT)*, GSM Association, 2014.

21. Bogdanov, Knudsen, L.R., Leander, G., Paar, C., Poschmann, A., Robshaw, M.J.B., Eurin, Y., Vikkelsoe, C., PRESENT: An Ultra-Lightweight Block Cipher, white paper.

22. Standaert, G., Gershenfeld, N., Quisquater, J.-J., The proceedings of ches, SEA a Scalable Encryption Algorithm for Small Embedded Applications, Springer, 2007.

23. https://www.cloudflare.com/learning/security/threats/owasp-top-10/.

24. Yi, X., Bouguettaya, A., Georgakopoulos, D., Song, A., Willemson, J., Privacy Protection for Wireless Medical Sensor Data. *IEEE Trans. Dependable Secure Comput.*, 2015.

25. Bose, Ulika, Bandyopadhyay, S., Ukil, A., Bhattacharyya, A., Pal, A., Why Not Keep Your Personal Data Secure Yet Private in IoT?: Our Lightweight Approach. *2015 IEEE Tenth International Conference on Intelligent Sensors, Sensor Networks and Information Processing (ISSNIP)*, Singapore, 7–9 April 2015.

26. Mohiuddin, J., Bhadram, V., Palli, S., Koshy, S.S., 6LoWPAN based Service Discovery and RESTful Web Accessibility for Internet of Things, IEEE, 2014.

27. Lamaazi, H., Benamar, N., Jara, A.J., Ladid, L., Ouadghiri, D.E., Challenges of the Internet of Things: IPv6 and Network Management. *Eighth International Conference on Innovative Mobile and Internet Services in Ubiquitous Computing*, 2014.

28. Yeole, A. and Kalbande, D., Security of 6LoWPAN IoT Networks in Hospitals for Medical Data Exchange. *International Conference on Pervasive Computing Advances and Applications – PerCAA, Procedia Computer Science*, Elsevier, 2019.

12

Empowering Secured Outsourcing in Cloud Storage Through Data Integrity Verification

C. Saranya Jothi*, Carmel Mary Belinda† and N. Rajkumar‡

*Department of Computer Science and Engineering, Vel Tech Rangarajan
Dr. Sagunthala R&D Institute of Science and Technology, Chennai, India*

Abstract

Cloud storage offers on-request information and cloud computing is the most anticipated domain because of its flexibility and low support cost. One important use of cloud storage is to store information for a long time, which can be accessed whenever required. However, security and privacy concerns emerge when information stockpiling is outsourced to an unauthorized person. Data Integrity includes keeping up the information safe and secure while ensuring the accuracy and consistency of data. In this paper, we describe a solution that will help cloud clients check and protect the integrity of their outsourced data in the event that their data is accidentally corrupted or compromised by attacks.

Keywords: Data integrity, secured outsourcing, cloud storage, privacy-preserving, cloud service provider, third-party auditor

12.1 Introduction

Toward the start during the 1990s the expression "cloud" was utilized to speak to the registering space between the supplier and the end user. In 1997 the term Cloud Computing (CC) was referenced by Professor

---

**Corresponding author*: saranyajothi22@gmail.com
†*Corresponding author*: carmelbelinda@veltech.edu.in
‡*Corresponding author*: sivarajkumar.n@gmail.com

Kolla Bhanu Prakash, G. R. Kanagachidambaresan, V. Srikanth, E. Vamsidhar (eds.) Cognitive Engineering for Next Generation Computing: A Practical Analytical Approach, (315–334) © 2021 Scrivener Publishing LLC

Ramnath K. Chellappa the first time. Cloud computing is a sort of handling the benefits rather than having neighborhood workers or individual devices to manage applications [9]. Through the internet it delivered the different services. It includes applications like servers, networking, software, and data storage.

Cloud storage stores the data on remote storage systems. In cloud storage, it protects the data along with data integrity checking and recovery is difficult. Some basic security requirements of cloud services are as follows.

12.1.1   Confidentiality

Data cannot be made accessible or disclosed to unapproved people, substances or procedures. The data should not be known to the unauthorized person even if they hack the information.

12.1.2   Availability

For any information structure to fill its need, the in-game plan must be available when it is required. This infers that the figuring structures used to store [12] and measure the information, the security controls used to guarantee it, and the comparing channels used to get to it should work adequately.

12.1.3   Information Uprightness

It must be ensured that when data lands at its goal, it hasn't been messed with or changed, either incidentally or purposely.

12.2   Literature Survey

To verify the integrity of a large scale we used the schemes like Functional Minimum Storage Regeneration (FMSR), Proof of data possession (PDP), High Availability and Integrity Layer (HAIL).

12.2.1   PDP

Provable data possession (PDP) offers [2] the accompanying advantages, as PDP is lightweight and robust. It provides data format independence. PDP uses efficient erasure codes [6]. Its performance is not affected by computational requirements, but has the following drawbacks: Cannot detect minimal loss or provide deterministic proof.

12.2.1.1 Privacy-Preserving PDP Schemes

The main role of this plan is to guarantee that the remote server effectively has the customer's information alongside the encryption key and to keep any data spillage to the TPA which is in charge of the auditing errand. In this manner, customers, particularly with compelling figuring assets and abilities, can go to outside audit social occasion to check the decency of redistributed data, and this pariah looking at strategy should secure no new weaknesses towards the protection of customer's information.

Notwithstanding the examining errand of the TPA, it has another essential undertaking which is the extraction of computerized substances [17]. This plan has the following advantages: The number of times a piece of specific information can be checked is constrained and should be settled in advance.

12.2.1.2 Efficient PDP

In light of KEA1 supposition (Knowledge of Exponent Assumption), EPDP concentrates on the issue that a direct mix of the document pieces is precisely figured by checking just the accumulated tag authenticator. EPDP has the following benefit: reviewing if an untrusted server stores a customer's information. Homomorphism Verifiable labels are unforgeable confirmation meta-information built from the document obstructs such that the verifier can be persuaded, EPDP has the following disadvantages: The E-PDP show gives weaker certification of information ownership. The E-PDP plot just ensures ownership of the entirety of record pieces and not of every single square being tested.

12.2.2 POR

In Proof of Irretrievability [4], it conspires the plan utilizing keyed hash function and is the least complex plan than some other plan for confirmation of derivability of informative documents. In this paper, the information that is to be stored in the distributed storage is pre-handled and protected by crypto-realistic hash [18]. In the wake of computing hash esteem, the record is stored in the distributed storage. The cryptographic key which is utilized to figure hash esteem is then discharged to the distributed storage

Table 12.1 High availability and integrity layer.

Parameters	Description
Error Correction Code	Integrity-protected ECC
Part of HAIL	Dispersal and Aggregation
Operations in HAIL	Challenge and Remediation

and verifier request to compute hash esteem once more [13]. At this point esteems are computed by the verifier and qualities.

Figured by the cloud storage are contrasted with each other is shown in the Table 12.1. From that examination, the last conclusion is considered.

12.2.3 HAIL

HAIL, is high accessibility and trustworthiness layer [3] that expands the basic standards of attack into the opposing setting of the Cloud. HAIL is far off record reliability checking show that offers capability, security, and exhibiting upgrades over clear multi-worker use of Proof of Retrievability (POR) [4] conventions and appropriated record accessibility recommendations. Through a watchful interleaving of various sorts of mistake adjusting layers, and propelled by proactive cryptographic models, HAIL guarantees record accessibility against a solid Byzantine portable enemy.

12.2.4 RACS

RACS [1] is a distributed storage intermediary that straightforwardly stripe information over different distributed storage suppliers. Striping information over different suppliers enables customers to endure blackouts and economic disappointments. Blackouts are a progression of far-fetched occasions that prompts information misfortune in the cloud. An adjustment in the commercial center renders it restrictively thoughtful for a distributed storage customer to keep on using a specific administration. The added repetition in RACS escapes the potential merchant security. In Merchant bolt the information is not secured so the supplier becomes bankrupt, then the clients will suffer.

12.2.5 FMSR

Down to earth information uprightness security (DIP) plot for practical least stockpiling recovering (FMSR) [5] codes under a multi-server setting

Table 12.2 Functional minimum storage regenerating.

Parameters	Description
Error Correction Code	FMSR-DIP codes
Parts of FMSR	DIP scheme,NC-Cloud
Operations in FMSR	Check, repair

are considered. Dive plot ensures the adjustment to non-basic disappointment and repair movement saving properties of FMSR. It permits a few parameters from FMSRDIP codes to adjust, to such an extent that customers can influence an exchange to off between performance and security is shown in the Table 12.2.

12.3   System Design

12.3.1   Design Considerations

The following considerations were influential in the design of the system:

Privacy Safeguarding: The TPA ought not to pick up information on the first client information during the examining cycle.

Unbound Number of Queries: The verifier may be allowed to utilize a boundless number of questions in the test reaction convention for information check.

Data Dynamics: The customers must have the option to perform procedure on information documents like addition, modify and erase while keeping up information rightness.

Public Verifiability: Anybody, not simply the customers, must be permitted to check the respectability of information [22].

Block Less Verification: Tested record squares ought not to be recovered by the verifier during the check cycle.

Recoverability: Aside from checking right ownership of information, some plan to recoup the lost or debased information is required.

Computational Complexity: As information honesty checking is basic, the information trustworthiness checking models must consider decreasing and steady complexities at customer and worker end. This is accomplished in some proposed models with the assistance of uncommon wordings. The computational intricacy can be diminished to a steady with the goal that customers can perform.Information confirmation intermittently with less computational prerequisites.

Communication or Network Overhead: The information confirmation incorporates sending and accepting information or a gathering of information among customer and capacity worker. This thus builds arranged traffic on the worker. For this situation, the models must attempt to lessen organize traffic however much as could be expected by diminishing system correspondence.

Stateless Confirmation: The verifier might not need to keep state information between surveys all through the long stretch of data amassing.

12.3.2 System Overview

The system aims to verify and protect the trustworthiness of information put away in the cloud utilizing regeneration codes. The system features are accessed through an interface that is controlled by the user. The architecture of the proposed framework is appeared in Figure 12.1.

12.3.3 Workflow

First, the User computes verifiable tags and uploads the data. Then data is striped, encoded using MSR-DIP and then distributed to cloud servers after updating the metadata. Then in the check process, we check the approximately selected rows of bytes of particles currently stored on servers.

We select the node to be checked and challenge it using metadata and verifiable tags. If some server fails to lose we trigger the repair process because there is all the data or data that is too bad to be recovered. We should locate the failed node, download required chunks from other nodes, and update metadata and configuration. To retrieve the entire file, the user has to check the metadata, download the required chunks, and decode the file.

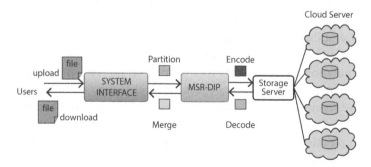

Figure 12.1 System architecture.

12.3.4 System Description

- System Encoding
- Decoding
- Repair and Check module

12.3.4.1 System Encoding

Firstly, we have to encode the files using any of the following coding schemes, for uploading. The way toward encoding changes over data from a source into symbols for communication or storage. The purpose of encoding is to transform information with the goal that it can be securely devoured by various parts of the framework. Encoding can be done using any of the coding schemes such as Reed–Solomon codes [7], Regeneration Codes [10].

12.3.4.1.1 Encoding in Reed–Solomon Codes

Eradication code is a forward error correction (FEC) code for the parallel deletion channel, which converts the message of k images into an extended message (code word) with n images with n images, to the extent that the first message can be retrieved from the subset of n images. This cycle is virtualized by Reed–Solomon codes, the coding uses the Vandermont architecture in a limited field [11]. The input file f is encoded using a Vandermonde matrix to give (n-k) parity chunks f.chunkk, f.chunkn. The file f is split into k chunks f.chunk0, f.chunkk-1. Each node will hold exactly one chunk. This encoding technique is shown in Figure 12.2.

12.3.4.1.2 Encoding in Regeneration Codes

Regenerative codes indicate the problem of recreating lost encrypted pieces from existing encrypted pieces. They are the new class of error

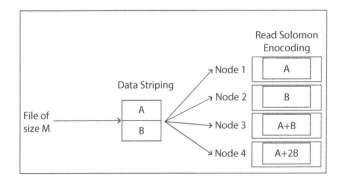

Figure 12.2 Encoding in Reed–Solomon codes.

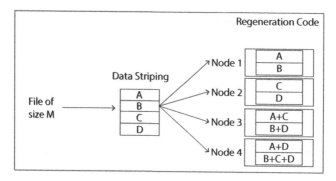

Figure 12.3 Encoding in regeneration codes.

correction codes. The input file f is encoded to give 2n code chunks f.chunk0, f.chunk2n. This encoding technique is shown in Figure 12.3.

12.3.4.2 Decoding

Interpreting is the way toward changing data from a hard to comprehend put away images arrangement to one that is more obvious. To retrieve the encoded file, we have to decode using the same encoding scheme with which the file is encoded. This is the reverse process of encoding which is done to download the file. Decoding can be done using any of the coding plans, for example, Reed–Solomon codes, Regeneration Codes.

12.3.4.2.1 Decoding in Reed–Solomon Codes
Decoding is done by decoding the k chunks downloaded from the first k accessible nodes. This is shown in Figure 12.4.

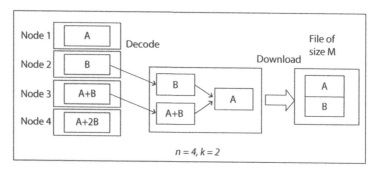

Figure 12.4 Decoding in Reed–Solomon codes.

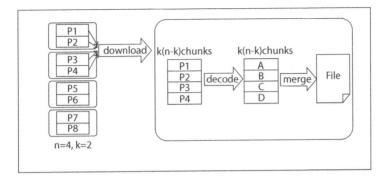

Figure 12.5 Decoding in regeneration codes.

12.3.4.2.2   Decoding in Regeneration Codes
Here, Decoding is done by decoding the 2k chunks downloaded from the first k accessible nodes. This is shown in Figure 12.5.

12.3.4.3   *Repair and Check*

Repairing is done by reconstructing the data at a failed node. A Check is performed on data, to check remotely, whether the information is in place or not. They are implemented specifically for codes [19].

12.3.4.3.1   Repair and Check-in Reed–Solomon Codes
In Reed–Solomon codes we repair by reconstructing data in new node, after downloading the entire file into temp [20]. This is shown in Figure 12.6. For checking on Reed–Solomon codes, we compute verification tag based on a secret key. If it is the same as old verification tag saved in server, the data intact.

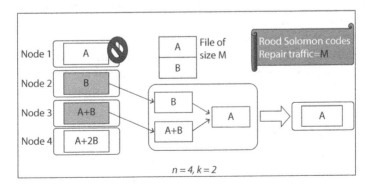

Figure 12.6 Repair in Reed–Solomon codes.

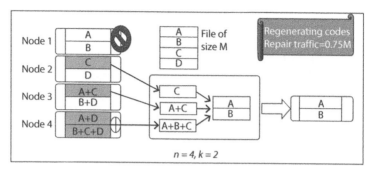

Figure 12.7 Repair in regeneration codes.

12.3.4.3.2   Repair and Checking Regeneration Codes

For repair in recovering codes we download one piece from every hub rather than entire document. Fix traffic: spare 25% for (n = 4, k = 2). This is shown in Figure 12.7. For checking in regenerating codes, we download a few percent of data from randomly chosen nodes. It is verified against its metadata to get a probabilistic proof.

12.4   Implementation and Result Discussion

It deals with the implementation of the proposed system. The implementation consists of namely System Encoding, Decoding and Repair and Check module. The tools [8], methods and algorithms involved in each module are discussed in detail.

12.4.1   Creating Containers

Containers are the user-space where the data of a user resides. Containers have directories which refer it as nodes. Based on the capacity of cloud storage provider there can be any number of containers. For implementation purpose, we consider only one user and one container. The number of nodes that is required is created. In our case, we create five. The nodes are named as Node0, Node1, and Node4. It can be increased if necessary are shown in Figure 12.8.

12.4.2   File Chunking

In the first step, the file is needed to be chunked. As we know that in regeneration coding, the operations are carried on file parts, rather than the file as a whole, we have to derive the required parts of the file. To divide a file

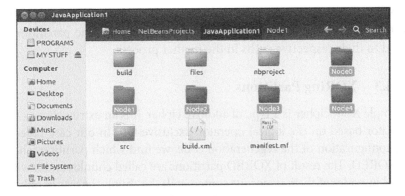

Figure 12.8 Creating containers for data.

first, we must find the total size of the file. In case of the input file is a text file. So we find the total number of bytes occupied by the input file. Then we have to divide the file into equal-sized n parts. Here n is the number of containers available.

By a simple division of total file size and number of containers, we estimate the size of a single partition. For convenience, let us name the partitions from partition0, partition1, and partition2. We now create byte chunks for the above which will be saved as files. Then we read the input file from its starting point to the size of the ordinary partition and copy its contents. Then we write the copied content to partition0. This above process is done for all the partitions other also except for the last one. The last partition needs special care as the read may reach the end of the file before covering ordinary file size. The last file chunk is padded with bits to make them equally sized shown in Figure 12.9.

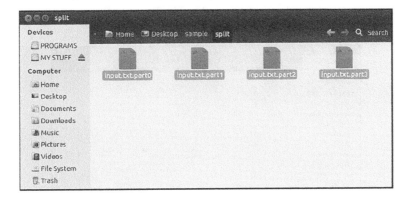

Figure 12.9 Chunking input file.

Now, after creating required number of partitions, we have to commit all the write operations and close all the opened files. The partitions are saved to their respective paths in the further process.

12.4.3 XORing Partitions

A simple XOR cipher is a type of additive cipher. It is an extremely common operator based on the logical operator Exclusive OR. In our case based on the configuration of the regeneration code, we find which partitions should be XORED. The result of XORED partitions are called chunks, and it will be saved in nodes of their respective container. If the chunk consists of only one partition, then no operation takes place and the partition is directly saved as a chunk and named with its partition number for identification purposes. If two partitions [14] have to be XORED for a chunk, the bits of the first partition are XORED with respective bits of another. This is possible as the partition of equal size. The numbers of both partitions are appended to chunk name. In case there are three partitions to be XORED into a chunk the process takes place linearly. Two partitions are XORED and their result is XORED with the third. Here the entire three partitions id is appended to chunk name.

Based on their respective nodes in the container on the configuration of the regeneration code, which is set by the user, these generated chunks are uploaded, by the user.

12.4.4 Regeneration of File

Get the operation that is required to be performed by the user. If he opts to regenerate the whole file, get the number of nodes from which the data is to be reconstructed. As per our configuration minimum of two nodes are required to reconstruct the whole file [21]. Get the distinct nodes. These nodes must not be the same. Read the chunks from each node shown in Figure 12.10.

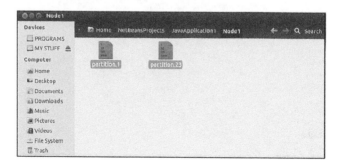

Figure 12.10 XOR-chunked files.

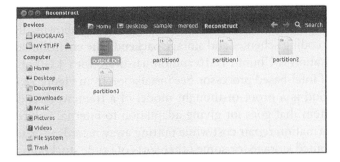

Figure 12.11 Regeneration of file from select nodes.

XOR these chunks against each other and find the original partitions. For example, if chunk0 and chunk01 are XOR-ED we get Partition1, due to the property of XOR. Likewise repeating the above process will result in the regeneration of all the partitions. To regenerate the whole file, we have to create a file and add the contents of these partitions to them as shown in Figure 12.11.

After finishing all the operations commit, the write and close files. Hence, we get the original data file the same as the input file.

12.4.5   Reconstructing a Node

If the user reconstructing a node when the node has failed. Get the other nodes from which the failed node has to be regenerated. They should be distinct and not the same failed node. Read the chunks from the inputted nodes. Same as in the regeneration of a whole file, XOR these chunks against each other and find the original partitions. After constructing all the partitions, check the configuration for the contents of the failed node. Based on these contents, reconstruct chunks for failing node and replace the data of failed nodes with computed data chunks with the same names. Thus we can reconstruct the failed node.

12.4.6   Cloud Storage

In a multi-cloud condition, the cloud configuration is comprised of multi-mists in which is a major cloud there are distinctive sub-mists or between mists [15]. The information from all the sub mists can be kept up and can be gotten to by the client from a control hub. We utilize Open stack's quick article stockpiling and neighbourhood stockpiling to give the necessary condition [16].

12.4.6.1   NC-Cloud

We actualize FMSR codes on NC-Cloud-A Network-Coding-Based Storage System depends on framework coding-based limit plans called recouping codes.

NC-Cloud is a proof-of-concept storage application written in C++ using Jerasure [11] and libfmsr [8]. It aims to be extensible, allowing the support of various coding schemes and storage backend. The environment used for implementation is Ubuntu 12.10 and on hardware with 4 GB of RAM and 2.0 GHz of Intel-based processor. See installation from Figure 12.12.

NC-Cloud is a proof-of-thought model of a framework coding-based report system that goes for giving adaptation to internal failure and lessening information repair cost while putting away records utilizing numerous distributed storage (or some other sorts of crude stockpiling gadgets). NC-Cloud is an intermediary-based document framework that interconnects various (cloud) stockpiling hubs. It can be loaded into a library on Linux, and moving/downloading the archive is done by reloading the records/reloading from the loaded list. NC-Cloud is based on FUSE, an open source, efficient grammar client space recording system that provides application programmable interfaces (APIs) for report configuration operations. From the point of view of customer applications, NC-Cloud presents a record structure layer that clearly stripe data transversely over limit centers. Framework codes for limit fix necessitate that capacity center points encode the set aside data in the midst of the fix methodology. Nevertheless, this may not be possible for some storing structures where center points simply give the major I/O functionalities yet don't have the encoding limit.

Our work is to change the upsides of framework codes in the limit fix of a handy stockpiling setting, by loosening up the encoding need of capacity centers. NC-Cloud supports a collection of coding plans, explicitly the Functional Minimum Storage Regenerating (F-MSR) codes. Contrasted with

```
jaga@ubuntu:~/Downloads/fmsrdip-0.2$ make
make -C Jerasure
make[1]: Entering directory '/home/jaga/Downloads/fmsrdip-0.2/Jerasure'
make -C Examples
make[2]: Entering directory '/home/jaga/Downloads/fmsrdip-0.2/Jerasure/Examples'
make[2]: Nothing to be done for 'all'.
make[2]: Leaving directory '/home/jaga/Downloads/fmsrdip-0.2/Jerasure/Examples'
make[1]: Leaving directory '/home/jaga/Downloads/fmsrdip-0.2/Jerasure'
make -C libfmsr
make[1]: Entering directory '/home/jaga/Downloads/fmsrdip-0.2/libfmsr'
make -C src
make[2]: Entering directory '/home/jaga/Downloads/fmsrdip-0.2/libfmsr/src'
mkdir -p ../include
cp fmsr.h ../include
make[2]: Leaving directory '/home/jaga/Downloads/fmsrdip-0.2/libfmsr/src'
make[1]: Leaving directory '/home/jaga/Downloads/fmsrdip-0.2/libfmsr'
make -C fmsrdip
make[1]: Entering directory '/home/jaga/Downloads/fmsrdip-0.2/fmsrdip'
make -C ../libfmsr
make[2]: Entering directory '/home/jaga/Downloads/fmsrdip-0.2/libfmsr'
make -C src
```

Figure 12.12 Installing NC-cloud.

```
jaga@ubuntu:~/Downloads/fmsrdip-0.2$ export LD_LIBRARY_PATH="../libfmsr
/lib:../Jerasure/lib:$LD_LIBRARY_PATH"
jaga@ubuntu:~/Downloads/fmsrdip-0.2$ cd fmsrdip
jaga@ubuntu:~/Downloads/fmsrdip-0.2/fmsrdip$ ls
bin          coding.o  config.cc  crypto.cc  docs       fileop.h  keys
list_repo.o  nccloud.o  README_NCCLOUD  storage.o  template
coding.cc  codings  config.h   crypto.h   Doxyfile   fileop.o  LICENSE
Makefile   NEWS       storage.cc  storages
coding.h   common.h  config.o   crypto.o   fileop.cc  jconfig   list_repo.cc
nccloud.cc  README     storage.h   store
jaga@ubuntu:~/Downloads/fmsrdip-0.2/fmsrdip$ bin/nccloud jconfig encode
README template/config_local
Coding type: 3
Encoding: README
Encoding: template/config_local
jaga@ubuntu:~/Downloads/fmsrdip-0.2/fmsrdip$ bin/nccloud jconfig decode README config_local
Coding type: 3
Decoding: README
Decoding: config_local
```

Figure 12.13 Working with NC-cloud.

```
jaga@ubuntu:~/Downloads/fmsrdip-0.2/fmsrdip$ bin/list_repo jconfig
On node 0:
config_local.meta
README.chunk1
README.meta
README.chunk0
config_local.chunk1
config_local.chunk0

On node 1:
config_local.meta
README.chunk3
README.meta
README.chunk2
config_local.chunk2
config_local.chunk3
```

Figure 12.14 Output of distributed chunks.

conventional ideal eradication codes (e.g., Reed–Solomon), FMSR codes maintain a similar stockpiling overhead under similar information repetition level yet utilizes less repair activity amid the recuperation of a solitary fizzled stockpiling hub. NC-Cloud acknowledges recovering codes in a common sense distributed storage framework that does not require any encoding translating insight on the distributed storage hubs. Scarcely any screenshots (Figures 12.13 and 12.14 of execution are connected underneath).

12.4.6.2 Open Swift

Open Stack gives an Infrastructure-as-a-Service game plan through a variety of complimentary organizations. Every organization offers an application programming interface (API) that energizes this coordination. Dissent Storage-Swift Stores and recuperates optional unstructured data objects using a Restful, HTTP based API [12]. It is incredibly accused open minded with its data replication and scale-out designing. Its use couldn't care less for an archive worker with mountable vaults. Thusly, the data trustworthiness is checked and made sure about.

12.5 Performance

The file is compiled and executed. The following Figures 12.15 and 12.16 are some screenshots of the execution and output.

An accomplished task needs to be measured against some standards to know the performance of the task. In the Data Integrity Verification system, the time predicted for the various operations of the system is compared for Reed–Solomon and regeneration codes.

Upload Operation: User encodes and uploads the data. Then data is striped, encoded using MSR-DIP and then distributed to cloud servers after updating the metadata. See Figure 12.17.

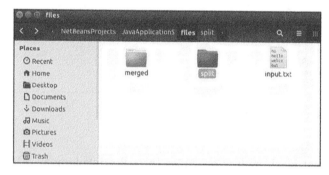

Figure 12.15 An input file and temp folders.

Figure 12.16 Executing the file.

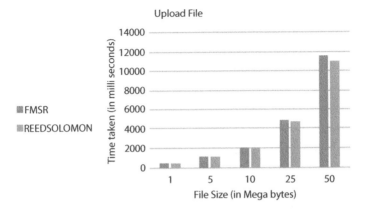

Figure 12.17 Time for the upload operation.

Repair operation: If some server comes up short losing all information or having excessively defiled information that can't be recouped, we trigger the Repair operation. We should locate the failed node, download required chunks from other nodes and update metadata and configuration. See Figure 12.18.

Check operation: This operation is to provide probabilistic proof on whether the data saved in a node are intact or not. If data is found to be compromised check is returned as data is compromised. The user has to initiate appropriate action is shown in Figure 12.19.

Download operation: To retrieve the entire file, check the user has to meta-data, download the required chunks, and decode the file is shown in Figure 12.20.

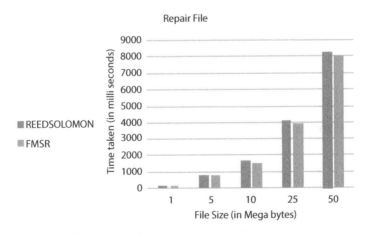

Figure 12.18 Time for the repair operation.

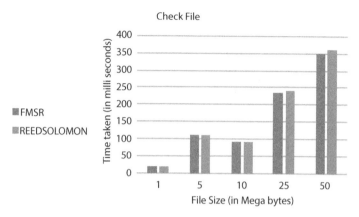

Figure 12.19 Time for check operation.

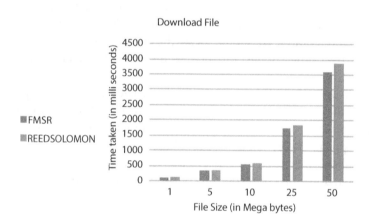

Figure 12.20 Time for download operation.

Thus, the performance measures are evaluated and the results produced are found to be satisfactory.

12.6 Conclusion

The data integrity is verified and preserved using this system. This enables the user to overcome any failure in data availability and integrity. The system provides a sense of ownership of data as the user directly controls the data.

The system takes into account privacy and security concerns. The data are not meaningfully read by others who don't have permission to view the data. Similarly any malicious change in data can be easily identified using verify operation. This system has a higher computational complexity than straight forward replication storage. But it is traded for saving cost in bandwidth usage and a higher level of replication factor with less memory space. The verify operation takes only a fraction of the cost when compared to downloading the entire file. Previously we found that Reed–Solomon and Regeneration codes have the almost same time for all operations except repair, where Regeneration codes are efficient.

When functional minimum storage, regeneration codes are used for data integrity verification, the system had a comparatively less usage of memory space. Hence, the future work will concentrate on improving the performance in terms of reducing the time taken for encoding and decoding operations. Additional features support for various commercial storage back ends can be provided. Various ways that allow exact repair using regeneration codes can also be explored.

References

1. AbuLibdeh, H., Princehouse, L., Weatherspoon, H., Races: A case for cloud storage diversity, in: *Proceedings of the 1st ACM Symposium on Cloud Computing, SoCC 10*, pp. 229–240, 2010.
2. Ateniese, G., Burns, R., Curtmola, R., Herring, J., Khan, O., Kissner, L., Peterson, Z., Song, D., Remote data checking using provable data possession. *ACM Trans. Inf. Syst. Secur.*, 12:1–12:34, 2011.
3. Bowers, K.D., Juels, A., Oprea, A., Hail: A high-availability and integrity layer for cloud storage, in: *Proceedings of the 16th ACM Conference on Computer and Communications Security, CCS '09*, pp. 187–198, 2009.
4. Bowers, K.D., Juels, A., Oprea, A., Proofs of retrievability: Theory and implementation, in: *Proceedings of the 2009 ACM Workshop on Cloud Computing Security, CCSW '09*, pp. 43–54, 2009.
5. Chen, H. and Lee, P., Enabling data integrity protection in regenerating coding based cloud storage: Theory and implementation. *IEEE Trans. Parallel Distrib. Syst.*, 407–416, 2014.
6. Curtmola, R., Khan, O., Burns, R., Ateniese, G., Mr-pdp: Multiple-replica provable data possession, in: *Proceedings of 28th International Conference on Distributed Computing Systems, ICDCS '08*, pp. 411–420, 2008.
7. Dimakis, A., Godfrey, P., Wu, Y., Wainwright, M., Ramchandran, K., Network coding for distributed storage systems. *IEEE Trans. Inf. Theory*, 4539–4551, 2010.
8. Hu, Y., Chen, H.C.H., Lee, P.P.C., Tang, Y., Mccloud: Applying network coding for the storage repair in a cloud-of-clouds, in: *Proceedings of the 10th USENIX Conference on File and Storage Technologies, FAST'12*, pp. 21–29, 2012.

9. Mell, P. and Grance, T., *The NIST definition of cloud computing*, Special Publication 800-145 of Computer Security Division, Information Technology Laboratory, National Institute of Standards and Technology, p. 2, 2011.

10. Papailiopoulos, D., Luo, J., Dimakis, A., Huang, C., Li, J., Simple regenerating codes: Network coding for cloud storage, in: *Proceedings of IEEE International Conference on Computer Communications, INFOCOM 2012*, pp. 2801–2805, 2012.

11. Plank, J.S., Simmerman, S., Schuman, C.D., *Jerasure: A library in c/c++ facilitating erasure coding for storage applications-version 1.2*, Technical report UT-CS-08-627, University of Tennessee, pp. 1–39, 2008.

12. Chen, Y., Li, L., Chen, Z., An Approach to Verifying Data Integrity for Cloud Storage. *2017 13th International Conference on Computational Intelligence and Security (CIS)*, IEEE.

13. Ye, J., Wang, Y., Liu, K., Code-Based Provable Data Possession Scheme for Integrity Verification in Cloud Storage. *International Conference on Network and Information Systems for Computers (ICNISC)*, 2016.

14. Zhang, Y., Xu, C., Liang, X., Li, H., Mu, Y., Zhang, X., Efficient Public Verification of Data Integrity for Cloud Storage Systems from Indistinguishability Obfuscation. *IEEE Trans. Inf. Forensics Secur.*, 12, 3, 2017.

15. Tang, X., Qi, Y., Huang, Y., ReputationAudit in Multi-cloud Storage through Integrity Verification and Data Dynamics. *IEEE 9th International Conference on Cloud Computing (CLOUD)*, 2016.

16. Zhang, Y., Xu, C., Li, H., Liang, X., Cryptographic Public Verification of Data Integrity for Cloud Storage Systems. *IEEE Cloud Comput. Year*, 3, 5, 2016.

17. Shen, W., Qin, J., Yu, J., Hao, R., Hu, J., Enabling Identity-Based Integrity Auditing and Data Sharing With Sensitive Information Hiding for Secure Cloud Storage. *EEE Trans. Inf. Forensics Secur.*, 14, 2, Feb. 2019.

18. Khedr, W.I., Khater, H.M., Mohamed, E.R., Cryptographic Accumulator-Based Scheme for Critical Data Integrity Verification in Cloud Storage. 65635–65651, IEEE, 17 May 2019.

19. Zhu, H., Yuan, Y., Chen, Y., Zha, Y., Xi, W., Jia, B., Xin, Y., A Secure and Efficient Data Integrity Verification Scheme for Cloud-IoT Based on Short Signature. *J. IEEE*, 7, 90036–90044, 2019.

20. Shao, B., Bian, G., Wang, Y., Su, S., Guo, C., Dynamic Data Integrity Auditing Method Supporting Privacy Protection in Vehicular Cloud Environment. *IEEE Access*, 6, 43785–43797, 08 August 2018.

21. Apolinário, F., Pardal, M., Correia, M., S-Audit: Efficient Data Integrity Verification for Cloud Storage, S-Audit: Efficient Data Integrity Verification for Cloud Storage.

22. Singh, P. and Saroj, S. Kr., A Secure Data Dynamics and Public Auditing Scheme for Cloud Storage. *6th International Conference on Advanced Computing and Communication Systems (ICACCS)*, 23 April 2020, IEEE.

Index

Printed and bound by CPI Group (UK) Ltd, Croydon, CR0 4YY

27/10/2024

14580469-0004